The Christian Leader Blueprint

Contact information for Blue Pioneer Publishing – bluepioneerpublishing@gmail.com

ISBN: 979-8-9878822-0-7 (paperback)
ISBN: 979-8-9878822-1-4 (ebook)
ISBN: 979-8-9878822-2-1 (hardcover)
ISBN: 979-8-9878822-3-8 (audiobook)

Library of Congress Control Number: 2023910309

All scripture quotations, unless otherwise indicated, are taken from the King James Version, KJV.

Any internet address (websites, blogs, etc.) in this book are offered as a resource. They are not intended in any way to be or imply an endorsement by Pioneering Publishing, nor do they vouch for the content of these sites for the life of this book.

Printed in Pineville, Louisiana

Ordering Information:
Special discounts are available on quantity purchases by corporations, associations, and others. For details, contact info@ryanfranklin.org

Cover design by Caleb Hogg.

The Christian Leader Blueprint

a step-by-step guide to leadership transformation

Ryan Franklin

"

Leadership is a high calling, but with the calling also comes great complexity, and often confusion. The responsibilities, risks and burdens can be overwhelming, and often seep into stresses in our families and personal lives. Ryan Franklin has created a clear, biblical and practical guide to helping the leader gain clarity of vision, be resourced well, and focus on the main things. His style is warm and his personal narratives are vulnerable, so that we can all identify with them. You will be glad you read this book.

—John Townsend, Ph.D.

Psychologist and author of the New York Times bestselling Boundaries book series

Founder, Townsend Institute and Townsend Leadership Program

Dedication:

To my wife, Angie, and my kids, Olivia and Neil. Thank you for being patient with me over the years as I grew (and continue to grow) as a husband, dad, and leader. I love you.

Special Note to Readers:

Feel free to read this book straight through. However, if you'd like to ingest the rich concepts more deeply, I recommend reading a chapter every week or even a chapter every month. Set a routine now and stick to it. Work through the concepts in your life slowly and thoroughly. Journal as you go and answer each of the thought-provoking questions. You can explore christianleader-madesimple.com to learn of the most current offerings, such as one-on-one coaching, group coaching, team coaching, community coaching, courses, workbooks, assessment, masterminds, and other opportunities to help you deepen these concepts in your life. If you will allow it, I promise this book and model will give you more clarity on what it takes to grow as a leader, and it will absolutely increase your effectiveness and enjoyment of leadership.

Contents

Part One: Establish a Better Rhythm of Life

Part Two: See Yourself More Clearly

Part Three: Leverage Your Strengths

Part Four: Build More Productive Relationships

A Blueprint for Success

† **JOHN 10:10:** *The thief cometh not, but for to steal, and to kill, and to destroy: I am come that they might have life, and that they might have it more abundantly.*

Do you feel trapped in the complexities of leadership? Are you struggling with a chaotic lifestyle and desperate for change?

When you hear those questions, do you immediately withdraw and think, "I'm supposed to be the one who helps others—what would people think if they knew I was struggling with my leadership ability?"

No one, especially a leader, wants to be stagnant—that sense of being confined to an island with no apparent way off. I've been there, and you are probably either feeling that despair now or may have experienced it in the past. The sensation of feeling unbalanced, ineffective, and yes, even a little frightened by your stage in life can leave you emotionally drained and empty. It can quickly take you down the path to burnout. If these words are resonating with you, you can find the answers you need as you progress through this book. I want to give you a direct path off that lonely island.

With so many uncertain internal and external challenges in the world, many leaders are unsure of their next step. They attend seminars, read books, and participate in team meetings, but they still feel confused on how to be an effective and healthy leader. Leadership feels too complicated and overwhelming. To provide a guide for your perplexing questions, I have created *The Christian Leader Blueprint.* Drawn from over 25 years of experience and education, these are concepts I have learned through trial, error, study, and dedicated work on these subjects. My hope is that when you reach the end of the final page of this book, you will walk away with a unique and life-changing model that will propel you to a new level of leadership—one that you have longed to have.

So how does *The Christian Leader Blueprint* work? It clearly and simply identifies and explains the components that will elevate a leader's life and organization. This structure gives a professional growth and developmental framework for leaders who have plateaued or need specific direction for growth. Organized into four, easy-to-approach parts, this guide will help you establish a better rhythm of life, see yourself more clearly, leverage your strengths, and build more productive relationships. By identifying and defining these crucial steps, *The Christian Leader Blueprint* propels you to become a more effective leader and ultimately guide your ministry or organization forward in a healthy and productive way.

Let's start the process with my personal journey, followed by the life-changing elements contained in this book.

A few years ago, my life felt stagnant. I had no definite vision. I was on the edge of burnout. I had no intentional rhythm of life, my work-life balance was out of sync, and I was struggling to embrace my calling and tap into my giftings. To add fuel to the fire, I was in a tremendous leadership role at a great church, but there were aspects of my leadership that were abrasive and caustic to others. I had routine prayer and devotion with the Lord; however, I was eroding the key relationships in my life—the very relationships that I really needed in order to be successful in life and ministry. My family would sometimes cringe when I got home from work because they didn't know what type of mood I would be in when I walked through the door. I blamed it on the fact that ministry is hard. I felt that I had to tough it out and do what was necessary to "do the work of the Lord."

Yet, there was a little scripture that spoke of something called "abundant life" (John 10:10). I had definitely experienced it to some degree, but I hadn't learned to live in it. I went through a great deal of counseling in my middle twenties to help overcome some deep-rooted issues, such as a fear of rejection and unresolved grief. It helped tremendously. I don't think I could have embraced the next phase of my journey without having had that foundation. In fact, it was so impactful that I chose to go back to school to get a Master of Arts in Christian Ministry with a focus in Pastoral Counseling. I wanted to be able to help guide others in the same way that I had been helped. However, I still felt like I was missing something.

As I read my Bible, scripture continued to speak of a life that seemed so much better than what I was experiencing. I found breadcrumbs throughout the Bible, referencing emotional health, clarity, purposeful living, and healthy relationships. I was still searching for something, however. I didn't know exactly what it was at the time, but I needed some sort of vision for personal growth. I wanted to live in that abundant life as I fulfilled my calling in the Kingdom of God. So, I jumped headfirst into analyzing and studying to try to find answers. I read scripture and books or whatever I could get my hands on, looking for the abundant life I sought. I talked to anyone I could find who would give me some insight. I was hungry for more, but I couldn't find what I was looking for.

One year at Because of the Times, an annual ministers' conference at The Pentecostals of Alexandria, I ran into an old friend. He told me about an executive coach who was changing his world. Of course, my friend had my attention! A few months later, I scheduled my first appointment with an executive coach, Dr. Brian Epperson. It was a tough decision to make that appointment because it was crazy expensive. To top it off, I had never even heard of an executive coach before that time.

A year later, after many sessions with my new executive coach, I reflected back and realized I had experienced one of the best years of growth of my entire life. I made amazing progress and enormous improvement in my personal life and discipleship process! I felt like I knew myself so much better. I had vision and purpose. I could feel a sense of healthy rhythm in life that I had rarely felt before. I was beginning to live in that scriptural, abundant life that I had longed for with an amazing sense of clarity and fulfillment.

As our coaching sessions neared the end of our agreed time together, I knew I had to learn how to do for others what Dr. Epperson had done for me. I wanted to share my experience with others. After three years of an adventure full of wonder and even some chaos—and after a great deal of mentoring from Dr. Epperson, receiving an executive coaching and consulting certificate from Townsend Institute, and just plain, old-fashioned trial and error while coaching others—I was beginning to see significant results in the lives of the people I coached. They, too, were experiencing this abundant life. These results were translating to their home life and to the organizations they led.

I also began to see a pattern. My clients were walking a path similar to my own. Many of the same challenges I experienced were surfacing in their lives. Everyone was unique and had individual deficiencies in their journeys, but there was a distinct pattern. By studying this distinct pattern and getting input from a few key people in my life, I eventually developed what is now called *The Christian Leader Blueprint*.

This blueprint is a personal-leadership growth model. Within this guide, readers have the opportunity to learn how to establish a better rhythm of life, see themselves more clearly, leverage the strengths within themselves, and ultimately build better and more productive relationships. *The Christian Leader Blueprint* clearly defines what is necessary to increase a person's capacity and become a deeper, healthier, and more effective leader. In addition, this resource will help leaders gain needed clarity to effectively lead a ministry or an organization forward.

Every leader has unique needs for his or her personal success. In *The Chris-

tian Leader Blueprint, I hope to have addressed this frustration by creating a fluid process that can be worked through from multiple angles. It is intended for you to find your personal area of greatest weakness: the thing that's keeping you from growing, having a good rhythm of life, or finding vision for your life. Whatever is holding you back from creating the relationships necessary to develop your ministry or organization is where you can start your journey of growth and leadership development.

The primary need of any organization today is effective leadership. Yet, effectiveness goes beyond just productivity and results. Organizations need Christian leaders who are also experiencing a healthy, fulfilled, and abundant life. The Lord wants an authentic, relational leader through which He can perform His greatest work.

If you desire to find this place of clarity and effectiveness in your leadership, I want to help. In the first and second chapters of this book, you'll read about the big picture of leadership and the role of pain in leadership growth. Then, in the following chapters, we'll get into the details of *The Christian Leader Blueprint* model broken down into four main parts. I can't express just how excited I am to introduce you to something that I *know* can drastically increase the effectiveness of your leadership. Let's get started!

chapter 1

The Making of an Effective Leader

† **MATTHEW 20:28**: *Even as the Son of Man came not to be ministered unto, but to minister, and to give his life a ransom for many.*

As evidenced by scripture, the Lord desires that we have healthy, fulfilled, and abundant lives as we pursue effective leadership. Jesus, the greatest leader in history, not only told us to make disciples, but He also gave us a leadership model to follow in our disciple-making efforts. I believe His methods are just as divine as His teachings. He exemplified the perfect fundamental methodology of healthily leading others. It's the big picture of leadership.

In Jesus' leadership, discipleship was always His emphasis; and relationships were always His method. Jesus invited 12 men into His life. He invested in them. Everywhere they went, He built His relationship with them by teaching and explaining His words and actions. He loved them, effectively led them, and communed with them. He taught them to be disciples. Then, He showed them how to make disciples.

The Apostle Paul did exactly the same thing. Paul didn't just lead a class once a week or occasionally preach a sermon to a large crowd. Paul focused on leading people in a healthy way, building relationships with people, and helping them grow. Paul led his followers to the next step, and then he helped them take that next step in their relationship with Jesus and others. *That* is the big picture of leadership.

Using the example of Jesus and Paul, the big picture of a leader is:

1. Developing yourself in a healthy, biblical way
2. Building productive relationships with others
3. Leading others to growth and greater influence

When we work hard to develop ourselves in a healthy, biblical way—when we establish a better rhythm of life, see ourselves more clearly, and leverage our strengths—there's no doubt we will build more productive relationships. This, in turn, will lead others to growth and greater influence. This healthy productivity with positive influence creates effective leadership.

The Big Picture

Having a clear vision of the big picture can help us stay on track during our long leadership journey. Sometimes as Christian leaders, it's easy for us to get bogged down in the weeds week in and week out. Our vision can get a little skewed and "pixelated" by the daily grind of life. Developing the ability to step back and refocus on the big picture of life helps us regain a clear and meaningful perspective.

I was reminded of that lesson in 2002, when I was 22 years old. My wife, Angie, and I had been married eight months. I was less than a year out of college and working as a registered nurse. An opportunity presented itself and we moved from Alexandria, LA, (population around 50,000) to Washington, DC, (metro population of over four million at the time) to help a new church. Angie and I were beyond excited—and nervous at the same time—to embark on this new season of life.

Those were the days before smartphones, and because we couldn't afford one, we didn't even own a camera to capture all the new places and exciting experiences. My stepmom, Laura, came to the rescue! For Christmas that same year, she bought Angie and I our first digital camera. It was a two-megapixel Sony Cyber-Shot, and state-of-the-art for 2002. We were excited to begin taking pictures of all our DC adventures.

One of the pictures shows Angie and I at the podium where the president of the United States gives press conferences at the White House. We took pictures of the Vietnam Veterans Memorial, Korean War Veterans Memorial, and many other sites. We also took pictures of our church in Alexandria, VA—you can see the basketball scoreboard in the background of those photos because, as a new church, we were conducting services in a school gym.

That little two-megapixel camera took some good shots. I flipped back through some of my old pictures while I was writing this, admiring my fancy handiwork but knowing, of course, it was the phenomenal quality of that two-megapixel camera that did all the work. Yeah right! Some of the pictures were so pixelated it was difficult to see what was in the image.

Let's consider another picture. It's a picture of Western Europe's highest mountain—Mont Blanc. A team of people led by alpinist/photographer Filippo Blengini in 2015 published an enormous photograph of the mountain. At the time, it was the largest photo that had ever been taken of something on Earth—365 gigapixels![1]

A five-member team gathered the data for this picture. They then pieced together over 70,000 photographs, a process that took over two months using high-tech equipment. If you were to print this picture at 300 dpi, it would be as large as an entire soccer field. It's a very large photograph. It's slightly bigger

---

1 Michael Zhang, "365-Gigapixel Panorama of Mont Blanc Becomes the World's Largest Photo," PetaPixel, May 24, 2015, https://petapixel.com/2015/05/24/365-gigapixel-panorama-of-mont-blanc-becomes-the-worlds-largest-photo/.

and clearer than my two-megapixel picture of the Capitol, to say the least.[2]

If you were to zoom way in on the center of the photo of Mont Blanc, you could actually see a couple of hikers who just happened to be on the mountain. It's amazing to be able to see that much detail and clarity from that many miles away. With a two-megapixel camera, I might be able to get an average view of the overall landscape of the mountain, but there's absolutely no way that I could zoom in 100% to these hikers. To say this photograph of Mont Blanc is a "big picture" is an understatement.

As leaders, it's so easy to allow the hustle and bustle of life to become paramount. Our vision may get a little skewed—"pixelated" if you will—by life's circumstances and the daily grind. Sometimes it helps to take a few steps back, reset the focus, and see the big picture of life. It does something to us. It allows us to be refreshed and regenerated; it helps us grab hold of a different and clearer perspective.

As a Christian leader called by God, I know where to find the "big picture" of my life in this world. It doesn't come from news reports and the media. I won't hear it in the voices of politics and current world events. I won't see it reflected in the face of a famous person. My "big picture" is clearly detailed in a book called the Bible. The Bible gives the details of exactly what I need to know. It tells me what to do. It helps me find my way when I'm lost. It gives me a clear perspective when confusion and chaos would attempt to rule my life. I trust and I believe every word of it, emphatically and without question.

I, personally, have bought into a leadership life that's full of the words of the Bible and of Jesus. I'm all in. There's nothing I want more in my life than to please my Lord and Savior! There's nothing I want more in my life than to be a greater disciple of Christ and to lead others to be greater disciples of Christ. I'm not happy with a pixelated, two-megapixel version of Jesus in my life. I want a clear, 365-gigapixel version of Jesus and His mission.

That's the big picture for my life.

---

2   Ibid.

With this big picture—this big mission—in mind, it is critical that we work to establish and maintain effective, biblical leadership. Before we dive into the rest of this book, I encourage you to evaluate your life by honestly answering this question:

What's the one overarching shift you think you need to make in your life in order to become a more effective Christian leader?

Don't answer that with the first thing that pops into your head and think you've finished the process. Make note of that first thing, then see what else may come to mind as we continue to journey through the concepts of *The Christian Leader Blueprint*. Ponder the real—big picture—answer to that question.

Jesus' Greatest Leadership Principle

There are a zillion books in print today that attempt to give the reader the big picture of leadership. It seems everyone has a different concept of what leadership is or should be. This model is different. I have taken in and used many of the same principles that other writers have, but I also have gained key concepts from the greatest leader of all time, Jesus, and the greatest book of all time, the Bible. The model and the organization of the content of this book is unlike that of any other Christian leadership book I've read. In an effort to bring some simplicity and clarity to the topic of leadership, I want to share with you in this section the one single thing that seemed to be the greatest leadership principle Jesus ever modeled.

Before we move forward, let's consider how "leadership" is defined.

Best-selling author and Christian leader John Maxwell has said, "Leadership is influence. That's it. Nothing more; nothing less." He went on to quote leadership authority James C. Georges, who said, "Leadership is the ability to obtain followers."[3]

Aubrey Malphurs, professor of pastoral ministries at Dallas Theological Seminary, says, "Christian leadership is the process whereby servants use their credibility and capability to influence people in a particular context to pursue their God-given direction."[4]

It is obvious from the repetition of these quotes that all of these well-known authors agree that leadership is influence with others.

Despite what many people may think, leadership is not a position. You may be a pastor, student pastor, department leader, CEO, manager, or hold some other position, but it doesn't mean you automatically become an effective leader. You may be a leader in title, but effective leadership is influence. Influence is gained by consistently doing the right things over time. Being influential is not something anyone can just give you, nor is it something you can randomly become.

As much as I would love to give everyone influence, I can't. I may be able to speak up for you. I may be able to show others that I believe in you, but eventually it circles back around to the influence you produce, the influence you have cultivated on your own, interacting with others.

Have you ever heard of a mantle of anointing? In the church world, we hear that phrase occasionally. Someone dies or steps aside from ministry in some way and reference will be made to the Old Testament prophets Elijah and Elisha. We say, "His mantle fell on..." There may be a spiritual mantle of anointing, however there can be no mantle of influence. Influence cannot be handed down nor can it be imparted or given to you. You may be assigned a position, yet influence must be earned by your credibility and your growth over time.

Some individuals are born with a natural ability to lead. Some people have

---

3 John C. Maxwell, *Developing the Leader within You 2.0* (Nashville: HarperCollins Christian Publishers, 2018), 1.
4 Aubrey Malphurs, *Being Leaders: The Nature of Authentic Christian Leadership* (Ada: Baker Books, 2003), 10.

a higher leadership energy than others. That's great if you're one of those people! However, leadership is not just for those born with natural ability. The traits that make a good leader or a good influencer can be learned and, in actuality, can and must be developed over time with consistency and intentionality. With that in mind, let's look at Jesus' methods in scripture:

Matthew 20:25–28 (KJV) says: "*But Jesus called them unto him, and said, Ye know that the princes of the Gentiles exercise dominion over them, and they that are great exercise authority upon them.*[26] *But it shall not be so among you: but whosoever will be great among you, let him be your minister;*[27] *And whosoever will be chief among you, let him be your servant:*[28] *Even as the Son of man came not to be ministered unto, but to minister, and to give his life a ransom for many.*"

Jesus is our perfect example of an influencer and the greatest example of an effective leader. He came to 1) minister, 2) serve, and 3) give His life for many.

If you think about it, Jesus' concept of leading and life in general is really a bit opposite of what our society says leadership and life are about. Scripture is full of opposites. It says the Kingdom of God is a place where the first are last and the last are first. It's a place where the poor are rich. It's a place where the foolish are wise. It's a place where the weak are strong. It's a place where death and failure lead to victory. That's the Kingdom of God. Just think about these biblical concepts and principles as we look to be effective Christian leaders.

Moses was filled with divine power and wisdom, as long as he questioned his own ability. When pride and arrogance and a sense of his own self-importance started sneaking in, that's when he made his life's biggest mistakes. Look at Gideon, Saul, Elijah, and Jeremiah—they were all in the same boat. They were men who were called of God to be leaders, yet each one had issues and tough things to overcome within themselves. There were risks and anxieties that came their way. No doubt, there were some sleepless nights, some things to be endured, not for personal gain, but for someone else's gain. That's true Christian leadership. The effective leader realizes genuine, biblical leadership is a matter of service and self-sacrifice to gain influence.

So, what's the big picture here?

You cannot seek leadership—especially Christian leadership—because you want a position, or you think it will bring you some level of power, or because it just sounds somehow exciting. If God calls you to lay down your life to serve and influence others, be ready to place yourself at His feet. Be ready to do it with an attitude of submission and sacrifice, with fear and trembling, because that is true leadership.

Christian leaders gain influence by giving of themselves to others. Jesus showed us this principle, so eloquently described in Philippians 2:7–8, when Paul wrote that He *"...made himself of no reputation, and took upon him the form of a servant, and was made in the likeness of men:⁸ And being found in fashion as a man, he humbled himself, and became obedient unto death, even the death of the cross."*

That is the big picture of leadership, exemplified by Jesus Christ. Humility, service, self-sacrifice—these things lead to true influence. That level of influence then leads to effective leadership and to making a huge impact in the lives of others.

That's the big picture of leadership.

I would like you to ponder this: Even in your service to others, how can you be more strategic—to serve with humility, to increase your influence—to become a more effective leader?

For a person to truly embrace the concept of humility and strategically increase influence, it's important to begin by reflecting on where he or she has come from—possibly even considering the pain that has been experienced and overcome in life. In the next chapter, we'll explore how the Lord often uses the pain in our lives to create opportunities for leadership growth.

chapter 2

Leadership Pain

✝ Psalms 23:4: *Yea, though I walk through the valley of the shadow of death, I will fear no evil: for thou art with me; thy rod and thy staff they comfort me.*

Effective leadership often comes from life's pain. Many times, the Lord grows us through His Word and through prayer, yet sometimes He chooses to use our pain to provide opportunities for growth. Not all of the time, but many times in my life, I probably could have avoided this pain if I had been a better person or better leader or if I had made better decisions. Regardless of the reason though, the Lord used these situations, these opportunities, to grow some internal parts of my being. And I must admit, many times the type of growth that happened would never have come without having walked down that tough road in my life. The majority of the lessons learned in this book have come through the pain that I have walked through.

Pain is inevitable. We all experience it; it is part of making progress in ministry and life. If we want to be where the Lord desires us to be, there is no way we can avoid the growth that pain helps us achieve.

I once worked with a person who was in a relational situation that felt hopeless. He was going through a season of rejection from one of his adult kids. Sadly, it also involved grandkids. In our conversation, he came to the realization there was nothing he could do to control the actions of his adult son. I could feel the deep agony and pain he was experiencing as he came to this realization.

Then, as we began to process that pain, the heaviness began to lift a little. He verbally asked himself the question: "What can I learn from this situation? How can it make me a better dad—and a better person in general?" This family pain allowed us to dive into some core issues that were holding him back in the way he interacted with people on his church leadership team.

There's no way we can control all the circumstances around us, so we cannot always control the pain that comes our way. However, we can control our response to that pain. We can decide if we are going to harbor the anxiety that comes along with it or if we will release it by processing and grieving the loss and ultimately allowing it to bring us to a greater place in life.

There are a lot of biblical examples of pain; I often think of Paul in this context. He was such a great leader who accomplished big things in the launch of the New Testament church. Paul wrote much of the New Testament and accomplished all sorts of amazing feats for the church. Yet, in truth, he did it all while experiencing persecution or prison or relational conflict. He produced significant things while going through some of the most extreme pressures imaginable. He did it while living with his undefined "thorn in the flesh."[5]

Paul writes in 2 Corinthians 12:7: "*And lest I should be exalted above measure through the abundance of the revelations, there was given to me a thorn in the flesh, the messenger of Satan to buffet me, lest I should be exalted above measure.*"

Paul calls this "thorn in the flesh" "the messenger of Satan." He felt certain it was put in his life to torment him. We don't know exactly what it was or why it was there. We don't know if it was physical or spiritual or emotional.

---

5   Reggie Kidd et al, "Paul's Imprisonment," Thirdmill, accessed January 8, 2023, https://thirdmill.org/seminary/lesson.asp/vid/17.

There really is not a lot of information on what that thorn in the flesh was, yet we do know it was the source of a ton of real pain in Paul's life. In fact, it was so bad we see in verse 8 that Paul asked the Lord three times to remove it from him. Many people like to look at Paul as some Superman. Yet, he was no less human than you and I. No one wants to live in pain, including the Apostle Paul.

The Lord was using these things to build Paul's character in a much greater way. Whatever the troubles were—whatever the thorn was—these things helped remove things like pride and provided a level of internal growth that couldn't come to Paul any other way.

Let's read his response to this pain in 2 Corinthians 12:9: "*And he said unto me, My grace is sufficient for thee: for my strength is made perfect in weakness. Most gladly therefore will I rather glory in my infirmities, that the power of Christ may rest upon me.*"

So instead of removing the pain, God gave Paul the grace and the strength to live through the pain. Paul learned firsthand how God's strength is made perfect in human weakness. He came to know that when we cannot fix or control or do, God will step in and become our strength.

Then in verse 10 we read: "*Therefore I take pleasure in infirmities, in reproaches, in necessities, in persecutions, in distresses for Christ's sake: for when I am weak, then am I strong.*"

Pain is inevitable. Pain is going to come. God gives us the strength and the fortitude and the grace to walk through the infirmities of life. He walks with us through the pain we experience. We come out on the other side better men and women of God because of it all.

Several years ago, when I transitioned in ministry from more of a pastoral support role to an actual pastoral role at The Pentecostals of Alexandria, I remember those first few months of transition. It was exciting on one hand; on the other hand, it was also extremely painful. I was excited to have the opportunity to be a pastor at one of the greatest churches in America. But even though I had assisted for many years with many of the duties I took on, there was still a very steep learning curve to handle the volume and complexity of tasks for which I was now responsible. This transition could not have come at a more challenging time in my life as I was in the middle of finishing an intense master's degree program. I felt like I had the weight of the world on my shoulders.

I remember one week three or four months in, I was burning the candle at both ends. My anxiety and stress were at an all-time high. I had to deal with a major leadership conflict in one of the ministries I oversaw. I felt like I was on the verge of collapse emotionally—and even physically—by this point. It seemed I was at my human limit of what I could handle. I admitted my feelings to a close friend and, amazingly, it was at that moment of admitting and acknowledging my limitations that I felt the hands of the Lord slide under my arms in a supernatural way. I knew He was with me. I knew everything was going to be okay. I knew He was going to give me the strength I needed. He did just that! He provided exactly what I needed through prayer and through strategically placed people in my life. The rest is history. I came out of that pain as a much better man and a better leader.

Pain is not fun. As human beings we seem to always try to escape pain. That's natural. Yet, we must remember our scars, our hurts, and our pains are literally preparing us for something bigger in our lives, something greater for the Kingdom of God.

I want you to consider a few questions before moving on:

1. What pain, anxiety, or negative experiences have you gone through in your life or ministry in the last few years?

2. What growth opportunity has this pain presented for you?

I encourage you to list your answers in writing. Put them in a place where they will be brought to the surface of your mind in a much greater way. As you find meaning in the middle of these experiences, writing and reflecting will help deepen the learning within you. The Lord could very well be using the pain in your life to shape and mold you into the leader He desires you to be. Let's continue forward to understand more about the positive effects pain can have on what the Lord desires of our lives.

The Pain of Doing Something Big

When you reflect on the pain you have experienced in your life, do you get the feeling that the Lord has a big, significant task ahead of you? The Lord is very calculating and intentional in His actions. When you feel the Lord call you to a specific task, there is usually a purposeful reason. He wouldn't have called you if He had not prepared you and equipped you for the task at hand.

However, it seems the Lord isn't in the business of making things easy for us. He wants us to do great things. He wants us to stretch and expand ourselves. He wants to see us get the best possible outcome for the Kingdom of God. Yet He also knows that it often requires pain for us to stretch and expand. It requires things that are out of our norm and even sometimes pushes the limits of what we think we are capable of handling. We must keep in mind it is not really about us; it is, in fact, all about the Kingdom of God.

I want you to push through the tough barriers in your life and do a greater work for the Kingdom of God. So, I am going to share with you my personal—and to some degree painful—experience of my first few months launching the YouTube channel, podcast, and blog that is a part of my Christian Leader Made Simple ministry.

On April 5, 2021, I publicly launched a YouTube channel, podcast, and a blog all at the same time. Some people thought I was crazy to do so much at one time. I had to learn all sorts of things in advance of the launch, such as videography, video editing, thumbnail creation, audio editing, and many other things. I had to rework my life by building efficient systems and routines—I'm tired just thinking about it all again.

To understand how truly difficult it was, I must explain the emotional side of the pain. Due to various hurts and pains in my life, I developed a fear of rejection and a fear of failure at an early age. Though I've worked hard to overcome these things, I knew that launching this leader content—putting myself "out there" and being transparent and vulnerable to whomever wanted to listen—certainly had the potential to stir some of those things in me.

Now, you must understand, I was happy living my life and conducting my ministry in the background. I really don't like the limelight. I don't like, nor do I want, people knowing my personal business. I had not been personally active on social media in over 10 years. However, I was following a prompting of the Holy Spirit in my life. I knew I had to do this if I wanted to help others learn some of the same things I had learned, so I began preparing for it.

The combined stress of working a busy pastoral job, launching a YouTube channel, as well as doing executive coaching on the side was a lot on my plate. Add to those things the emotional toll of a fear of rejection and fear of failure, and the entirety really was a little overwhelming.

This experience was different than the unbearable seasons I had experienced in the past. I could sense the internal growth of my character this time. I could feel the positive effects of all the work I had done on my internal self over the past few years. Sure, it was lots of pressure. Sure, there were insecurities surfacing. Yet when I look back now, they were things that needed to surface. Instead of feeling burnout or depression or seeking approval or trying to medicate myself in unhealthy ways, this time I knew what to do with the pain I was experiencing. I knew how to process it in a positive way. I knew, too, that I needed others in my life to help me through the pain.

When high levels of stress and anxiety like this surrounded me in years past, I could easily be triggered and spiral emotionally—sometimes for days at a time. My energy levels would dip. I would get moody with my family and those closest to me. I would feel the urge to move away from people and just be alone. Sometimes those feelings would last for days, not just an hour or two.

When I publicly launched the YouTube channel and podcast on April 5th, it all happened as anticipated on some level. Lowered energy levels, moodiness, detachment from people—all the components were there. However, something was significantly different this time. This time, when it happened, it only lasted a few hours instead of a few days. You may be wondering why such a change took place in me. Let me tell you the biggest reason why: First and foremost, it was through the Spirit of God, through prayer, and the Lord's help. Outside of that, the biggest reason was because of the productive relationships in my life.

For the last couple of years, I've spent a considerable amount of time building a small team of people around me that I can resource from. From these individuals I can gain the connection, love, and support that all humans need. These are the people with whom I can process things, people to whom I can voice my most vulnerable emotions. And they just contain it—providing encouragement, empathy, or whatever is necessary in the moment.

During an amazingly difficult and somewhat painful time of growth in my life—and here's a big key, I want you to get this—I had a group of people around me that could meet my needs.

Another major difference was I knew how to ask for my relational needs to be met. It made all the difference in the world in how I came through that pain.

I want you to process a few questions as you evaluate your own life and leadership:

1. What big role, task, or undertaking has the Lord called you to do that you haven't started preparing for yet?

2. Now, ask yourself, "Why?" Why haven't you pursued the direction the Lord has called you to?

3. What's one thing you can do this week to begin preparing for it?

Don't let the potential pain of the situation or process worry you or derail you from making it happen. Embrace the things necessary and take a significant step toward success! This pain has a significant role in helping you become an effective leader.

The Role of Pain in Effective Leadership

I trust by now you are beginning to see how the pain in our lives has shaped us to be the people the Lord desires us to be. It has or will help us to fulfill the plan the Lord desires of us. Pain is part of the process that helps us make progress. I have no idea what you've had to endure in your past or perhaps are enduring right now. I am definitely not saying the Lord made you go through those things. However, I am saying the Lord is using those things, regardless of what they are or how they came about, to bring you closer to Him and closer to the person/leader He wants you to be. He can use the pain in your life to place in you the key ingredients necessary to make you the leader He's called you to be.

I had a grandmother named Mawmaw Eggie—at least that's what all us grandkids called her. Mawmaw Eggie made some of the best cornbread you could ever wrap your lips around. It was crispy, it was buttery, it was delicious! She made it in a cast iron skillet and baked it to perfection. I can almost taste it—I wish I could taste it right now!

She passed away several years ago. I miss her, of course; I really missed her cornbread, too. Every year at family gatherings we would talk about that cornbread. My mom would try to reproduce it. Her cornbread was good, don't get me wrong, but it just wasn't quite the same as Mawmaw Eggie's. She couldn't figure out why it wouldn't turn out the same. Somehow, she felt certain she was missing something. She kept trying different things and different ways and one day, she finally figured it out. My mom got the right combination of the right ingredients to make my grandmother's cornbread—and *that* cornbread was really good—as good as Mawmaw Eggie's!

Ingredients are very important. One wrong ingredient can completely change the end result. It works the same way for leadership. The insertion of the correct ingredients is essential, and this is one of the ways that pain can benefit us. In some cases, it identifies areas where we are deficient. In other ways, it instills in us the things that are needed for effective leadership. For instance, if a leader doesn't know how to build productive relationships, the effectiveness of the leader will be limited. Having the proper ingredients in a leader's life is critical if you're seeking a specific end result. You must understand you were made for an intended, specific purpose in the Kingdom of God.

It's sort of like a key that fits into a lock. You are the only person that can fulfill the perfectly shaped purpose you were designed to fulfill. Here's the deal, though. You weren't necessarily born that way. You may have been born with some of the necessary elements, but not all of them. Life is what equips you. The good things in life and also the pain of life give you the key ingredients to be that man or woman of God He's called you to be.

Think about the Apostle Peter. He fulfilled his mission even after failing miserably. His failures taught him some important things in life. They gave him some of the key ingredients he needed to become an intricate part of the Kingdom of God. Wild-man Simon Peter, the man who was a loose cannon at times, later became a trusted apostle in the church. He became a man people listened to, looked up to and respected. He was a tremendous example of growth and temperance, accomplished through the pain of his life.

2 Peter 1:5 says: "*And beside this, giving all diligence, add to your faith…*"

Let's stop there for a minute—"*add to your faith…*". Faith means you have trust or confidence in someone or something, but this scripture is saying *add* to your faith. So, I can have trust and confidence in Jesus Christ, the one true God, and it's still not enough? Complete faith in Christ alone is just not going to cut it? Really, Peter? Yet, we hear Peter saying to us all—listen up people! You must help yourselves. You must take advantage of some of the opportunities the Lord has provided for you to learn, opportunities He's provided for you to grow. Even the tough opportunities—even the painful opportunities—they are from Him.

2 Peter 1:5–7: "*And beside this, giving all diligence, add to your faith virtue; and to virtue knowledge; *6*And to knowledge temperance; and to temperance patience; and to patience godliness; *7*And to godliness brotherly kindness; and to brotherly kindness charity.*"

When talking about things like virtue and knowledge and temperance and patience and love, these things don't come easy. Character-based growth and learning experiences are sometimes extremely difficult.

2 Peter 1:8: "*For if these things be in you, and abound, they make you that ye shall neither be barren nor unfruitful in the knowledge of our Lord Jesus Christ.*"

Do you know what barren means? Barren means something or someone is too poor to produce anything. Barrenness is bleak; it is lifeless. We all know those people in our lives. These are the individuals who just seem lifeless. They are not producing anything worth talking about. They are not making any progress in any area of their lives. They have no joy. They have no peace or contentment. Their lives don't seem to be leading to anything. Their existence is bleak—it's unfruitful—it's lifeless. It is barren.

If we can be honest with ourselves right now, it's amazing how often we, too, can find ourselves in this same or a similar situation. We feel like we have no fruit in our lives. We are existing but not really living. We're just going through the motions. We love God with all our hearts, yet there's something about life that's just missing. Have you ever been there before?

Again, 2 Peter 1:8: "*For if these things be in you, and abound (or thrive), they make you that ye shall neither be barren nor unfruitful in the knowledge of our Lord Jesus Christ.*"

It's promised! You are not going to be barren. You are not going to be unfruitful. Peter is saying there are certain ingredients every one of us must pursue in the power of the Spirit. If you add these things to your faith —if you work hard to grow—if you're not passive in your approach to God, it will happen. If you don't just rely on your faith, and instead pursue some of these hard and painful things in your life, you will find effectiveness. You will produce some amazing things for the Kingdom!

I want you to notice how Peter brings together God's work and our responsibility. God calls us, God saves us, God gives us everything we need for life. Yet at the same time, He calls us to act. He calls us to embrace these hard things. He says for this very reason *"…add to your faith…virtue and knowledge and temperance…"* and the list goes on.

These are key ingredients to life. That cornbread isn't going to come out quite right if you don't have certain key ingredients in it. Likewise, leadership won't be as effective without particular ingredients. Many times, these key ingredients come through hard and painful things in our lives. These key ingredients will keep you anchored to the calling and election God has placed before you.

In 2007, I was in the middle of removing some of the unhealthy ingredients in my life. I was in counseling working to overcome my approval addiction and the unforgiveness I carried with me most of my life. I learned how to communicate with my wife more effectively. I truly learned all sorts of things. At that time though, I didn't really understand the big picture of what God was trying to do in my life. It was hard and painful stuff. I knew the Lord was directing me down that road, I just didn't understand it all.

I felt like I was a man after God's heart. I loved God. I gave him my time and my energy and my finances and my resources. I had faith. Still, though, there was something missing. I couldn't put my finger on it, I just knew I was not feeling as complete as scripture said I should be feeling, as complete in Him as I wanted to be. Full of faith, God was leading me on a journey to incorporate some other key ingredients in my life. I was adding to my faith.

I didn't realize it then, yet I can look back on it now and realize God brought me on that journey. He was pruning unwanted things and adding those key ingredients to my life, all for the purpose of learning to love Him and serve Him more effectively. He also wanted me to learn how to love others more effectively. He was shaping me and molding me, preparing me for the tasks ahead of me. I am still on that journey. Sometimes it is still not all pleasant. There are painful things I go through even now and painful things I will go through in the future. It is all for His Kingdom.

It's possible that you have had to endure some pretty horrific things in your childhood or adult life. As I said before, I'm not saying the Lord made you go through those things. However, I can say the Lord is using those things, regardless of what they may be or how they got there. He is using that pain in your life to make you a better man or woman of God for the purpose He has set before you. He is making you a more effective leader.

Before you move forward, I encourage you to spend a few minutes in prayer and reflect on how the Lord is using pain in your life to add to your faith. What key ingredients is He adding to your life to make you an effective leader? When you settle on the answers, write them down and remember He is at work within you!

As you reflect on the key ingredients He has added to your life, we will now begin to look forward at what's to come. Considering where you've been, where is He now taking you? What more does He desire to do in you? What growth opportunities are before you? It could be that you need a better rhythm of life. You may need to see and understand yourself in a greater way. Maybe you understand yourself really well, but don't know how to fully leverage the God-given strengths within you. You may have all of the aforementioned things in order, but you're struggling to build those productive relationships that really make you an effective leader.

This is where *The Christian Leader Blueprint* model comes into play. I encourage you to take some time to review and familiarize yourself with the blueprint diagram before moving forward to Section 1: Establish a Better Rhythm of Life. These are the components that will use the ingredients you are made of today and continue the work within you—the making of an effective leader.

The Christian Leader Blueprint

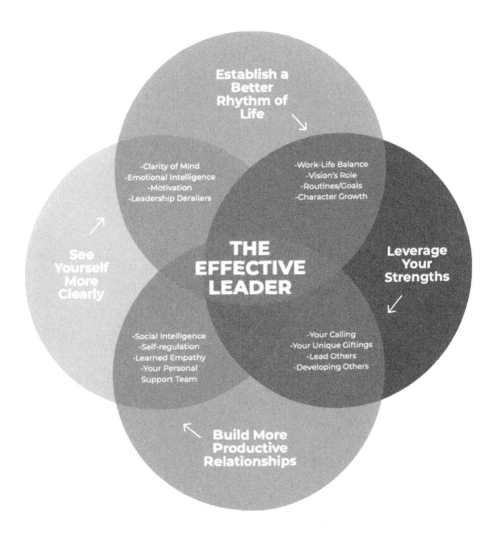

Establish a Better Rhythm of Life

-Clarity of Mind
-Emotional Intelligence
-Motivation
-Leadership Derailers

-Work-Life Balance
-Vision's Role
-Routines/Goals
-Character Growth

See Yourself More Clearly

THE EFFECTIVE LEADER

Leverage Your Strengths

-Social Intelligence
-Self-regulation
-Learned Empathy
-Your Personal Support Team

-Your Calling
-Your Unique Giftings
-Lead Others
-Developing Others

Build More Productive Relationships

Part One

Establish a Better Rhythm of Life

Does life feel chaotic as you keep up with all that is demanded of you? You may be thinking, "My goodness, my life is mayhem." Or you may succeed at various things, but you experience a short period of success before that old emptiness returns to your life. It seems so difficult to keep the big picture in mind while dealing with the general chaos and responsibilities of life. For some reason, it seems like something is missing inside of you. You may feel like you are working harder than you ever have to keep up with the demands of life. The pressure is relentless. There's no space for quality time with family or friends. There's no time for solitude or self. Your life feels too crowded for even God to work.

You may try to be all things to all people and think to yourself, "I'm struggling to find a rhythm in life. There's no balance between work and rest. I feel out of sync." The thought of doing what is necessary to develop a good rhythm in life may sound appealing to you, but you may still have difficulty taking time to do it. In reality, the majority of people who really need to make a change will not take the time needed to create that change. If you are feeling these struggles that I have described, I've got great news for you. Life really doesn't have to be a constant, competitive struggle.

In the following chapters of Part 1, we will dive deeper into these four components that will help you establish a better rhythm of life:

1. Healthy Life Balance

2. Vision's Role in a Leader's Rhythm

3. Effective Routines/Goals for Productivity

4. Grow Your Character

Scripture speaks of abundant life in John 10:10: *"... I am come that they might have life, and that they might have it more abundantly."* If we will commit to working on these four components, I believe that, even in the midst of the various disruptions of life, we are capable of experiencing this abundant life. When there is rhythm in a leader's life, there is usually consistent success evidenced by personal growth and productivity. Ultimately, this rhythm of life leads to greater leadership fulfillment. We will start with healthy life balance, which is one of the most challenging aspects of this rhythm of life.

chapter 3

Healthy Life Balance

✝ Philippians 4:11: *Not that I speak in respect of want: for I have learned, in whatso-ever state I am, therewith to be content.*

Even Jesus shared our same human life struggles, or at least the Gospels seem to suggest that. Rhythm of life was a constant negotiation. In Mark 3:7, Jesus withdrew Himself from the crowds and went out to sea with his disciples. He withdrew Himself with those who were closest to Him to sort of regain His balance in life. This was part of His method of getting back into a good rhythm.

Jesus actually had to "grind through life," kind of like we do. He had demands from people and His "work-life"; and all of these things were pulling at Him. It's evident that it was causing Him to feel a sense of burnout. His answer to all of these internal and external struggles was for Him to simply withdraw to the sea to rest. Jesus knew what brought Him back into rhythm. He knew that life would have chaotic moments, but He also knew what would bring Him back into balance.

Sometimes it can be extremely difficult to live a healthy "balanced" life.

Believe it or not, few people accomplish that feat, especially in a complex and ever-changing world like we live in today. Life is full of chaos. Yet, because of this chaos, it's becoming much more important to learn to create and to manage a healthy rhythm for your life.

When life is in rhythm, there's a persistent and consistent look and feel to it. Have you ever seen a metronome? A metronome is the device that's used by musicians to practice playing to a regular beat. A metronome swings out, sure, but it always swings back in. There's a particular rhythm to it. When we're in a rhythm in life, there's a smooth flow. We sometimes swing out, but we always swing back in—and it feels smooth and purposeful.

It's okay to occasionally get out of rhythm if you're able to eventually come back to the things that keep you in that rhythm; when you swing out and you don't figure out how to come back, you may begin to experience burnout. This can often lead to a feeling of distress in your life. It is important that you guard against getting to this place in life because it will eventually lead to a derailment of what God originally planned for your life.

I did a webinar a while back with a pastor named Dan Reiland, an author and church leadership coach. I've gained wisdom from his leadership blog for over 20 years. There happened to be only about 10 people in attendance, which meant I was able to interact with him and ask him a few personal questions. One of the questions I asked was, "What have you attributed your success to?"

His answer was simple, but it resonated with me in a deep way. He said, "The only way to be successful in this crazy fast-paced world is to properly manage your life-rhythm."

Dan initially introduced me to the metronome example. He said that he finds his rhythm with daily morning prayer and exercise. He said, "If I can get my devotion and exercise in to start my day—every morning—I know that my day with work and family and fun—whatever the day beholds—my day is gonna go well…because it brings all of the parts of my life into rhythm."

He went on to say that his life occasionally gets out of rhythm. If he's in the middle of finishing writing a book, working on a big project, or working on something his church has going on that's out of the norm, he will sometimes swing out of balance. It is okay to be temporarily out of balance at times as long as we can swing back to what keeps us in our rhythm. For Dan, it starts with his daily prayer and exercise.

Think about when you go on vacation. There is nothing balanced about sleeping late, riding amusement park rides all day, or going on a big outdoor adventure. However, it is still okay to go on vacation if afterward you can come back to a normal working rhythm that keeps all parts of your life in sync.

Occasional unbalanced life is permissible if it doesn't burn us out or derail us from what God has planned for us. Ecclesiastes 3:1 says, "*To every thing there is a season, and a time to every purpose under the heaven.*" It's important that we come back to the normal rhythm of healthy life.

Emotional intelligence, which will be covered later in the book, is something that greatly impacts being in sync in life. If you notice, Dan Reiland's sense of rhythm starts with his awareness of what keeps him in sync. Are you self-aware enough to know your strengths, weaknesses, energy levels, and things that can drain you or fill you? When you're tired and stressed, what are those defense mechanisms that raise their heads? Most of us have those blind spots that only show up when we're exhausted. Can you self-regulate when you're having a tough, emotional time or does it throw you into a bad emotional state? This was something I battled with throughout my life until the past few years. Do you know what motivates you? These are things that have the ability to impact our life balance.

In these questions, I'm describing emotional and social intelligence. If you can learn more about yourself, there's no doubt that it will greatly impact the rhythm of your life. When Jesus withdrew from the crowd to be on the sea, this wasn't a cowardly or lazy act. It was His awareness of His own internal makeup. He knew that He needed rest. It was an intentional part of His rhythm.

In the next few sections, I will share with you four major components that will help you create a normal rhythm and an overall healthy life balance.

Before moving on, I encourage you to evaluate yourself with a few questions:

1. What is your greatest frustration right now and what's the source of it?

2. What negative emotional fruit are you seeing in your life and why are you seeing that?

3. How is your work/life balance? Are you getting adequate physical and mental rest? Are you working too many hours?

4. Are your most important relationships—with God, your spouse, and your close friendships—getting adequate attention? If they aren't, ask yourself why.

Work-Life in Rhythm

Work-life balance is the first of the four major components of a healthy life balance. So often, work takes precedence over everything else in our lives. Our personal desire to succeed and do a good job often pushes us to disregard our own well-being and the relationships we value the most. However, if we truly want to experience good productivity and avoid burnout, it's critical that we find a healthy work-life balance. Our physical, emotional, mental, and relational health depend on whether we find this balance.

What is a work-life balance? In short, it is the state of equilibrium between the demands of a person's work or ministry and the demands of their personal life. But it goes beyond this dynamic as a person tries to balance work, rest, play, and worship. Keep in mind, it's not realistic to stay perfectly balanced all the time. Thankfully, we were built with endurance to withstand certain variables, but we must know that there are limits. No matter how hard we push, those limits do not disappear.

Work is a necessity to our livelihood and the balance that we seek to achieve.

Work isn't all good, nor is it all bad. It's really what we personally make of it and how we negotiate through it. Some people make their life about work. They push those limits and sacrifice everything, including their friends and their family. They're driven to achieve money, position, fame, or whatever they may be chasing.

I was driven to achieve in an unhealthy manner at one time in my life. I was a workaholic and allowed work to interfere with the time that was needed to create healthy relationships. My grandfather used to tell me, "Ryan, if you don't work hard, you're never gonna amount to anything." So, what do you think I did? I worked hard. I sacrificed relationships and internal Godly fulfillment to work even harder. This was an unhealthy work mindset that pushed my limits and ultimately led to feelings of emptiness and unhappiness.

Working too hard isn't the only extreme approach to work. Some people are the opposite; they're lazy and struggle to work at all. So, where is the middle ground? What does health look like? Within the various extremes, God calls us to be a good steward of our time and energy resources. He desires for us to be obedient to His Word instead of overly ambitious. And He desires for us to be committed to His cause instead of overly competitive. The result of this biblical mindset is a person who is free to maintain a good rhythm—and who is free to balance work with the other areas of life.

Let's consider a work-life imbalance for a moment. Most leaders generally lean toward being workaholics. We're obsessed with busyness. It's almost like a medication for us. For me, the approval that I received from working hard, for most of my life, was sort of like a drug to me.

So how can you tell if you're a workaholic? Here are some questions you can ask yourself:

1. Is work the primary source of your identity? Is work where you find your value and self-worth?

2. Do you believe that work is good, so the more work you do the better person you are? In other words, do you occasionally "brag" about

how many hours you work in casual conversation?

3. Do you feel that you are not giving the Lord your all unless you push yourself to the point of fatigue? You may have adopted the line that you would "rather burn out than rust out."

4. Will you be judged based on what you have done for the Lord or what He has done for you?

5. Do you control your work, or does it control you?

If you answered "yes" to several of these questions, work is probably a bit out of balance in your life. You're either a workaholic or you're well on your way to becoming one. Here's the problem with this type of mindset: there is often the feeling of a void present. Success in the form of money, position, power, etc. is achieved without experiencing that true, long-lasting fulfillment.

It's been said that the writer of Ecclesiastes may have been a workaholic. Ecclesiastes 2:4-6 says, "*I made me great works; I builded me houses; I planted me vineyards:*[5] *made me gardens and orchards, and I planted trees in them of all kind of fruits:*[6] *made me pools of water, to water therewith the wood that bringeth forth trees.*"

It goes on about work in verses 11, 18, 20, and 23. If he wasn't a workaholic, he was certainly an overachiever. However, listen to verse 22, "*For what hath man of all his labour, and of the vexation of his heart, wherein he hath laboured under the sun?*" He's basically saying that all of the work he did was meaningless! Can you believe that? He had tons of successes in life, but he didn't have true fulfillment.

There was something missing. There's not enough success, power, or wealth in the world to satisfy a heart's longing for relationships. At the core of work, the writer in Ecclesiastes was looking for this exact fulfillment. I guess you could say he was experiencing a relational nutrient deficiency. A person may struggle with self-deception and rationalize this unbalance or deficiency for the good of his family, but in the end there's always a sense of emptiness. It creates a longing for a balance and a life that's in rhythm.

According to his blog, Dr. James Dobson, founder of Focus on the Family, said the number one marriage killer is busyness and overcommitment.[6] I believe this statement represents all significant relationships in our lives. The bottom line is when we worship our work—even good work like ministry—at the sacrifice of everything else, it gets us out of rhythm and we're setting ourselves up for devastating losses in our personal relationships. Unbalanced work steals time and energy that's meant for relationships in your life. Relationships require time for communication and for closeness; therefore, unhealthy work balance is usually consistent with unhealthy relationships in a person's life.

Ask yourself this question: Are you living the kind of work-life that'll leave you fulfilled in the most important area of your life, the area of relationships? If you're not, you've got to get honest with yourself today. What can you change this week to move closer to a healthy rhythm in your work-life so you can be in rhythm in other areas of your life as well?

A Rhythm of Rest

As our work-life comes into more balance and healthiness, we are able to move into a better rhythm of rest. The first thing we need to remember about rest is that it was God's idea to begin with. God invented it and He called it the Sabbath. It's a biblical principle and God's gift of rest. To clarify, rest is more than just sleep. Rest is a time when we sort of push life's demands aside for a moment and we remember who we really are. It could be a few minutes of solitude in a hectic day. It could be a time when we just pause in the crazy busyness of life and reflect on something good in the past. Rest helps to clear our minds and restore our physical being. Rest renews our emotional and

6   James Dobson, "12 Marriage Killers," Dr. James Dobson Family Institute, August 29, 2015, https://www.drjamesdobson.org/blogs/12-marriage-killers.

spiritual energy.

When we make the decision not to rest, we're not only draining our physical energy, but also risking our spiritual and emotional wholeness as well. Exodus 34:21 says, "*Six days thou shalt work, but on the seventh day thou shalt rest: in earing time and in harvest thou shalt rest.*" During biblical times, the plowing season and harvest time were critical to the life cycle of that culture. Just one missed day could mean the difference in feast and famine for those people. However, God said that even in the harvest season, they must rest. It is evident that God designed humanity with limitations and the need for rest.

Do you feel physically and emotionally drained on a regular basis? There's a good chance you have exceeded your limits and you must admit that you can't do everything. We all need to understand the blessings and limitations of the gifts God has given us to lead our churches and organizations. We must learn to live within our emotional and our physical limits. Like budgeting finances, we can learn to budget our emotional, spiritual, and physical resources as well. Despite what some people may assume, there's not an endless supply of those resources within us. If you give out more than you take in, you can become overdrawn. However, if we budget our rest well, then we'll move closer to a life that's in rhythm and we'll be able to make regular deposits. We'll return to our public-life duties each day with renewed energy and effectiveness.

Just as when He and His disciples retreated, Jesus knew when He needed time to rest. We, also, need to learn to retreat when it's time. This will allow us to experience that renewing power of God in our lives. The Lord gave us the responsibility to be good stewards of our lives—body, soul, and spirit. This starts with learning to care for our own bodies.

Let's talk about sleep for a moment. According to *Huffington Post* founder, Arianna Huffington, in *The Sleep Revolution*, scientists are confirming there is an intense neurological renewal and cleansing that happens while we sleep.[7]

---

7   Arianna Huffington, *The Sleep Revolution: Transforming Your Life, One Night at a Time* (New York: Harmony Books, 2017), 17.

She goes on to say that the right amount of sleep enhances the quality of the hours we spend awake. Despite what some people may think, sleep is not an empty, wasted time.

Inadequate sleep can easily get us out of rhythm in other areas of life as well. How much sleep do you need to feel rested? How much sleep do you need so you don't feel tired and fatigued all the time? Most people need seven to eight hours of sleep a night. If we fail to get those seven to eight hours of sleep regularly, we will eventually end up in a place of fatigue. Then, fatigue can easily lead to failure in other areas of our lives.

There are two major barriers when it comes to getting rest or being rested. The first hindrance is psychological. Most people subconsciously think of rest as a waste of time or a weakness. Productivity, for many people, is a coping mechanism for life's anxieties. They go to bed late, get up early, and run hard all day long. The second hindrance is lifestyle. Many people overextend and overcommit themselves. They continually pack events and obligations into their days to a point that it's almost impossible to have adequate, good-quality rest. Though there are legitimate busy times in life, we often can choose to eliminate some things and not seriously affect our overall productivity and satisfaction.

In today's culture, work has become a god, and rest is God's answer to that. It's a counterbalance designed to protect us from the dangers of physical exhaustion, stress overload, relational alienation, and all sorts of other issues. Life is renewed day by day by the rhythm of rest. It's renewed by silence, solitude, reflection, mini-vacations, close friends in our lives, time with God, AND deep sleep. These things renew us day by day. Isaiah 40:31 says, "*But they that wait upon the LORD shall renew their strength; they shall mount up with wings as eagles; they shall run, and not be weary; and they shall walk, and not faint.*" Healthy life balance requires rest. With a good work-life balance and a rhythm of rest, it also gives us the time and energy to effectively manage a rhythm of play.

A Rhythm of Play

When people struggle to balance the first two components of work and rest, it will usually lead to an unhealthy or nonexistent rhythm of play. Rhythm of play is the third major component of life that is required for a healthy life balance. Play is simply engaging in activity for the purpose of fun and recreation.

Of the four components, play is the one that I have personally struggled with the most. I've had an unhealthy perspective toward play for most of my life. I have not made adequate time for it. In fact, I've often felt guilt during or after my times of engaging in fun things. Because of our work-oriented society, play often receives a bad reputation. Most of us are geared for production, and we've talked ourselves into believing that even our play must make us more productive. I know this because I have personally had this mindset most of my life. I was taught this concept throughout my childhood, and I still struggle with this problem today.

As I mentioned earlier, my grandfather was one of the most respected voices in my life growing up. After his passing, as I grieved and processed, I realized that he instilled a concept in me at a very early age that affected my ability to engage in a healthy, rhythm of play. I have often reflected back on the statement I mentioned earlier, "Ryan, you'll never amount to anything if you don't work hard." I know he meant well, and I believe we all need to work hard. The message of this statement, however, made me believe that my self-worth was somehow attached to how hard I worked versus how little I played.

After this realization, I became aware that I didn't even really know how to put all work aside and simply play. All of my play had to be linked to productivity in some way. I love to hunt, but I'm not sure I ever truly enjoyed the hobby in the past for what it was—a hobby! I can remember coming home after a morning hunt and experiencing a negative, depressive feeling. I didn't realize then, but I know now that this feeling was linked to my lack of productivity with how I was spending my time. I wasn't giving myself permission to simply play; I felt that I always had to be productive. It's important to understand that for fun activities to be considered play, there must be no goal in mind.

The intended goal of play is, simply, to be ourselves and enjoy ourselves. We may have some physical or emotional benefits from our play, but that's not the goal of play—only a consequence of it. Jesus was very focused on His work and His mission (John 9:4), but even Jesus knew He needed to play and have fun. In fact, He socialized with people so much that the religious leaders accused Him of shirking His responsibilities. Jesus realized rest and pleasure were necessary for a successful, balanced life. He modeled it with His life, and He wants us to experience this as well. Nothing eliminates enjoyment more quickly than a guilty conscience; therefore, it is important you maintain the mindset of play as a necessary priority in maintaining a good, healthy life balance.

When the motivation for play becomes competitive, a means to reach a goal—or something other than fun—play becomes work. Consider the woman who loves photography as a hobby. She is hired to take family pictures and photograph weddings. The quality of her work is so good that she eventually finds herself shooting a wedding nearly every weekend and her evenings are filled with family photo shoots. On the days when she is not taking photos, she spends hours editing. The woman even becomes dependent on the income to help support her spending habits. Suddenly, the hobby that she once loved is now like a second job that drains her energy. At this point, the hobby that she used to do for fun is no longer fun. If your play becomes work, it's important that you find another source of play.

Proverbs 17:22 teaches us, *"A merry heart doeth good like a medicine: but a broken spirit drieth the bones."* Balance in play is like medicine in your life. It will allow you to face the other areas of life that are difficult and stressful. Play has the ability to renew your mind and spirit.

I was working recently when my son, Neil, asked me to play football with him. I was deep in thought and wanted to continue working, but I considered the reality that in a few years I'll long to have these moments back. This phase of his life is going by in the blink of an eye. I stopped what I was doing and I went to play football. We even talked my daughter, Olivia, into coming out to play with us! Before long, we were engrossed in a family football game, making a tremendous occasion to remember, and all because I stopped my work for a moment and simply played.

Do you create routine opportunities in your life for play? We must realize that God wants us to have fun. He designed it as a vital part of the rhythm and revitalization of life, and it's often on the field of play that many of our key relationships are made or rekindled. There's a time and a season in which we need to simply enjoy life. I encourage you to get intentional with creating those fun times in your life.

The next component, a rhythm of worship, brings all four components of a healthy life balance together. Without worship, the components of work, rest, and play are deficient in creating that balance. As a Christian leader, worship becomes a necessity. Read on for more explanation.

A Rhythm of Worship

Worship is the fourth and final component to a healthy rhythm and balance of a leader's life. Though it's listed as the "fourth" component, it shouldn't be considered any less important. In fact, I would consider it to be the most important. Worship is personal prayer and devotion as well as gathering with a body of believers and giving glory and honor to God. Worship can take place in many ways, but for the purpose of this book, I want to accentuate the fact that worship is essentially enjoying the wonder of life with God and with others.

A personal relationship with Jesus will allow you to maintain a certain level of rhythm in your life despite your circumstances or imbalances in other areas. When life is grueling and oppressive, you can still rest in the knowledge that Christ will never leave you or forsake you. Matthew 28:20 says, "*...I am with you always, even unto the end of the world.*"

Genesis 32:30 says, "...*for I have seen God face to face, and my life is preserved.*" This scripture shows the foundation of worship, which is seeing God face to face so that our lives are preserved. Worship includes many things, but at its core it's the cry of our hearts for the Creator. It is the expression of reverence for our God. Without worship in our lives, we will never have true rhythm. We will continue to experience feelings of emptiness and insignificance. We can achieve all the money in the world, the perfect family situation, a great balance of work, rest, and play, but if you don't have a relationship with Jesus, your life will always be a bit out of rhythm.

When we enter a relationship with God, He gives us the capacity for abundant life. Without Him, however, we can never truly have it. The reality of abundant life happening is our responsibility. Preacher and author Richard Exley has written, "Abundant Life...is both a gift and a discipline."[8]

I can remember as a 16-year-old kid sitting behind a closed muffler business on the tailgate of my new-to-me truck. I was smoking a cigarette with one of my closest friends before we finished the drive to school one morning. I had just had a life-changing experience with God a few days before in a church service, and the conviction of the lifestyle I was living was pressing in on me. I remember throwing that cigarette down and telling my friend that I couldn't live that life anymore. From that day forward, I committed to worshipping God. I began a journey of service to the Kingdom of God that eventually led to my love for leadership. I've made many mistakes since then, but I determined in my mind to live a life of worship to Jesus Christ every single day.

When we have a daily rhythm of worship in our lives, we are allowed to forget ourselves for a little while and simply remember who God is. Think about these questions: How do you approach God? Are you approaching Him authentically, in the right way with the right things? Are you giving Him

---

8 Richard Exley, *Living in Harmony: Moving to a Better Place in Your Life* (Green Forest: New Leaf Publishing Group, 2003), 106.

your best religious voice that you can muster up, or are you talking to Him like He's your best friend? Your answers to those questions will probably reveal how you truly perceive God. Your answers determine whether you're just checking the box of a religious lifestyle or you truly long for a deep, personal communion and relationship with God.

If you find yourself checking the boxes of devotion as a Christian leader, I want to encourage you to make a shift today and develop a true relationship with Christ, where you know God personally and intimately. The result of such a relationship is a much greater rhythm of life for you and a supernatural power to endure through the tough things in life and leadership. Be real, transparent, and vulnerable with God.

God is present in all of life. Even in the toughest experiences, we can find opportunities for worship unto God. Worship is an act of faith. It renews us and helps us overcome the most challenging circumstances. I want you to take a moment now and think about the small moments that give life its greatest meaning. Think about how all of those small moments pull you into worship.

In what ways do you enjoy worship? I love spending time in prayer in the sanctuary at my church. I usually pray at home most mornings, but when I get to the church, I spend another 45 minutes to an hour praying in our sanctuary. I usually enter into that time of prayer with thanksgiving and praise, eventually transitioning into worship. These are grounding moments in my day for me. They anchor me while still helping me move in the right direction. It seems like no matter how my day starts, I know that if I can experience that short time of worship before work, everything will flow so much smoother throughout my day. I feel the presence of God, and it brings a rhythm to my life and my day like nothing else can. I'm so thankful for those moments.

Referring to the book of Ecclesiastes, it was written by King Solomon who had succeeded with wealth, power, and fame; he had it all. At first glance, Ecclesiastes appears to be a book about the meaninglessness of life, but a deeper look shows that the author of Ecclesiastes found God and His blessings in the midst of reality. The author longed for peace and comfort but couldn't find it in the riches of this world. His search led him to a deep yearning for God. We also have this same deep yearning inside of us, and nothing will satisfy it except the power of the Holy Ghost in our lives.

Isaiah 2:8 tells us, *"Their land also is full of idols; they worship the work of their hands, that which their own fingers have made…"*. When chaos interrupts our lives, we get out of rhythm and begin to wander aimlessly. Our human flesh tends to drift toward idols and the work of our own hands. Humanity did this in the Bible, and we do it today. We can easily become selfish in our motives and lose focus for whom we are serving. We can begin seeking fortune and fame, and the only sure way to combat the temptations of life is to worship God every single day.

I want you to consider this question: What do you need to do today, tomorrow, this week to make sure that you include worship as a daily part of your leadership rhythm? I imagine that some ideas have already come to mind; but, as I told you once before, if you truly want to transform your life, you must be willing to make the needed changes. I know you have what it takes deep inside to establish a tremendous, healthy life balance with work, rest, play, and worship.

Because worship is a spiritual matter, I would like to end this topic with a simple prayer. Here's my prayer for you and me:

Lord, I thank You for Your presence that I feel today as I write this content. You've always been the reliable anchor in my life that keeps me stable while helping me move in the right direction. You keep me focused on the things in my life that are necessary for rhythm. Lord, I pray for the person reading this book. I pray that you allow us to live within the freedom of our limits, biblical limits that ground us and protect us from doing harm to ourselves and others. I pray, Jesus, that You give us the necessary fortitude to make significant changes in our lives in the areas of work, rest, play, and worship. Give us self-awareness as well as the energy to reestablish a healthy life balance. In Jesus' name I pray.

Even with a healthy balance of work, rest, play, and worship, we must embrace the fact that chaotic times will come. Circumstances will still get tough and create challenges as we attempt to navigate through life and leadership. In this next section, I want to share with you some tips to care for yourself during those chaotic times. Effective coping is necessary if we truly want to be effective leaders.

How to Care for Yourself First When Chaos Comes

What is the worst chaos you've ever been through in your life? Go ahead. Think about it. The thing that comes to your mind is probably something that was incredibly tough and life altering. No matter how healthy our life balance seems to be, we are not exempt from chaos arising in our personal and professional life. You may be going through circumstances right now that feel like the toughest thing you've ever been through. Over the past few years, we've all been impacted by the effects of COVID-19, sicknesses, deaths, the economy, and other life changes. The list could go on and on. These challenges impact our routines, our character, our responses, and yes, even our faith in God.

This is simply our reality. We all go through things. I know you could tell a story of some major chaos that disrupted your life at some point. You could probably tell of a time when you didn't know how you were going to get through some circumstance; yet here you are. You are making time to read this. You made it through. Give yourself a pat on the back. In this section, I want to give you tips that will help you learn how to go through those really tough things in life—not just make it through them, but successfully navigate through them in a timely manner.

What we thought was a temporary disruption in March of 2020 quickly became a way of life, at least for the foreseeable future. We kept thinking things were going to get back to normal, only to realize our lives were forever changed. In fact, people became more divided as the months went by on what was right and what was wrong concerning masks, vaccinations, and many present world issues. For leaders, people were divided on how the church or organizations should be structured and operated. These created a deep sense of emotional weariness and physical fatigue that people experienced as they realized there was not an end in sight to our circumstances. It was exhausting and discouraging.

I later realized that not everything was bad. Our churches certainly helped people through the increased anxiety in their lives as they sought answers to the chaos. We now have some tremendous stories of life changes. However, many people had—and are possibly still having—to endure incredible hardship because of the world's chaos.

We're living in difficult times, the most difficult times of my 40-plus years of life. But I want to give you a few things that have helped me deal with the difficulties that we encounter in leadership—tips that I hope will offer you some light at the end of your tunnel if you are currently enduring chaos that is disrupting your healthy life balance. If you're one of the few that rarely feel stressed, you may still want to take notes because stress and chaos will eventually come. Life is full of surprises.

I was surprised the first time I got on a plane after the COVID pandemic began. I had not flown for almost a year and several flight policies had changed to adapt to the world's circumstances. You'll never guess what the flight attendant told me! She said, "Sir, just sit down and shut up!" Can you believe that?

I'm kidding! The flight attendant didn't say that. If you've ever flown, you know exactly what she said. "In the event of an emergency, you must put on your own oxygen mask first before you can help anyone else."

As a frequent flier, I sometimes get annoyed by hearing this over and over. However, there is so much wisdom in that statement. Life is not a sprint, it's a marathon. If you want to go the distance and live life well no matter what chaos comes your way, you've got to take care of yourself first.

Perhaps you might say, "But, Ryan, scripture speaks of serving others, helping the less fortunate, delivering the Gospel at all costs." You're right. Life is about all of those things; but if you don't help yourself first—if you don't put your own oxygen mask on first—you're likely not going to be present to be the servant that the Lord has called you to be. You need to help yourself so that you can help others. Helping yourself is a means to an end, not an end in itself. I help myself so that I can serve others. I seek a healthy life balance so that I can be an effective leader in the Kingdom of God.

During the first year of COVID, I read a blog post by Dan Reiland that listed the five signs of being over-stressed. I have seen myself in each of these five things many times in my life. In fact, I think I've experienced all five at the same time on several occasions. I want you to evaluate your life through Dan's list:

1. Sleep doesn't bring you rest. You sleep, but you wake up tired.

2. Play doesn't bring you joy. Vacation doesn't work anymore; you feel like you still need a vacation when you get back from what was supposed to be a restful vacation.

3. Work doesn't bring you significant results. You work really hard, but it's just not moving the ball. Your work is not productive.

4. Prayer doesn't bring you peace. Even when you attempt to give your burdens to the Lord, you keep carrying them. You can't seem to let those burdens go.

5. Relationships don't bring you a sense of fulfillment. You have time with friends, but you still feel disconnected from people (this is a prominent one that I see regularly with pastors and Christian leaders).[9]

---

9   Dan Reiland, "5 Ways to Invest in Your Soul Care," Dan Reiland: The Pastor's Coach, accessed November 28, 2022, https://danreiland.com/5-ways-to-invest-in-your-soul-care/.

I want you to think about these statements. How many of them are you seeing in your life? Is it one or several or maybe all of these things? I know I've personally experienced all of these issues at one time or another in my life, and I've recently experienced a couple of them. I've been there.

Jesus said in Matthew 11:28–30, "*Come unto me, all ye that labour and are heavy laden, and I will give you rest.* [29] *Take my yoke upon you, and learn of me; for I am meek and lowly in heart: and ye shall find rest unto your souls.* [30] *For my yoke is easy, and my burden is light.*"

If your yoke is hard—if you're regularly carrying unnecessary burdens in your life—there's no way you can be an effective Christian leader. Today, if you're not serious about putting your oxygen mask on first, you can forget about helping others for the long haul because the burden and the weight we're carrying is much too heavy.

How, then, can you put your oxygen mask on first? One good way is to create margin in your life. In simple terms, margin is your breathing room. It's the difference between your limits and your responsibilities. Margin allows us to have space in our day so that we're not stressed and worn out all of the time. In the event of an unexpected opportunity or emergency, we'll have the space and capacity to respond to those things. It's necessary that you put the most important things in your life first and guard them from those least important things. If daily devotion is important to you, and it really should be, do it first. If church or small groups are important to you, put them in first. Once you put the most important things in, be sure to add margin next. Treat margin likes it's one of the "most important things."

Another way to put on your oxygen mask first is to grieve your losses. If you live a normal leadership life, you are routinely and consistently experiencing losses. We may experience the loss of people, the loss of what is normal, the loss of jobs, the loss of relationships, the loss of health, and even at times the lack of progress in life and leadership. When chaos hits, many times some form of loss will come.

I want you to sit for a minute or two and think about some of the losses you've experienced in the past few years of life. I want you to bring some awareness to those losses. At one time in my life, I did a terrible job of grieving my losses, and those emotions built up until I began to experience feelings of burnout. Many other negative emotions also came to the surface. I've learned that it's extremely important to grieve my losses as I go.

When I feel those negative emotions arise, I know I've got to figure out what's going on inside of me. I realize it may sound odd to some, but when we are grieving, it's important we admit that a loss really does hurt and that we're sad. We must remain honest with ourselves. No human alive is immune to the grieving process, especially leaders who intend to live healthily. We must grieve and experience that sadness, and when it lifts, we can move on with life. We can't, however, push the grieving away or medicate the impact of that grief. We have to embrace it. We have to grieve our losses, and that's part of putting on our own oxygen masks first.

If you're struggling with grieving the losses in your life, I want to encourage you to find a professional who can help you. It's so very important for your emotional and physical health. I also want to encourage you to give yourself permission to take care of yourself first. These are extremely tough times in which we're living and leading. There is much chaos around us. Give yourself permission to take care of yourself first—because if you take care of yourself first, you'll be able to successfully endure difficult times and have the energy to serve others around you. Eventually, life will swing back to a place of joy and fulfillment.

How to Enjoy Life in the Present

Thankfully, life is not always chaotic. There should be times of balance and success as well, which, hopefully, is the rule and not the exception to the rule for you. As leaders, even when things are not chaotic, we often either don't know how to enjoy life or are so driven to succeed that we struggle to enjoy life in the present.

Enjoying life in the present is something I struggled with until the last couple of years. I believe there are many leaders who struggle with the same thing. One of the reasons I struggled with this issue is that I was driven by the future as well as my tendency toward prudence and productivity. These qualities motivated me to move forward every day at the expense of living in the present moment. I would struggle to enjoy the process of the work that I was doing. If it was a project that took weeks or months, I would go to work on that project with focus and persistence. On many occasions I would struggle to slow down and enjoy the moment as well as the people I had the privilege of working with.

I had tunnel vision at times, and I would work hard to accomplish the tasks I was responsible for. I experienced an artificial high when I completed a task and looked back at what I had accomplished, but then I would crash emotionally. I hate to say it, but I was addicted to the thrill of getting the job done. I failed to realize just how important it was for me to slow down and enjoy the relationships in my life. I struggled with focusing on each step of the process of my work and the pleasure of interacting with the people of God.

One time, my executive coach told me that I live in a world of structure that doesn't exist for anyone else. That has stuck with me for years now. He was trying to tell me that the unhealthy use of my God-given ability to have vision and prudence to work toward that vision really gave me no quality of life at all. I was missing the big picture of what scripture shows as a successful life. My work ethic was interfering with my ability to love like I should.

1 Corinthians 13:1–3 says, "*Though I speak with the tongues of men and of angels, and have not (love), I am become as sounding brass, or a tinkling cymbal.² And though I have the gift of prophecy, and understand all mysteries, and all knowledge; and though I have all faith, so that I could remove mountains, and have not (love), I am nothing.³ And though I bestow all my goods to feed the poor, and though I give my body to be burned, and have not (love), it profiteth me nothing.*"

If we don't have the love of Christ or the love of people in our lives or the ability to slow down our incessant need to accomplish things, even good things, we will eventually deteriorate the very relationships that bring us the most biblical fulfillment.

My coach told me that I had to soften that drive within me so that I could begin to implement balance. Balance is what helps me slow down and mentally process what is going on around me. It helps me enjoy what I am doing each day and allows me to minister to the people that may cross my path. The process of finding balance was hard for me, but it was important for long-term fulfillment.

There's also another side to this issue which I've experienced in another season of my life. Despite my tendency to dream about the future and to work toward my vision, there have actually been times when I didn't have a clue about the future, and I struggled for direction and vision.

I can remember, several years ago, praying for direction in the prayer room of our church. I cried out to the Lord because I felt like I was just waking up every morning, living my life, taking care of kids, working at my job, earning a paycheck, going through the motions of life while doing my best to live in the present. Although that wasn't necessarily a bad thing, I felt miserable inside because I knew there was more to life. I was living so much in the present that there was no excitement for the future. I didn't have anything good to work toward; my life felt mundane, and I felt lost. I really needed vision for my life. Perhaps you're thinking, "Okay, Ryan, what are you trying to tell me?" I'm trying to tell you that if you find yourself in either of these circumstances where you're so busy working toward your vision that you aren't living in the moment or you're miserable because you're not working toward anything, something must change if you desire to have long-lasting fulfillment in your life.

The key to enjoying life in the present is having balance between those two extremes. There's a sweet spot where you strive to accomplish a God-given vision for your life in a healthy way while living in the present, enjoying each moment. Though it may feel impossible at times, it is possible to have both. Let me give you a few steps to take so that you can find a balance between both.

Step 1: Discover a God-given vision for your life.

Proverbs 29:18 says, *"Where there is no vision, the people perish."* It is critical that we find something in our future to work toward. Vision is so important for motivation and fulfillment in life. If you have no vision, you're not going to enjoy life. I will cover this in much more detail in the next section. Even if you feel that you have vision, I encourage you to read that portion of the book and review the vision for your life.

Also, let me warn you that not everyone is good at forward thinking; not everyone has that gift. If you struggle with this area of your life after reading that section, be sure to find help from someone, such as an executive coach, mentor, or capable peer.

Step 2: Enjoy the moment.

How do you enjoy the moment? There are many ways, but here's the way I do it. First, every week when I do my "Start of the Week Sight" (see Chapter 5—Effective Routines/Goals for Productivity for more details), I ask myself this question: What successes did I have in the previous week? Then, I slow down and thank God for what's been accomplished. For the times when I don't have a strong answer to that question, I celebrate the fact that I was okay with having a slower, more restful week.

Another thing I do to help me live in the moment and enjoy each day is to meditate each morning during prayer. I sit in the presence of the Lord and reflect on what's going on in my life. I give God the opportunity to speak into my life as I give Him my full attention.

Last, as I previously mentioned, I try to live my life with margin. This isn't possible all the time, but I try not to cram my life so full that I can't be there if someone important in my life needs me or wants to talk to me. Because I am so structured, I have to force myself to take time for those key relationships in my life. For help with margin, refer to Chapter 5—Effective Routines/Goals for Productivity.

Step 3: Find balance.

It is important that you find balance between establishing your vision for the future and enjoying the moment. When you find this balance, or that sweet spot, it's amazing how fully you can enjoy life in the present.

When you enjoy life in the present, you can begin to live life in a healthy and fulfilled way, and that's exactly where I want to be. In our next chapter, we'll explore the topic of vision that can help give us motivation to pursue this healthy life balance. It's a critical part of establishing a better rhythm of life.

chapter 4

Vision's Role in a
Leader's Rhythm

✝ Proverbs 29:18: *Where there is no vision, the people perish: but he that keepeth the law, happy is he.*

To generate the motivation needed for a good rhythm of life and healthy work-life balance, it's imperative to clearly define what you're working toward. If you want or need something to change in your life but don't have a vision for how to implement that change or what the end result will be once you make the change, the likelihood of you accomplishing your goal is minimal. If you don't have an intentional vision for your life, you will probably struggle to have a healthy rhythm or God-centered life.

Proverbs 29:18 says, *"Where there is no vision, the people perish."* Where there is no dream, no revelation, no sense of our created purpose, there's no passion to live life abundantly and do purposeful work. People with no vision struggle living beyond their everyday responsibilities of life. You and I were made for so much more!

Vision shouldn't be confused with a person's calling and gifting, which we'll discuss more in Part 3. Calling is the purpose or reason an individual exists. A person's gifting is the lens through which that purpose is projected into the world. Finally, vision is the ability to imagine a future that doesn't yet exist. When a person's calling and giftings come together, the individual can better align with a vision that's true to him or her. In essence, a vision is what will make the difference in defining the necessary rhythm for your life.

Find Your God-Given Vision for Life

In your final years, I hope you can look back on a life well lived. I want you to close your eyes for a moment. Imagine that you're 90 years old, sitting in your recliner thinking about all of the years you've lived. You ask yourself, "Did I do anything significant? Did my life really matter? What did I live for? Did I fulfill what the Lord wanted me to do? Why was it important that I live my life?" The Lord isn't going to force you to find your calling or His vision for your life. He's not going to twist your arm or stand over you until you make a move, waiting for you to fulfill His will. I want you to think about this truth: The decisions you're making right now are creating the answers to those questions that you'll answer at the end of your life and will determine whether you've lived life well.

I don't want you to have to sit in your recliner when you're 90 and question your effectiveness. You were created by an intentional God who saw purpose for your life. In Psalm 139:14–16, David wrote, *"I will praise thee; for I am fearfully and wonderfully made: marvellous are thy works; and that my soul knoweth right well.*[15] *My substance was not hid from thee, when I was made in secret, and curiously wrought in the lowest parts of the earth.*[16] *Thine eyes did see my substance..."* God created *you* with a divine vision. Even in your mother's womb, God knew you, and He knew what He wanted your life to be like.

If He's really such a purposeful God, what is His vision for your life? That's the big question that so many are wrestling with today. Most people simply move through life hoping they'll find that vision in time. They don't know what the plan is; they simply wake up each day accomplishing whatever they see to do. Although there's a bit of success even in that, you don't need to stop there. There's so much more left for you to accomplish. You can live your life on purpose and strategically fulfill your God-given vision.

The wisest man on Earth, King Solomon, said in Proverbs 29:18, *"Where there is no vision, the people perish."* You may not literally perish if you don't access your vision, but you will suffer emotionally. Without a God-given vision, your life will be dull, and you'll lack passion to pursue the life God intends for you to live. With vision, you can have energy, motivation, endurance, and joy. John 10:10 summarizes this point, *"I am come that they might have life, and that they might have it more abundantly."* What has the Lord uniquely designed *you* to do?

To illustrate what a focused vision will do for a leader, I'll share a unique story of a church. As a person born into this church, I've witnessed the last 40 years of this story myself. In July of 1950, evangelist G. A. Mangun and his wife, Vesta, pulled into Alexandria, LA. They began pastoring and leading a group of about 40 people at what was then called the First Pentecostal Church of Alexandria (now called The Pentecostals of Alexandria, POA). G. A. Mangun had a clear vision. He wasn't just dedicated to the cause, but he was sold out to prayer and fasting. His life's vision was simply to reach the people of Alexandria with the Gospel message. Within six short years, the church multiplied beyond what was ever expected. Over 280 people attended the church.[10]

Through the 1960s and '70s, the church experienced astronomical change and growth, but there still remained one purpose, one drive, and one vision. Anthony Mangun, G. A. Mangun's son, became the pastor of POA in the 1980s and remained focused and passionate about continuing that same vi-

---

10 "Our Story," The Pentecostals of Alexandria, accessed January 5, 2023, https://www.poa. church/our-story.

sion. As a result of that vision, the church today has a membership role of thousands of people and has had a life-changing impact on many thousands more around the world.[11]

I had the tremendous privilege of working around Bishop G. A. at POA in his last few years of life. I can still remember passing him in the hallways. I would usually see him coming from the prayer room when he would often tell me his famous words, "Don't look to the left, and don't look to the right." This was his way of saying, "Don't get distracted with the things around you. Just keep moving forward to accomplish the vision the Lord has called you to do."

God has a vision for *your* life! When you discover it, I promise it will make all the difference in your motivation, energy, and rhythm as you accomplish something significant. Just imagine what you'll be able to achieve! Now that we've talked about the importance of having this vision, I'm going to offer some practical tips that you can follow to bring clarity to that vision.

Assessments are one method of delving into your personality and giving you a clearer understanding of how God designed you. This is one of the easiest and fastest ways to begin to bring clarity to the vision that God has for your life. Not everyone has the opportunity to take an assessment because of finances or other personal reasons, so I'm going to give you a few helpful suggestions that are more organic and practical.

1. Calling/Motivation

The Lord has placed something unique within you. It's what drives you. It's what motivates you. It's what gets you up every day. It's the calling within you (see Chapter 11—Discover Your Calling). I want you to take a few minutes and think about what motivates and drives you. What feels rewarding to you? What subject keeps you up at night because you can't get it off your mind? What do you need in your life in order to be happy and fulfilled?

It's interesting how many people don't tune-in to their natural motivations,

---

11 Ibid.

but those motivations are there for a reason (see Chapter 9—Understand Your Motivation). The unique circumstances in your life, your DNA, your childhood, your family of origin, and other factors shape this within you. When you are determining God's vision for your life, give adequate time to thinking about your motivations and calling.

2. Gifting (Strengths)

Romans 12:6 says, *"Having then gifts differing according to the grace that is given to us..."* The word "differing" in this scripture means different and excellent. We all have unique gifts that are needed in the Kingdom of God. I'm speaking of gifts in respect to the natural strengths that God has given you for the purpose of serving others.

Most people usually have some remote idea of their strengths and weaknesses, but it's often difficult to confirm and build confidence in them. There are a variety of online assessments available to help identify strengths, but I want to give you a few questions you can ask yourself that may help you organically narrow those down.

When considering your weaknesses, what are the things you wish you could give up? What drains you and leaves you feeling empty? We all do things we don't enjoy for the sake of our jobs, but the things that completely expend you are the things that you want to try to move away from as much as possible.

There are many other questions I could ask you, but spend considerable time thinking about this: What parts of your work do you enjoy the most and do the best? What kinds of activities make you the happiest? What types of tasks would you secretly enjoy doing that you've never had the chance to do in your church or organization? If you were to ask those closest to you what they think you do best, what would they say?

Hopefully, as you wrestle with some of these questions, you will better understand your strengths and weaknesses. Although we want to acknowledge our weaknesses enough to not harm others or the organization in which we serve, we maximize our efforts when we pour our time, energy, and growth into our strengths.

3. Your Personal History

What have you gone through in life? What hardships have you faced? What education do you have? What jobs have you worked? What has the Lord equipped you for as you've journeyed through life? There's probably a reason you've endured some of the things you've gone through.

Your calling in life is the motivation, the purpose, or the reason you exist. Your gifting is your strengths. It's the lens through which that purpose is projected into the world. Your personal history is the training ground that has equipped you to best use those gifts and fulfill your calling.

Your vision for life comes when your calling, gifting, and personal history collide. Those three subjects point to the sweet spot in life. They'll help determine how your calling and gifting is manifested into the world. They are the projected image of what's to come. Vision should only be considered through the lens of prayer and fasting, but the more you pay attention to the calling of God, the gifts that He's given you, and the personal history that He's allowed you to live, the better you're able to align to the God-given vision that's true to you.

I have one final exercise for this section to get you started. Prayerfully ask yourself this question based on your calling, your gifting, and your personal history: "In a perfect world, what do I want my life and ministry to look like in the next three to five years?" Write down a detailed answer to this question and write it in present tense as if you're already living it. Using your imagination, think about what you want each area of your life to look like. What are you seeing? What are you feeling? What are you hearing? Get specific, get prayerful, and start writing down the God-centered vision for your life. Don't let perfection stifle your progress. The more specific you can be with your thoughts, the better. Once you determine your answer to this question, you'll have a better understanding of God's vision for your life.

After you've written down your dreams and desires, edit and modify what you've written—regularly. Keep in mind that this vision is never actually settled. As the months and years go by, things are going to change. Perspectives will change. Revelation will change. Awareness will change. Don't be afraid to tweak and adjust this vision as you live your life.

Learn How to Give Vision to Your Week

Vision is not just beneficial for years down the road. It's important to have vision for the shorter timeframes of your life as well. For a while now, one of the best things I've done to help increase my productivity and establish a better rhythm of life is to pause once a week for about 15 minutes and give vision to my week. It has literally revolutionized the focus that I have in my week, and I think it could help you tremendously as well. I call it "Start of the Week Sight."

I would recommend you do this exercise each week on Sunday evening or early on Monday morning. Think about it from a practical standpoint with your long-term vision in mind. Knowing the vision that you want to work toward is important as you ask yourself these questions.

1. What notable successes or God moments did I have last week?
   This first question is very important because most productivity-driven people don't celebrate their successes enough. Like keeping a journal, recording your victories can be a valuable practice.

2. What are the most important spiritual goals to accomplish this week?
   You might want to push yourself to pray more this week or spend more time in devotion.

3. What are the most important family/relationship goals this week?

   Do you need to ensure that you have individual, intentional

conversations with your kids? Do you need to connect with an individual this week that you would consider vital to your relational life? List those things.

4. What are the most important ministry or business goals/tasks to accomplish this week?
   What do you need to accomplish this week to make your future goals happen later on down the road?

5. What is required of you this week?
   Do you have to teach on Wednesday? Lead a small group on Friday? Meet with a group of leaders on Saturday? What's required of you that may need some preparation ahead of time?

6. What is an important health goal to accomplish this week?
   If health is important to you, what do you need to make sure happens this week? Going to the gym? Biking? Eating differently? What's important to you this week?

7. What is one thing you will do for fun this week?
   Fun is something I personally struggle with fitting into my schedule because I love to work; but it's important that I have fun, and asking myself this question will ensure that I give it some thought each week.

8. What will you do this week for intellectual growth that is related to your goals?
   If I'm going to be a good leader, minister, and family man, it's imperative that I keep growing. I ask myself, "What will I read this week? What podcasts will I listen to? What YouTube videos will I watch?" I usually keep a running list and check them off as I go through them.

If you'll ask yourself these eight questions, I can almost guarantee you'll begin to create a vision for your week. All of your planned time, and even some of your unplanned time, can go toward working on these specific goals that you set with these questions. You may need to adjust the questions to better fit what you need for your life, but you must remember to ask the questions *every* week to get the most out of this process.

When I started doing "Start of the Week Sight" a few years back, it changed my life. My productivity increased at least 30 to 40 percent, maybe more. That's significant for a guy who was already structured.

I had to get honest with myself and ask if I really wanted to do something great for the Lord—if I *really* wanted to accomplish the vision that I felt He had put before me. If I did, I had to make a few needed changes and get even more intentional with the limited amount of time I had in my week. If I truly desired a good rhythm of life and truly wanted to accomplish many good things in a healthy manner, I knew it all had to happen in the context of my normal routine and in my normal week. I knew that if I continued to enter my week with no foresight, my chances of being focused and productive were minimal.

If you're not intentional with your week, I can guarantee that you'll waste your time on unnecessary things. It's hard enough to be productive when you're intentional with your time; but without intentionality, you won't even have a chance at success. We also need to tune-in to the Spirit of God because it's the Holy Spirit that's going to help us structure ourselves in the right way. The Lord will lead us to the road that we need to go down if we listen. John 16:13 tells us, *"Howbeit when he, the Spirit of truth, is come, he will guide you into all truth..."* If you will listen to His leading, the Lord will guide you to the right place, allowing you to be effective in His Kingdom. In fact, I have to believe that some of you are even consuming this book today based on the Lord's leading and direction in your life.

Though I've given you some basic routines here, this section is primarily focused on the role of vision in a leader's life. In this next section, I want to share the routines and goals that have been very effective in creating time and space for productivity in my life. Without vision, these routines are just empty rituals, but without routines your vision will never become a reality. So, dream big, but be sure to engage in creating effective routines that will make your vision a reality.

chapter 5

Effective Routines/Goals for Productivity

✝ Ephesians 5:15–16: *See then that ye walk circumspectly, not as fools, but as wise, 16Redeeming the time, because the days are evil.*

To achieve your God-given vision in leadership, it's vital that you practice routines and set clear goals that accomplish these objectives. You need to discover new ways to think and operate. You need new skills that will allow you to reach your goals and create the success that you want in your church or ministry. I like to categorize my goals by week and even by day. Your daily routines will allow you to accomplish your vision and ultimately give you a successful and effective week.

What do your daily routines look like? Have you implemented habits that help you prioritize the most important aspects of your day? If not, I guarantee that you are not accomplishing your goals. Think about what is important to you. Is it your devotion? Is it personal or intellectual growth? Physical exercise? If you deem something critical for life function, you must identify a specific part of your day—every day—to accomplish that thing. Otherwise, the pressures of the day will divert your attention and take away opportunities for you to accomplish your goals.

As a popular saying suggests, "The man who removes a mountain begins by carrying away small stones." We must concentrate on the simple, daily routines and objectives of our lives in order to be effective leaders.

Routines in Leader Rhythm

If you've worked through creating your vision from the previous section, you will need to ask yourself what is reasonable for you to accomplish this year. Focus on what you want to accomplish by setting goals for this year, this month, this week, and ultimately today. If you're going to accomplish "X" this year, what do you need to complete by the end of the month? If you're going to accomplish "X" by the end of the month, what do you need to do before the end of the week? What does your day need to look like for you to reach your weekly goal?

Your mission, once you've finally developed your vision, is to make that vision a reality. Making the vision a reality is where establishing a better rhythm of life all comes together. The vision becomes your motivation to move toward a greater rhythm, making positive changes in the way you're living your life. As you move toward that vision, you will become more productive in life as well.

Think about what your daily and weekly routines look like. These routines are going to determine how effective your week is. It's amazing how one day can make a great difference in where you are at the end of the month, year, or several years.

Dr. Brian Epperson, my executive coach and a good friend of mine, introduced me to a concept called "the one percent ladder." It reinforces the need to master each and every day. He told me about a man by the name of Sir Dave Brailsford who won the Tour de France bike race in 2012. Prior to his winning, no British team had ever won. His popular quote says, "If you broke down everything you could think of that goes into riding a bike, and then improved it by one percent, you will get a significant increase when you put them all together."[12]

Brailsford wholeheartedly followed a strategy that he referred to as "the aggregation of marginal gains." James Clear, the author of *Atomic Habits*, explains, "In the beginning, there's basically no difference between making a choice that is one percent better or one percent worse... It won't impact you very much today. But as time goes on, these small improvements, or declines, compound and you suddenly find a very big gap between people who make slightly better decisions on a daily basis and those who don't."[13] The difference in whether or not you have a good rhythm in life and whether you're able to effectively negotiate through work, ministry, and life in general may all hinge on what you do in those one percent increments every single day. A person can climb the ladder of success one percent at a time. This is why it is vitally important you make every day your masterpiece.

If you're struggling with your rhythm of life, it's important that you start small with the one percent. If you want a good rhythm, you must think about the small things you do every day that influence that rhythm. Ultimately, we need to tune into the Spirit of God because it's the Holy Spirit that helps us change ourselves in the right ways. Listen to His leading; I promise that He will guide you. In addition to the guidance of the Holy Spirit, I encourage you to review the practical weekly exercise from the last chapter called "Start of the Week Sight" to help bring clear vision to the daily routine. When you give vision to your week, it creates motivation to follow through because you know exactly what you're working toward with your daily routine.

---

12 Matt Slater, "Olympics Cycling: Marginal Gains Underpin Team GB Dominance," BBC Sport, August 2012, https://www.bbc.co.uk/sport/olympics/19174302.
13 James Clear, "This Coach Improved Every Tiny Thing by 1 Percent and Here's What Happened," James Clear, accessed January 5, 2022, https://jamesclear.com/marginal-gains.

I want you to consider your daily rhythm or routine. Many people don't realize this, but your day actually starts with the routine you implement the night before. If you don't establish a nightly routine that prepares you for the next day, you're liable to struggle with your morning routine.

You must ask yourself, "What do I need to do to get ready tonight so that I can have a successful morning?" Think practically. Lay out your workout clothes as well as the other things you know you'll need so you don't have to think about them when you're half asleep in the morning. Also, think about who you need to tell that you're changing your routine so they can be on board with what you're doing. You should do this for accountability but also so the people in your home know what you're doing and why you're doing it. Perhaps they will become invested in your life changes as well.

Think about what time you need to go to sleep to make sure you get adequate rest. Most studies say that we need seven to eight hours of sleep. I'm an eight-hour kind of guy, so I have to think about what time I should go to bed to make certain I get to sleep on time. Your nightly routine could involve turning the lights low, reading a book, or doing other low-key activities to ensure that you rest mentally. Keep in mind, your morning routine is only as good as your nightly routine. Your success starts the night before.

You also might need to move your alarm clock to the other side of the room. I have one of my old cell phones that I use solely as an alarm clock. If you snooze your alarm, you lose valuable time every morning. You're wasting 30 to 40 minutes of your morning, and you're not getting quality sleep. Set your clock for the time you actually want to get up, place it across the room, and make yourself get out of bed. Now, I know that's easier said than done, but I believe you can get back some valuable time by doing this.

Here is an example of what most mornings look like for me. My alarm clock goes off at 5:00 a.m. I wake up and immediately put on my exercise clothes, brush my teeth, splash some water on my face, drink half a cup of water, then go for a run. If it's cold outside, I have an indoor bike I like to use. I listen to an audiobook for about 30 minutes while I'm doing cardio. The book that I listen to usually relates specifically to what I'm currently working on that week.

After I finished exercising, I go inside, take a shower, and get dressed for work. I then eat breakfast, get a cup of coffee, and do part of my devotion for about 30 to 40 minutes. Next, I spend about an hour reading, studying, or writing something of my choice, usually related to my particular goals for that week. I take my son, Neil, to school, then I go to the church. I finish praying in the sanctuary for about 45 minutes. At 9:00, I begin my workday. By that time, I've checked the boxes on most of the major components I need to accomplish in my day to have a successful week.

It's important that you think through the things you need in your day, how much time you have, and how much time you want to dedicate to those goals, whether they be your devotion time, exercise, intellectual growth, or other important tasks. If you want to read a book that will give you motivation and ideas for your morning routine, I suggest *The Miracle Morning* by Hal Elrod.[14] This book was instrumental in giving me ideas to incorporate into my own morning routine.

I do realize that there are a variety of seasons in life, and it's important that you regularly adjust your schedule depending on those seasons. My obligations and routines must change fairly often. In fact, it's best to evaluate most of these areas once a week, especially the goals that you want to accomplish. Evaluating your goals will keep you focused on accomplishing tasks and investing in personal development.

I also realize that life can bring regular and unpredictable interruptions. Distractions happen nearly every week for me, but for the most part, the previously mentioned schedule is what I follow every weekday. By doing the same things almost every day, I've developed a flow or rhythm to my schedule. When my routine gets interrupted, it's not a problem, but as soon as

---

14 Hal Elrod, *The Miracle Morning: The Not-So-Obvious Secret Guaranteed to Transform Your Life (Before 8AM)*, Self-published, Hal Elrod International Inc., 2012.

I can, I try to get back to that same rhythm. Remember the metronome that I talked about in the first part of this section? It's okay to swing out of balance occasionally as long as you come back to the routines that keep you in rhythm.

The more routine I can create in my morning, the less emotional and physical energy I have to spend trying to decide what to do with my day and where to start. This practice definitely makes my day more productive and successful which ultimately makes my week more productive and successful as well.

We all have limited amounts of time and energy, so it's important that we budget our resources wisely. The less time we spend thinking through what we need to do next, the more time and energy we can invest into the things that really matter the most, such as our inner being, relationships, spiritual lives, and productivity.

In this next section, I want to give you five of my best personal organization tools that help keep me productive. They are a big part of keeping my effective routines and goals. Keep in mind as you go through them that there are many other resources that are just as effective. These are simply the ones that have helped me in this season of my life.

Five Tools That Keep Me Organized

Personalities and character traits play a huge role in whether a person thrives or struggles with personal organization. Some people, like me, love this subject, and other people dread it. Regardless of what side of the spectrum you're on, I believe that personal organization can directly impact the effectiveness of your leadership. I'll share with you the five things that keep me organized throughout my week. It may surprise you how simple they are.

None of us are perfect, but personal organization, or the lack thereof, directly impacts the effectiveness of our routines and goals in life. I want to dispel what could be a misconception as we get started. I am naturally prudent; therefore, I am usually structured and organized. However, if you feel that you struggle with personal organization, please take a deep breath right now and relax. I want you to know up front that prudence and structure don't have to be a natural gift for you to be highly productive, and you don't have to be perfect.

Ephesians 5:15–17 (KJV): *"See then that ye walk circumspectly, not as fools, but as wise,*[16] *Redeeming the time, because the days are evil.*[17] *Wherefore be ye not unwise, but understanding what the will of the Lord is."*

Notice in this scripture, it's not about your internal wiring. It's about deciding to walk circumspectly. It's about deciding to redeem the time well. This scripture prompts us to live carefully. We must make the most of every opportunity the Lord gives us because the days are evil. We can find ourselves busy "doing." We can always do something, but that doesn't mean that we're accomplishing the Lord's will. Our time is limited so we must be wise and make sure that we're doing what the Lord wants us to do. This is first and foremost.

There's a quote that I've used for years that says, "Tame today and you will transform tomorrow." I know it's simple, but it's so powerful. If you're willing to tame today, there's no doubt that your tomorrow will be better. You don't need to make today perfect. All you need to do today is tame it. Add a little organization to your day or allow others around you to help you add organization, and over time, I know it'll change your future in a huge way.

Now, let's get extremely simple and practical for a moment. We'll cover a few things that have the potential to impact all our lives. Keep in mind that most of my suggestions are going to be electronic because I love my electronic world. I would assume that many of you do as well considering the day and age we live in. If you don't, you can just make the adjustment to whatever method you prefer. The principles still apply. We'll start with "to-dos."

1. To-dos

We must have a method of keeping up with the massive number of things we do. It doesn't matter if it's personal, ministerial, business, or another type of responsibility. We must have a method of keeping up with the tasks that we've got to get done.

Some people have a phenomenal memory and can keep up with all of their obligations in their heads. I'm not that fortunate, so I use a to-do app that integrates with all my electronic devices. There's a million of them out there to choose from. You will have to find what works for you. Again, I don't have the strongest memory, so this is an easy way for me to ensure that I remember everything I need to do.

I use my to-do app to remind me to do things like pray for someone on a particular day, send someone a card after they've experienced a major challenge, schedule an oil change for my car, or remind myself that I have to speak on a certain day for a certain event. Anything and everything from personal to ministry that I must remember to do I can put in this app. I schedule the to-do item to come due on a certain day, then I don't have to spend the mental energy trying to remember all the numerous things I need to do.

The key is that I must work the system. If I fail to use the app and put the needed information into it, I find myself spending unnecessary mental energy trying to remember those things that I didn't put in my to-do system. You may do better with paper and pencil or some other type of method. Do what's most comfortable for you. The key is to remember to do what you need to do when you need to do it without letting important things slip through the cracks.

2. Miscellaneous Lists and Notes

The second topic that is necessary to consider is how to keep up with miscellaneous lists, notes, and information. There are a ton of different options, but for this I use a program called Evernote.

If you meet with certain people regularly, you may have a list of things that you need to discuss with them. You also may need to keep notes of a meeting to remember what was said when you meet with that person again. If you're working on a project, you may have a brainstorming list or a task list that you need to record. This is where a good note-taking app comes into use. I use one that is available on all my electronic devices.

Within the note-taking app, I establish folders of all sorts depending on what I'm working on. I've got a folder for sermon thoughts, leader content, leadership coaching topics, personal vision notes, POA ministry notes, and more.

3. Filing Systems

Next, let's talk about filing systems. This includes things that you need to store just because you may need to reference them one day. Over 10 years ago, I scanned all my hard copy files. I got rid of the three-drawer filing cabinet, and I've moved to an all-electronic filing system. Today, I hardly ever keep paper. I simply scan the document and file it on my computer. It really doesn't matter whether you use an old metal filing cabinet or an electronic method. The key is to be able to retrieve what you want when you need it.

My personal filing cabinet is a program called Dropbox. Some people use Google Drive. There are many other cloud storage options, but Dropbox seems to work best for me. I can retrieve files from my computer, iPad, iPhone, or any other device that has an internet connection. If you've ever used a jump drive, cloud storage is very similar to this except it's all online in the cloud. I create a simple nest of folders and store things like documents, pictures, and all sorts of files. The files then sync to the cloud, and they are available on any of my computers or devices wherever I may need them.

It's amazing to think about the fact that I literally carry around my old three-drawer filing cabinet in my smartphone. I can access any of that information any time at any place. It's incredible to me.

4. Email

Let's move along to the email monster. Email can be very intimidating at times because most of us probably get a ton of emails throughout the week. I use one app for mail. For my needs, I use the Apple mail app. This one app keeps all my email accounts in one place.

I could probably do an entire section on email, but here's the main thing about email that's important to share. I try to keep my email inbox as clear as possible. Unless I'm going to act on something later in the same day, I try to do something with every email that I read. If it's a to-do item, I put it in my to-do app and delete the email. If it's a calendar item, I put it in my calendar app and delete the email. If it's something I need to keep for reference later, I have a series of folders in my email to store those types of emails for later. I occasionally even make the email into a PDF and store it in my Dropbox or Evernote for easy retrieval later.

The key to managing email is to avoid reading the same email repeatedly before you delete it or act on it. It's important to carve out some time every day to deal with your email. You may need to put it as an appointment on your calendar. Then, when you sit down to work on email, read it, act on it, and then delete it or store it. When I take the time to check my email, my goal is to leave the end of the session with zero emails in my inbox. Amazingly, most of the time I'm successful in making that happen.

5. Calendar

The last thing I'll mention is the calendar. If we can't manage time, then there's no way that we can be efficient. Unless you have a photographic memory, you should have a calendar that you look at on a routine basis.

The primary solution to time management is that we must control our priorities. You have probably heard of the "jar and the rocks" illustration. You must put the big rocks in first. As old and worn out as that illustration is, it provides relevant wisdom. We must be intentional about making sure we schedule those big items, the most important items, in our lives first. You must ask yourself, "What's most important in my life?" For me, it starts with God first, family second, and ministry or work-life third. What is most important in your life?

This is a tough statement, but so true: If you don't stop spending your time on the least important things in your life, you'll continue to get the least important results. We must get crystal clear on the priorities that make the greatest impact in our organizations and our lives. When we clarify those priorities, we must schedule those things first.

I know myself well, so I've strategically structured my schedule to build in time for meeting with people. However, as an introvert I must intentionally schedule downtime in my office to work alone at times throughout my day and week. If I don't structure my time to best fit me, there'll always be someone else who has a better thought of what I can do with my time. I don't want that or need that. As much as I possibly can, I want to redeem my time the way I feel the Lord desires me to redeem it so that I can be the most productive in His Kingdom.

There are many books, blogs, and classes that can help with the calendar, such as time blocking techniques and other time management methods. However, if you don't figure out how to plan your time in advance with a calendar, the chances are great that you'll never schedule time for all the most important things that need to get done.

So, there you have it. These are the methods and tools that keep me organized and productive throughout my week. They keep me engaged in my routines and moving toward my goals. I try to keep my personal organization methods as simple as possible. The simpler I can keep them, the greater the chance that I will continue to use them.

If you're struggling with personal organization or even if you're not struggling, I would like to encourage you to simply raise your standards a notch. Raise the bar in your life. If you need a to-do app, get one this week and start using it. If you need to better organize your files so you can retrieve what you need when you need it, start it this week.

Ask yourself this question: What's one thing I can do to raise the personal organization bar in my life this week?

I promise it will make a tremendous difference in your effectiveness in the Kingdom of God. Tame today, and you'll transform tomorrow. In this next section, I'll dive a little deeper in how to conquer time management.

The Absolute Most Important Tip to Conquer Time Management

The lack of good time management is one of the major obstacles that keeps us from accomplishing great things in our lives. It seems like it's so easy to get distracted and lose focus of what's most important. This kills our productivity. In this section, I want to share with you the absolute most important tip that will help you conquer the time management beast.

At certain times in most of our lives under certain circumstances, we can sort of "lock in" and "burn the candle at both ends." We can do what's necessary to get whatever we need to get done. We know just how to push through the fatigue, burnout, and dissatisfaction of whatever we're having to do. We just "get it done." We don't even think about those things when we're cramming at the last minute. Most of us just have the innate ability to make it happen and that's a positive thing.

My question for you today, though, is: How are you doing on a routine basis? Before you get to the final hours of the deadline in your daily and weekly routines, what does time management look like for you?

What symptoms are coming to the surface when life is in routine? Are you feeling fatigue or burnout? Are you feeling unhappiness and lack of satisfaction? Are there light feelings of depression? Are you just sort of meandering through the day "faking it until you make it?" These are all symptoms of time management issues.

We all want to accomplish big things. We want to know that our day has had meaning and we've accomplished something great for the Lord. There's something in every one of us that makes us want to pursue those things. So, how do we maximize our time to position us to accomplish big, God-directed things?

You can't manage time. You can only manage your priorities within that time. I've heard this statement most of my life. However, I want to take it one step forward. There are a million different options in your day, but an important principal with time management is not to try to do everything you can do in a day. It's to do the things that you *should* do in a day.

What's going to drive the mission that the Lord has you pursuing? What's going to move the needle in small increments toward what the Lord has you specifically doing in your life? It's not about doing all you can do. It's about doing what you should do. What critical priorities do you have to do in this season of your life? This week? Today? That's what you've got to focus on.

There is a principle that has helped me so much in the last few years of my life. This principle will literally change your life! Are you ready for it? The key to time management is all about energy management. Time management is more about energy management than anything else.

Dr. Henry Cloud, who is a leading psychologist and best-selling author, says, "The most important resources you have are your time and energy. So, who's getting the benefit of your resources?"[15] I love this question. You only have so much energy in your day to do great work. There is no way you can do intense, great work all day long. It's just not possible. There are certain times in the day, usually the morning time for most people, that you have the highest focus. You think so much clearer during this time, and you experience your highest energy levels. So, you must ask yourself: What am I giving my best energy to?

There's a ton of practical how-tos of organization and time management. There are hundreds of applications on just about any platform. There are a million different people who will tell you a million different good ways to organize your time. However, the principle always comes back to how you are managing your energy.

It starts with the right vision in life (see Chapter 4—Vision's Role in a Leader's Rhythm). If you don't have the right God-given vision, then you're not going to be as motivated. Once you're clear on what you're working toward,

15 "Burnout Doesn't Have to be the End Result," Boundaries.me, accessed January 5, 2023, https://www.boundaries.me/burnout-doesnt-have-to-be-the-end-result.

it all funnels down to your week and to your day and what you're giving your best energy to. It's easy to cut out menial tasks in your week and your day when you've got your eyes set on something bigger. It's so much easier when you know what your purpose is. So, what are you giving your best energy to?

A few questions to ponder as you think about energy management:

1. In what part of the day do I have my best energy?
2. What are the most important things that I need to be focused on with my best energy?

When we figure out the best times of our day and week and we know what to focus those best times on, we have to intentionally build margin into our routines. Margin is what will give us the needed rest and relief from the pressures of life. Margin will help ensure that we have our best energy at certain times of our day.

How to Create Margin in Your Life

It's amazing how life can just get cluttered with too many things. And when life gets cluttered and there's so much going on that we don't have time to breathe, we sometimes tend to eliminate the things that actually bring relief to us. The stress builds and turns into anxiety and emotional tiredness. Then, those things begin to manifest as moodiness, passive-aggressive behavior, cynicism, and all sorts of negative ways.

Therefore, it's extremely important to create margin in your daily and weekly routines. Most people struggle with this. Most productive people really struggle with this. To be transparent, I often struggle to create and keep margin in my life as well. I want to give you some thoughts that have helped me and I believe will help you create the needed margin in your life.

When I say margin, what does that mean to you? In simple terms, margin is your breathing room. It's the difference between your limits and your responsibilities. Margin allows us to have space in our day so we're not so stressed and worn out all the time. In the event of an unexpected opportunity or emergency that happens from time to time, we'll have the space and capacity to respond to those things. There are a few principles that I want to give you today that'll help you create this margin needed in your life.

1. Recognize your limits.

Sometimes it's so hard for us to admit that we have limits. It has been for me—I would push through and just make it happen. I did this most of my life until I eventually learned that if I recognized that I had limits, I could work smarter and not harder.

It becomes difficult when we must admit that we're in over our heads. It's hard when we get to a place that we must ask for help. We sometimes need to swallow our pride and get someone else to come in close and rescue us from the situation. However, when we are willing to recognize our limits, we're making room for others to use their gifts.

Only leaders and individuals who are aware of their limits can make room for others. We must recognize and admit that our success is not about us anyway. Lean on the Spirit of God to get you to a place where you can admit that it's not about you anyway. I must decrease and He must increase. Recognize your limits—that's the first step in creating margin in your life.

2. Respect your limits.

When you admit that you've reached your limits, it brings a level of accountability with the people around you that helps you respect your limits. You don't have to pretend any more. You have limits and those closest to you are aware of your limits. And those that truly love and care for you are going to respect your limits as well.

You don't have to remove everything from your plate. In fact, that wouldn't help things anyway. The important thing is to get your load down to a pressure that is manageable. When this happens, you can get focused on the things that you are good at. When you've reached your limits, it's so important that you respect those limits. You've got to make time to replenish yourself, have fun, and rest. The only way you will have time in your life for these things is to respect your limits and create margin.

If you've been running on fumes for way too long and you're doing way too much, you're not going to just jump into a healthy margin. So, it's important to start by finding small pockets of margin. Where can I find some quick wins? How can I start moving toward respecting my limits and creating that margin?

Isaiah 26:12 says, *"LORD, thou wilt ordain peace for us: for thou also hast wrought all our works in us."* The Lord's desire is for us to have peace, but we can't have peace without some level of space and margin. If you'll start somewhere, I can guarantee the Lord is going to help you find those small pockets of margin. He helps you find those small things that will eventually add up over time and make a tremendous difference in your life.

3. Get others involved in your relief.

Don't try to create margin alone. In fact, there's not much in life that we need to do alone. Galatians 6:2 says, *"Bear ye one another's burdens, and so fulfil the law of Christ."* It is not impossible, but most people will struggle if they try to do it alone. Find a few people that you can admit your needs to and use them for accountability to make it a lasting change.

You can also find people who you can delegate to (See "Improve Your Ability to Delegate" in Chapter 13—Lead Others Well). You may not even realize how many people around you are just waiting on the opportunity to serve your church or organization in some significant way. When you release those things and get them off your plate, it creates margin in your life, but it also brings fulfillment in someone else's life. You must understand that you're not "using" those individuals. Though it may feel like that sometimes, you're bringing fulfillment to them and allowing someone else to step into what the Lord has called them to do.

4. Make it last.

When you find margin in your work and in your life, you must guard it as best you can—and then slowly add to it. Continue to look for ways to focus on the things that you're good at and make attempts to eliminate the things that are just weighing you down. I would love to tell you that there's some special formula, but there's not. This is something that takes effort and hard work, but it is very important.

If you're struggling with keeping margin, I would encourage you to make it a matter of prayer every day. If you'll make it a matter of prayer, I guarantee the Lord will begin to show you opportunities to increase your margin and to make it last.

The goal is not to be doing nothing. The goal is not to be stress free. Stress can be a good thing. Stress helps give us motivation to do hard things. However, when we don't have margin, the stress and pressure in our lives will usually rise to an unnecessary and even harmful place. Then, ultimately, our productivity can go down. We think that making our plate full is going to help us accomplish more things, but all it really does is add additional stress. When we don't have margin, we usually struggle to gain the traction we want in whatever we're trying to accomplish.

Regardless of how hard we work with the goal of accomplishing big things, there's a limit to our productivity if we don't figure out a way to build margin into our lives. If you desire to lead effectively over a long period of time without burning out, it's important to build in margin.

I would like you to consider these questions before moving on:

1. On a scale of 0–10, how would you rate your level of margin (0 being no margin and 10 being healthy margin)?

2. What would it take to move that number one point?

If you're a 2, what would it take to move to a 3? If you're a 4, what would it take to move to a 5? I challenge you today to create some margin in your life.

When we're considering effective routines and goals for productivity, sometimes the best thing we can do is just do nothing. In line with creating margin, doing nothing can sometimes increase our overall productivity significantly. Keep reading for more.

Why the Most Productive People Do Nothing

Sometimes doing nothing is the most productive thing you can do in your day. Now, if you read that first line and you were excited because you now have permission to sit on the couch and play video games, this section is not for you. I'm writing to all of you workaholics out there (you know who you are) for whom work is like a drug. The thought of just doing *nothing* gives you the heebie-jeebies. You don't like doing nothing. I know, I know. You're a driven person. You have an enormous amount of ambition. Your schedule is hectic. But there are still times in your life when you *need* to just do nothing. I'm going to give you permission to push against your natural instincts and find some time every day to do nothing. Read until the end, and I'll leave you with a huge practical tip that will help you do nothing!

Leaders, especially church leaders, are known to struggle in one specific area of their lives. They don't take time to rest. We can't help ourselves! With the "always-on" nature of church ministry and our drive to make disciples of Christ pushing us forward, taking time to rest and recharge every day is often the last thing we make space for. Many other Christian organizations struggle with this same dynamic.

Here's the problem, scripture is very clear that we *need* to rest occasionally. In fact, there are times that we not only need to rest, but we also need to do absolutely nothing. Psalms 46:10 says, *"Be still, and know that I am God."* You see, when we try to over-cram our lives to a point that we don't have time to simply be still and know that He is God, we can quickly find ourselves in a physical, spiritual, and possibly even an emotional crisis, especially if this behavior goes on long enough.

I believe that taking breaks and scheduling *intentional* routines of rest throughout the day is critical for the health of Christian leaders. When you take time to properly rest, you feel refreshed, energized, and ready to continue to serve in the Kingdom of God. I'll repeat what I said earlier—sometimes doing absolutely nothing is the most productive thing you can do.

There are incredible spiritual advantages to resting, but let's talk about the other benefits. Most of you are overworking your minds in a way that, if you aren't careful, will negatively affect your performance. This pattern will lead to burnout and, in the most extreme cases, depression and other mental and physical sicknesses. Your mind *must* rest. It's critical for the longevity of your ministry and leadership.

For you church leaders, I know the mission of the Gospel drives you. I know it causes you to want to push yourself to the extreme. You love the people of God, and you also love the many people in your community who need Jesus. These burdens cause you to wake up every morning, helping you to take on loads and do things that most people can't do, but I want you to stop for just a moment. You've got to switch off your mind on a regular basis and allow yourself to simply "be" with Jesus, even if it's just for a few minutes every day. This will give you the God connection that you may be missing, but it will also give you the mental refreshing that you need to keep moving forward for the weeks, months, and years to come.

There are many ways to stop and rest. You can take time in your prayer closet if that's close by, but you could also take a walk out in nature or sit in your favorite easy chair. Maybe you have a place where you can go to sit in your backyard or a private location at work. Go to your car if you need to. Whatever it takes to give your mind and soul time to relax and do nothing, do that thing.

Here's what doing nothing does: With the Lord's help, it increases your focus and your ability to perform well when you get back to the daily grind of work. So, if you can, why not do absolutely nothing multiple times a day? Studies have shown that most people only have a window of about two to three hours of focused work before they need a significant break. For some people, it's even less time. Taking time to rest has the potential to give you the focus you need to be highly productive when you get back to what is next on your agenda. Just be still and *know* that He is God.

Let me leave you with one of the biggest practical tips that I can give you. Get rid of the phone distraction. It's so tough to do nothing if your phone is buzzing in your pocket or on the table beside you. This is one of *my* biggest distractions, and I bet that you probably struggle with it as well. You can either leave it in another room or place it on "do not disturb" mode. It doesn't matter how important you *think* you are, I promise you that the world can live without you responding to your phone for a few moments so that you can have solitude with yourself and with Jesus. My challenge to you is to figure out how to build some time into your day to do absolutely nothing. I promise it will make a difference in your ministry.

When a person begins to develop healthy life balance, vision, and effective routines/goals, it's amazing how much smoother the rhythm of life begins to feel. It's a compounding effect that impacts all areas of life. It also will give a person the capacity to dig into even harder growth opportunities, such as character growth. In this next chapter, we will cover concepts to help grow your character and continue the work of establishing a better rhythm of life.

chapter 6

Grow Your Character

✝ Matthew 7:16–20: *Ye shall know them by their fruits. Do men gather grapes of thorns, or figs of thistles?[17] Even so every good tree bringeth forth good fruit; but a corrupt tree bringeth forth evil fruit.[18] A good tree cannot bring forth evil fruit, neither can a corrupt tree bring forth good fruit.[19] Every tree that bringeth not forth good fruit is hewn down, and cast into the fire.[20] Wherefore by their fruits ye shall know them.*

V ision, routines, pursuit of goals, and other things that are parts of our rhythm of life can all be impacted by the stability of our character. There are so many challenges and painful things that can come at us at any point, and the way we interpret these challenges has a drastic impact on our character. Dr. John Townsend defines character as "having a set of abilities required to meet the demands of reality."[16] We can't always control what's happening around us, but we can change the way we navigate those circumstances. The more we work to improve our character, the better our reactions during

---

16 John Townsend, "4 Components of Good Character," Townsend, July 23, 2018, https://drtownsend.com/4-components-good-character.

tough situations. The person you are on the inside is who you will portray on the outside.

There's More to Character Than What You Think

Character is the point where emotional health, leadership, and discipleship converge. Character is shaped by the good stuff in life, but it's shaped by the tough things as well. I'm curious, have you ever noticed that life is really hard at times? Of course, you have. Everyone experiences difficulties. There are many challenges and painful circumstances that come at us, and it's usually during the toughest of times that the worst comes out of us. I've witnessed this in my own life.

Scripture is very clear: Following Christ doesn't make all of the hard things of life go away. Consider what Paul said about some of his hardships in 2 Corinthians 11:23, *"Are they ministers of Christ? (I speak as a fool) I am more; in labours more abundant, in stripes above measure, in prisons more frequent, in deaths oft."* Paul graciously suffered these many difficulties even while taking care of the New Testament churches.

Paul endured much as a leader and a minister of the Gospel, yet he still retained his love for Christ (2 Corinthians 11:31). How could he respond to these amazingly difficult circumstances and still maintain such a good and healthy response? How could he struggle in life and in service to Christ and still express his love for Christ and others? What did he know that we don't? What is the solution to going through the tough stuff in life and leadership and continuing to produce phenomenal fruit? I'll give you a hint: Most of Paul's success has to do with his character.

In the next few sections, I'm going to share some insight with you about character that has the potential to change your life. Specifically, in this section, I'll introduce the topic of character, but I'm going show you a different side of character. Most people think that character is about morality, but there is quite a bit more to character than that.

Carey Nieuwhof, a leadership expert and author, once said, "Ultimately your character, not your competency, determines your capacity."[17] He went on to say that your talent may get you in the room, but your character is what is going to keep you in the room. For me personally, my character growth has been one of the hardest and yet one of the most important parts of my leadership journey. As Carey put it, I've had to wrestle down my character issues, blind spots, and leadership risks so that I can lead better and, ultimately, live better.

The way we interpret the challenges of life has a drastic impact on our character. We can't always control what's happening around us, but we can change the way we navigate through difficult circumstances. The more we work to improve our character, the better our reactions are going to be during those tough situations. The person you are on the inside is the person you will eventually portray on the outside. You can fool most people for a period of time, but ultimately, when you're under extreme stress, tired, and filled to capacity, you won't be able to hide those internal struggles. The character flaws on the inside of you will start to become visible on the outside of you.

This is the point where our pain surfaces, revealing the negative fruit in our lives. Negative fruit can manifest a number of different ways. We may begin to detach from people, pushing them away. We may become temperamental, cynical, anxious, or passive-aggressive. We may develop into people-pleasers or even acquire narcissistic behaviors, becoming egotistical and arrogant; however, the negative fruit in our lives is deeply rooted in our character.

Almost everything I know about character structures comes from scripture first, but also from Townsend Institute at Concordia University, Dr. John Townsend's institute for executive coaching. Character structure was

---

17 Carey Nieuwhof, "The 6 Biggest Factors That Cause People to Ignore Your Ideas and Influence," Carey Nieuwhof, accessed November 28, 2022, https://careynieuwhof. com/6-non-negotiable-traits-you-need-to-increase-your-leadership-influence.

drilled into my head through this great program. You may have heard of Dr. Townsend and Dr. Henry Cloud through their popular work on boundaries. These men have written many phenomenal resources that have helped me better understand the concept of character. Two of my favorite books from them on this subject are *Hiding from Love* by John Townsend[18] and *Changes that Heal* by Henry Cloud.[19]

Character is more than just morals, because character is what defines the internal morals of a person. As previously mentioned, Townsend explains character as "having a set of abilities required to meet the demands of reality." In other words, character is the personality traits that determine how you respond to people, circumstances, and environments. The Bible would probably define character as the heart or the soul of a person. Matthew 15:19–20 states, *"For out of the heart proceed evil thoughts, murders, adulteries, fornications, thefts, false witness, blasphemies: 20These are the things which defile a man..."* Matthew 7:16–17 says, *"Ye shall know them by their fruits. Do men gather grapes of thorns, or figs of thistles?17 Even so every good tree bringeth forth good fruit; but a corrupt tree bringeth forth evil fruit."* And in verse 20, Matthew states, *"Wherefore by their fruits ye shall know them."*

Character is the deep-rooted soil of a person's life that either produces positive fruit or negative fruit. Some of you may not feel that you struggle with negative fruit in your life. In fact, you may be thinking that this topic doesn't apply to you, but hold on just a minute. I can also say, with confidence, there's not a person who doesn't occasionally see unwanted, negative fruit rise to the surface in his or her life. I know this is true because I know that only Jesus is perfect. I believe that every one of us has opportunities for growth in our lives. We are all in a process of growth, and we'll remain that way until the day we die.

---

18 John Townsend, *Hiding from Love: How to Change the Withdrawal Patterns That Isolate and Imprison You* (Grand Rapids: Zondervan), 1996.

19 Henry Cloud, *Changes That Heal: Four Practical Steps to a Happier, Healthier You* (Grand Rapids: Zondervan), 1993.

What if you could understand your character and this growth process enough to help expedite your growth? What if I were able to give you a few aspects of character that could help you identify specific opportunities for growth within you? Would you want to hear that? I'm going to wrap up this section by giving you the big picture for character growth; and in the next few sections, I'll breakdown each of these components one at a time, going into a little more depth.

In their books, both Townsend and Cloud agree that there are four major components of good character. They back up their claims and research with scripture. I've changed the names of these components somewhat to make them better fit my preferences. They are listed below.

1. Healthy relational connection (bonding): The ability to trust and be vulnerable as well as bond to important people in your life.

2. Healthy separation (boundaries): The ability to have your own voice, make your own choices, and freely express yourself.

3. Integration (reality): The ability to embrace the truth that there are both positive and negative realities in your life.

4. Adulthood (maturity, authority, or emotional capacity): The ability to be confident in who you are and why you exist.

Again, I'm going to break these components down further, but I want to share with you how these elements have impacted my life. Character is vital to leadership. I've worked on these issues for many years now, but it wasn't until I was provided this character model that I developed focus and clarity around the growth that was needed in my life. This model revealed the deficits that created those occasional sore spots in my leadership. I couldn't figure out why I would sometimes go days with a downturn in my emotions. I couldn't understand why I would occasionally become so moody that my family couldn't stand to be around me. I didn't know why there were periods of time that I would want to detach from the key relationships in my life, even though those relationships were vital to my ministry and leadership.

It wasn't until I understood and learned how to lessen the impact of my deficits in these four character structures that I started seeing significant and routine growth in my life. I began overcoming things that I didn't think were possible. When I started out, healthy integration was my most glaring deficit. After growing in integration for a few months, I realized that adulthood was then my greatest deficit. This went on for several years back and forth between the four character components until I felt significant growth in my life. I felt transformed into a much better and healthier person.

The beautiful thing about all of this truth is that it is deeply rooted in scripture. Paul modeled character growth and wrote about it. At its core, character growth is simply a deeper level of discipleship and maturity. Understanding the issues involved with character growth allows us to overcome those deep-rooted problems that sin has brought upon us and to live whole and fruitful lives as Christ intended.

In this next section, I'll discuss healthy relational connections. This area of my personal character growth has drastically changed the way that I relate and bond to others; and I've learned to use these healthy relational connections to recover from the most stressful things in my life.

How to Have Healthy Relational Connections

Learning how to have healthy relational connections is an enormous part of growing your character. In this section, I'll provide insight on how to foster those connections. To start, I'll give you a personal story to help you understand the positive impact that a healthy relational connection has given me.

I had just gone through several stressful days at work at the church, and I wasn't feeling well physically. I'd helped counsel someone through a crisis in his life, and I was mentally exhausted. On top of these challenges, someone with good intentions at work had given me some "constructive criticism." Though this usually wouldn't have bothered me, for some reason, this time it caused me to spiral emotionally. Under normal circumstances, not one of these things alone would have drained me emotionally, but since they all happened together, it created a perfect storm. In years past, this spiral could have negatively affected me for two or three days. Perhaps you can relate to this sort of experience.

This scenario was much different from experiences I'd had in the past. This time, I had exactly what I needed in order to quickly make it through this situation and still remain emotionally stable. One thing that helped me was the healthy relational connections I have in my life. I've invested the time needed to create those healthy attachments with people I can trust, people I can be vulnerable with and bond to during critical times.

A few years ago, I was doing leadership coaching for a pastor with a congregation of about 150 members. From the outside, it seemed like he had a thriving and growing church; but on the inside, he was on the edge of burnout. He was even on the verge of resigning his church and looking for a secular job. I find this burnout is especially common among church leaders.

As I began asking him questions to determine the root of his problem, I quickly realized that his work-life balance was out of sync. There was something more to his issues than that, though. He shouldn't have been experiencing such severe dissatisfaction simply because he was working too much. I dug a little deeper and found the real issue. He was a pastor surrounded by relationships: a pastoral team, many volunteers, and a good-sized congregation; but he wouldn't allow anyone to enter his inner circle before he turned them away. He was a dynamic, people-person on the outside, but on the inside, he was isolated and lonely. The only person who ever saw a glimpse of vulnerability was his wife. Over the next few months, we worked hard to help him understand why he was struggling to bond with others in a deep way and to begin making steps to develop healthy need-based relationships.

As I mentioned previously, healthy relational connection is the ability to trust, be vulnerable, and bond to important people in your life. Many times, pastors and leaders are really good at helping others with their emotional baggage, but they themselves do not open up and trust others with their own issues, leaving them feeling empty and alone. These are the same type of people who often say, "It's lonely at the top." I'm here to tell you today that it doesn't have to be lonely at the top. That's a choice. If a leader wants to be healthy and thrive, he or she must realize that vulnerable bonding is one of humanity's greatest needs. Relationships are vital for every one of us, not just relationships that we give to, but also relationships that we receive from.

Ecclesiastes 4:9–10 says, *"Two are better than one; because they have a good reward for their labour.*[10] *For if they fall, the one will lift up his fellow: but woe to him that is alone when he falleth; for he hath not another to help him up."* This is a warning from Solomon for those who want to isolate themselves when things are difficult instead of drawing into healthy, need-based relationships.

Paul said in Galatians 5:14, *"For all the law is fulfilled in one word, even in this; Thou shalt love thy neighbour as thyself."* The Lord created us for bonding; He created us for relationships. However, in order to truly share a bond, we must have mutual engagements. We can't simply give to a person and consider it bonding. We have to receive from our relationships as well. We must be aware of our needs and experiences and be able to ask for those needs to be met.

How do you know if you struggle with this part of your character? How do you know if you need more healthy relational connections in your life? Scripture says, *"For where your treasure is, there will your heart be also"* (Luke 12:34). So, I ask you, where is your heart? What do you give your greatest energy and resources to? If it's something other than relationships, that's where your heart is. Those are the things replacing the key relationships in your life. It may be work, money, or something much worse. God designed us with two natural voids. One is a void that can only be filled by the Spirit of God, and the other is a void that can only be filled by healthy, human relationships. If you're experiencing a void in your life, I encourage you to practice two steps.

1.   Find at least two safe people who you think will love you

unconditionally, without judgment, no matter what you tell them. Choose people other than your spouse. I say choose two people, if possible, because having two confidants helps spread the load of your burdens. No one person, including your spouse, should feel the weight of all of your emotional needs.

2. Take a risk and be transparent and vulnerable with these people. Talk about some of the difficult emotional things that may be challenging to you. Sharing your heart with a safe person will undoubtedly help lift the load of whatever you're carrying. Those individuals will have the opportunity to feel a closeness to you that truly draws them in and bonds you to them in a way that's needed for healthy relational connection.

It's amazing how hard-hearted people can melt in the presence of empathy. When you allow someone to empathize with you, you receive healing, and they also receive healing as well. Your hurt and loneliness is impacted, and their hurt and loneliness is impacted.

Vulnerability opens the heart and allows us to exchange love between one another. When you admit that you have needs and ask for those needs to be met, your life can be transformed and the chains that have held you back from experiencing that healthy attachment can break. I have personally experienced this bonding transformation time and time again in the last few years as I've chosen to be vulnerable with safe people with the toughest parts of my life.

If you're struggling to bring people in close, I encourage you to ask the Lord to change this area of your life. Revelation 3:20 tells us, *"Behold, I stand at the door, and knock: if any man hear my voice, and open the door, I will come in to him, and will sup with him, and he with me."* Take a risk and ask God to soften those defenses that have likely plagued you most of your life. Ask Him for the courage to take these steps toward healthy relational connections that will ultimately lead to a huge growth in your character.

The difficulty with making these relational connections is that if you take the risk to make them once, you have to take this risk again and again because you can't do life alone. You need Jesus, but you also need human relationships in your life. Push past your desire to detach from people and eliminate whatever you're using to push people away. I challenge you to engage with healthy relational connections. You will see your character grow like never before.

Next, is a subject that has changed not only my leadership life, but also my personal home life as well. My first introduction to boundaries was from one of Cloud and Townsend's books, *Boundaries in Marriage*, years ago.[20] I remember that it literally shaped the way my wife and I interacted with one another. In this next section, you'll see that I've learned to extend boundaries into all relational areas of my life, especially in leadership environments.

Learn How to Establish Healthy Boundaries

When I was 16 years old, I felt a divine call to the ministry. There was nothing that I wanted more than to be in pastoral leadership at a church. I remember giving everything to the church, including doing everything the leadership of the church asked of me for many years. I led ministry teams, taught Bible studies, and did manual labor at the church facilities. In my early twenties, I eventually received an opportunity to move across the nation and help a small church plant as an assistant pastor.

The opportunity was exciting for the first few months, but then it started to become work—a great deal of work. I was also working a full-time secular job as well as fulfilling a full-time ministry role. There weren't enough people involved in the small church to spread the load. There were Bible studies to teach, staff meetings to lead, new members' classes to instruct, youth ministry to organize as well as preaching, service organization, ministry work, and

20 Henry Cloud and John Townsend, *Boundaries in Marriage* (Grand Rapids: Zondervan), 1999.

counseling. Before long, I had almost no margin to do any of the things I enjoyed. A little bit of resentment began to creep into my heart and mind. So much was demanded of me, but I didn't feel as appreciated as I thought I deserved.

The situation I found myself in was no one's fault but my own. I was struggling with boundaries in my life, but at the time, I didn't even know what a boundary was.

Because I lacked boundaries in my role as assistant pastor at that new church in Virginia, the relational side of my life suffered. My personality revolves around productivity; therefore, I thought if I did more and achieved more that I would gain the approval of those in authority around me. I sacrificed my relational needs to work harder. My poor wife felt the brunt of my lack of boundaries, as I undoubtedly missed the cues of some of her relational needs, but others in my life suffered as well. Even more importantly, I didn't obtain the key relational nutrients that I desperately needed in my own life for growth.

Drs. John Townsend and Henry Cloud define a boundary as the place that one person's property line ends, and another person's property line begins.[21] Boundaries are essentially the realization that we are our own person apart from others. Boundaries teach us how to love others but also how to avoid entangling our will with the will of others.

Having healthy boundaries allows you to have your own voice, make your own choices, express yourself freely while still allowing the people around you to have their own voices, choices, and expressions as well. A person with boundaries has the ability to say "no" while still being able to confront others in appropriate and caring ways. A person with healthy boundaries doesn't handle things in a passive way but has the ability to take care of his or her own needs while still having a strong approach to life. God created us in His image

---

21 Henry Cloud and John Townsend, "What Do You Mean 'Boundaries?'" Cloud-Townsend Resources, March 9, 2016, https://www.cloudtownsend.com/what-do-you-mean-boundaries-by-dr-henry-cloud-and-dr-john-townsend/.

with the ability to freely make choices and have boundaries. If you're struggling with boundaries in your life, there's no doubt in my mind that the Lord can restore this area of your character and repair your damaged boundaries.

Paul commands us in 2 Corinthians 10:5, *"Casting down imaginations, and every high thing that exalteth itself against the knowledge of God and bringing into captivity every thought to the obedience of Christ."* It's important that we learn to take responsibility for our thoughts. We should not repress our thoughts but own them and examine them. This is more than just a right that God has given us; it's a responsibility. When we begin to take responsibility for our own thoughts, we will begin to take ownership of our feelings, attitudes, desires, and even behaviors.

One of the major things we need to learn regarding boundaries is that they must be established within the context of love. Even though we may need to say "no" or set boundaries with someone, it doesn't mean that we don't love those people. In fact, the act of setting boundaries ensures that we're able to continue to have those healthy relational connections. In his book *Changes That Heal*, Dr. Henry Cloud writes, "Love cannot exist without freedom, and freedom can't exist without responsibility."[22] It's so important that we take responsibility for the issues that are ours and deal with them accordingly. Boundaries are critical for freedom, and freedom is critical for healthy relational connections.

Another important aspect of boundaries is allowing other people to take responsibility for how they feel personally. We want to be sensitive to others and the way they feel; we want to be aware of their feelings, but ultimately, it's their responsibility to own their own emotions. In another words, if someone is angry or sad and tries to use those emotions to control your actions, they've crossed over the line of your boundaries. We all have the right to be angry or experience other negative emotions, but we can't try to control others with

---

22 Henry Cloud, *Changes That Heal: Four Practical Steps to a Happier, Healthier You* (Grand Rapids: Zondervan, 1993), 142.

those emotions. We have to allow people to be who they are, and we have to learn to love and accept others the way that they are.

Boundaries are a deeply rooted subject with many components to consider. If you're struggling in this area of your life, you're not alone. Establishing boundaries is something that is difficult to learn and implement. I want you to know that the result of not having boundaries can create all kinds of problems. Lacking boundaries can cause resentment and passive-aggressive behavior or even worse issues like panic attacks, depression, and addictions.

It's not always easy to learn how to set boundaries, and if you can't seem to make headway with this topic, please consider getting outside help from a friend, a counselor, or a coach. It will be hard work putting the time and effort into strengthening the healthy boundaries in your life, but I promise it will be worth it. Having the ability to take responsibility for ourselves determines the quality and the significance of our lives.

As important as the subject of boundaries is, the next topic of character growth is just as important. Embracing reality, or integrating the good and bad parts of your life, is something that was my greatest weakness when I originally started studying character structures. I want to share more in this next part.

Learn How to Embrace Reality

A few years ago, one of my clients was struggling to settle into his ministry role. He would spend a short time working in one place before becoming bored with that job and moving on to the next, often uncovering some sort of "issue" that would make him want to consider changing positions and locations. In reality, he was simply running from his internal struggles.

He continually wrestled with the same problems. As we worked to uncover the cause for his discontentment, we realized he was struggling with integration and the reality that there is no perfect situation or environment. He was continually dissatisfied with his inability to achieve perfection. He was also frustrated with the lack of perfection from those around him.

The reality is that we live in a fallen world, a world that's sinful and flawed. We are all flawed. I really think we know this deep within, but sometimes it's hard for us to accept this truth, especially when it comes to our own lives. I want to give you some insight on how to embrace the truth that there are both positive and negative realities in your life.

The negative things in life that people experience such as weakness, loss, mistakes, or failures often trigger shame and guilt within them. These are internal triggers that make it hard to face the disappointments of life and still experience successes and happiness.

We must learn to embrace the good and the bad together. When we can't embrace the good and bad simultaneously, we can't accept our imperfections and the imperfections of others. We seek perfectionism, which many times leads us to place performance and achievements ahead of the important relationships in our lives.

My pursuit of perfectionism has been the number one challenge to overcome in my life and leadership. I've struggled with it since I was a kid. My drug of choice for most of my life has been the pursuit of achievement. I would work hard to achieve things in my ministry for the unhealthy approval of the important people in my life. Getting a pat on the back would give me a "high" that would keep me continually seeking achievements and perfection.

Have you ever felt such a competitive drive within you that it created an unreasonably high standard for you and others? I have often experienced that. For me, the idea of failing or being less than perfect would send me spiraling emotionally and once again cause me to pursue achievements in an unhealthy way. Through much counseling, coaching, and learning about integration, I've been able to do some significant work toward overcoming these challenges. I've learned to experience loss, failure, weakness, and even mediocrity while still maintaining a love for myself. It's impossible to be all good, and I'm okay with that. I recognize that I have limits, and I accept those limits.

Our world and the people of this world have good and bad in them. Because of our sinful nature, we all have good parts and bad parts. It's not possible for any of us to be all good. We have a combination of good and bad inside of us, and the world around us has a combination of the good and bad as well.

In the case of my client, he required perfectionism from whatever environment he was working in; and when the church or his job failed to meet those expectations, he would become frustrated and devalue the group. He would then withdraw emotionally and eventually withdraw physically as he moved on to a new job, a new church, or a new group of people who could try to meet his expectations.

Here's one of the major issues with this pattern of behavior. When we are unable to accept the good and the bad together within us or within the world we live, we develop inconsistent emotions within ourselves and inconsistent relationships with others around us. This behavior creates a roller coaster effect on our relationships. Our relationships become strained, and we then push the people most important to us away.

So, what's the solution? What does it take to overcome these various integration issues and come into some sense of health? Though it is much easier said than done, the solution is to embrace reality. Paul understood reality all too well. In Romans 7:14 he says, *"For we know that the law is spiritual: but I am carnal, sold under sin."* Paul knew he was weak and fallen. That's reality, but he also knew that when he was weak physically, he was strong spiritually. In 2 Corinthians 12:10 he said, *"Therefore I take pleasure in infirmities, in reproaches, in necessities, in persecutions, in distresses for Christ's sake: for when I am weak, then am I strong."*

We must embrace the fact that we're fallen and weak, and we must realize that it's through our relationship with Christ that we become strong. We were created in the image of God and because of that we have significant value and strength. We're both weak and strong. It's when we embrace this reality that we can accept that there is good and bad in life, but life is mostly good. Learning to embrace reality is vital to the growth of our character.

Character growth requires us to give attention to four major areas of our lives. Like embracing reality, setting boundaries, and creating healthy relational connections, the next structure is just as significant to the growth of our character. In this next section, we will unpack the fourth and final character structure, which is emotional capacity. It makes a huge difference in our interpretation of authority in our life and can greatly impact our ability to lead.

Increase Your Emotional Capacity

I wrote a little bit in the last section about my unhealthy desire to seek approval from certain influencers in my life. Though those unhealthy attachments had a great deal to do with my lack of ability to embrace reality, essentially, they represented my issues with emotional capacity.

Dr. John Townsend calls this issue "the adulthood character structure."[23] Others may simply call it maturity, and I also refer to it as emotional capacity. Truthfully, however, as adults, we have the freedom to make our own decisions without permission from other adults. We can judge our own abilities. We can choose what we value. We can have opinions of our own. We can disagree with other people, including people who are important to us and those we respect. We also have the responsibility to approach other adults with the same mutual respect and freedom.

Why can we do all of these things? Here's the simple answer: We're adults. I think you would be shocked at how many people struggle with this particular part of their character. I hope this section really opens your eyes to some important aspects of emotional capacity.

As children, we're extremely dependent on our parents and caretakers to provide for us and give us guidance in just about everything we do. It's a "one-up and one-down" relationship. We look up to our parents and caretakers.

---

23 John Townsend, *Hiding from Love: How to Change the Withdrawal Patterns That Isolate and Imprison You* (Grand Rapids: Zondervan), 1996.

They guide us in decision-making and life in general.

Hopefully, as we grow, we become less dependent on others. I think about my 12-year-old son, Neil. His capacity now is more than it was five years ago. He's capable of doing so much more now than he used to be able to do, but he's still not capable of doing some of the things that my 15-year-old daughter, Olivia, is capable of. Even Olivia has a capacity limitation at 15.

To become an adult, we have to constantly move through the process of growth in those early years. It's a physical, mental, and emotional developmental process until we ultimately move out of the "one-up and one-down" parental relationship and eventually move into mutual peer relationships with other adults, including our parents and the other influencers in our lives. We may respect and honor their positions, but we become mutual adults with them, having the same potential capacity and the same responsibilities.

Genesis 1:27 tells us, *"So God created man in his own image, in the image of God created he him; male and female created he them."* We were created in the image of God; and if we are going to operate in the image of God, we have to walk in the authority and dominion that the Lord has given us over our own lives. This includes being able to step up and do all that He asks of us. I also need to say this: He has either equipped you or He will equip you for whatever He may ask of you. The Lord has never called a person to something that He has not prepared them for. When we embrace this call and responsibility, we are truly able to submit to God and others in healthy and productive ways.

I'm sure you know of someone in your life who has gotten stuck in their developmental process. Sometimes, people never actually "grow up," so they feel one-down to others; or, out of a defensive posture, they take the role of one-up to others. They may even become rebellious in some way. Any of these approaches are unhealthy. A person may struggle with small aspects of relational issues; they may even act appropriately at home with their spouse and kids, but at work, when they're around certain people, problems arise. These problems can manifest in different ways in our lives and can easily seep into other areas of our lives.

In adulthood, we should submit to God; He's our heavenly Father. Every other adult in our life, including those who may hold a position higher than ours, we are equal to. They are our siblings, our brothers and sisters. Now, this doesn't mean that we don't submit to people in authority over us. I'm absolutely going to submit to my pastor or my boss or the other leaders in my life. I'm going to submit to whoever is in organizational authority over me. It doesn't matter if they're older than me or younger than me; that's irrelevant. I'll submit to organizational and spiritual authority. However, we are still mutual adults, and I can be confident in who I am and what the Lord has called me to do. I have a voice, I have an opinion, and I even have a responsibility to exercise my voice and opinion in my life.

Dr. Cloud, in his book *Changes That Heal,* points out through scripture that Jesus calls us out of the one-down relationship to other people, but at the same time encourages us to have respect for those in authority (Matthew 23:2–5, 7–10).[24] Here's the bottom line: If you're an adult, you don't need permission from anyone else to think, feel particular emotions, or even act. As adults, we have the freedom to do those things; and more importantly, we have the God-given responsibility to think, feel, and act individually.

I was working with a client not too long ago who was struggling with the responsibilities of adulthood and his emotional capacity. His father had been a hardworking, prayerful man. He had good morals, went to church, did all the "right" things. He loved his family, but just didn't show it much. Emotionally, his father had been a hard man, especially when he worked all day and came home tired at night. He expected his kids to wait on him hand and foot. He barked orders from his recliner, and when the kids did just as he expected, he showed approval and love. When they slacked a little and acted like normal children, he would become angry and punish them.

As my client grew older, he developed an unhealthy need to please people

---

24 Henry Cloud, *Changes That Heal: Four Practical Steps to a Happier, Healthier You* (Grand Rapids: Zondervan, 1993), 266-268.

in authority. In fact, this approval addiction and unhealthy desire to please affected many parts of his life, including his relationships with his spouse, the leaders in his life, and even the people he led. This made it amazingly hard for him to tell people difficult things. He hated even healthy confrontation, and he struggled to voice his opinions and personal desires to people in authority. These issues produced enormous challenges as he progressed in leadership, creating blind spots that hindered his growth. Thankfully, we were able to illuminate what was happening and even develop tactics to make significant progress in growing his assertiveness and building his adulthood character structure.

The issues within this client were challenging because of the multidimensional nature of emotional capacity and adulthood. Many times, the issues we face are deeply rooted in the challenges of our past. To simplify, I'm going to give you the three most common ways in which this aspect of character can impact a leader.

1. Some people take a one-down approach with authority. This is an unhealthy form of submission in which people view those in authority positions as superior.

2. Some people develop a one-up approach with authority. This is an egotistical or "better than" approach to authority in which people feel they are superior both to those they lead and to authority figures.

3. Some people develop a rebellious or defiant approach to authority. In this approach, people often take on a defensive posture in their relationships or feel victimized by others.

If you're struggling with one of these aspects of emotional capacity in your life, having an awareness and acceptance that you are struggling in this area will help in a tremendous way. Awareness is a powerful thing, but there are also some actions that you can take to help in your development. I want to give you some steps to help you begin moving in the right direction.

Let's talk about the one-down approach. If you're feeling one-down to certain adults in your life, here are some things you can apply to help you grow in this area. First, realize that your opinion does matter and begin to express that opinion to the safe authority figures in your life. Also, you need to begin making a few safe decisions beyond what you would normally do without seeking the approval from someone in authority.

I realize this may sound a bit simple, but if you are struggling in this area, these are easy steps to push you out of your comfort zone and create growth. You need small steps in the right direction to get you started.

For those of you who revert to the one-up mentality, here are some simple suggestions you can apply to your relationships. First, be aware of how you're talking to the people you lead. Lead them with care and empathy rather than telling them what they "should do" or shaming them for not doing a task as well as you think they should. Also, recognize that you too have limits. Admit that you need other people to make a complete and productive team.

When you have conversations with authority figures, unlike with the one-down mentality, you may need to actually back down a little with your demands. Be aware of your tone of voice and body language and be willing to submit to the authority in your life.

Finally, let's discuss the rebellious or defiant approach. One of the biggest challenges for those who struggle with this mentality is recognizing that you're struggling. You must also realize that you can't do everything, that you do have limits, and that it's okay to submit to authority. Remember that not everyone is out to wound or take advantage of you. It may be helpful to find someone with whom you regularly push limits and purposely submit to that person no matter what they request of you. Follow through with their request, purposely yielding to authority rather than pushing against what they ask of you.

Although everything I've told you may sound simple, there's nothing easy about overcoming any one of these three relational problems. It takes work, and it usually requires seeking help in some way. I realize that I'm covering a very complicated topic in a very short way, but I do hope I've at least opened your eyes to the subject. Again, these things are extremely difficult to process, but they're important if you truly desire to grow your emotional capacity and ultimately grow your character. The Lord designed you for a specific purpose on this Earth. It is possible for you to have confidence in who you are and why you exist.

The four character structures, including creating healthy relational connections, setting boundaries, embracing reality, and increasing emotional capacity, have become a vital part of the growth of my life and the lives of the clients I have worked with. In this next session, I want to give you some final thoughts about growing your character with these structures.

Final Thoughts About Character

Most people think that character is merely good morals. As simply as I possibly can, I want to show you in this chapter that character is much more than what you may think. In fact, character is the foundation of everything we do, good or bad. Character is the soil of our lives. It is the place where the fruit we produce—whether good or bad—originates. So, I encourage you to keep reading as I give you my final thoughts on the subject of character and wrap up this Grow Your Character chapter.

Scripture confirms that we're known by the fruit we produce. People know us by the outward fruit they see, but that fruit grows from something deep within us. That fruit is produced from the soil of our character. Our emotions, reactions, dedication, and all good external leadership comes from deep within us.

The nutrients in the soil of your character will determine the type of fruit that you produce; the soil of your character will determine the type of external results you see in your life. Scripture says that other people will know you by your fruit. That fruit will manifest in your life in a relational way, either for good or bad. If you like the fruit you're seeing in your life, the soil of your character is good and healthy. Many times, however, you may not like the fruit you're seeing. If that's the case, you can more than likely trace your issues to the poor soil of your character. The negative fruit identifies a need for growth in that particular area of your character.

It is the negative, deep-rooted things of our character that I believe the Lord desires to set us free from. Think about this. Luke 4:18 tells us, *"The Spirit of the Lord is upon me, because he hath anointed me to preach the gospel to the poor; he hath sent me to heal the brokenhearted, to preach deliverance to the captives, and recovering of sight to the blind, to set at liberty them that are bruised."* When the Lord speaks of healing the brokenhearted, delivering the captives, giving sight to the blind, setting at liberty those who are bruised, He is speaking of a spiritual and emotional healing for us. These issues are deep-rooted soil issues, and the Lord has given us the tools to work through these problems. The result is better relational and external fruit in our lives.

Learning how to produce positive fruit is what this chapter is all about; that's what character growth is all about. The Lord desires to help us repair the hidden, broken parts of our character. He has called us out of darkness into His marvelous light, and that light will help us finish the process of growth in our lives. We shouldn't have to learn to live and cope with negative fruit. I believe Christ desires to repair and grow those deep-rooted negative issues in our character so that we can ultimately produce better, more Godly fruit.

You might be wondering what is at stake if you don't pay attention to character growth in your life? I'm glad you asked. Let me explain. We all have wounds and dark places in our pasts that come from sin. It is the sin that taints our soil and character. Not one of us on Earth can avoid this. Psalms 51:5 tells us, *"Behold, I was shapen in iniquity; and in sin did my mother conceive me."* Sin and "soil" issues are a fact of life for us today, but consider the next few verses. Psalms 51:6–7 says, *"Behold, thou desirest truth in the inward parts: and in the hidden part thou shalt make me to know wisdom.*[7] *Purge me with hyssop, and I shall be clean: wash me, and I shall be whiter than snow."* Sanctification is a process. The purging, cleansing, and developing of the inward parts of our character take time.

In this day and age, it's so easy for a person's platform to grow faster than their character. A person may have the charisma, the degrees, and the knowledge to perform a job, but if their character is not healed or developed properly, then it's easy for the sinful, dark areas of their life to manifest during the most inopportune times. Negative character traits can affect the way you interact with your family as well as the way you lead people. Negative character can even cause devastating moral failure.

Really, this is how the lack of character kills careers and destroys friendships. It splinters families and lessens influence, but you don't just wake up one day in a morally compromising situation. Those situations come from years of neglecting the deep-rooted soil issues in your life. Talent and competency may get you on the platform of your choice, but character is what's going keep you there. If you really want to expand your leadership and personal capacity, it's incredibly important that you learn to deepen and grow your character.

The four structures that I've gone through in this chapter are the primary aspects of our character. These are the points that will deepen and grow your character. I encourage you to go back and read those sections if you need a review, but here they are again in short definition:

1. Healthy relational connections: The ability to trust, be vulnerable, and bond to important people in your life.

2. Healthy boundaries: The ability to have your own voice, make your own choices, and freely express yourself.

3. Embracing reality: The ability to accept the truth that there are both positive and negative things in your life.

4. Emotional capacity: The ability in adulthood to be confident in who you are and why you exist.

By working on these issues in my life for several years now, I've been able to create a tremendous focus and clarity around the goal of growth. I have found the sore spots in my life and leadership and identified and worked on the character structures that coincide with my negative fruit. It has taken a great deal of time, effort, and vulnerability with key people in my life, but I've seen significant internal growth. I'll be the first to tell you that I'm still not perfect and I'm still growing, but implementing this process has made all the difference in the world for me. I call this another level of maturity; I call it my discipleship process. Character is such a vital part of our leadership. It is important to work hard at growing your character!

As you work to establish a better rhythm of life, you must give significant attention to your healthy life balance, vision's role, effective routines and goals, and growing your character. When you take action to establish a better rhythm, it begins to create margin and opportunity to focus on gaining a greater understanding of yourself. In Part 2 of *The Christian Leader Blueprint*, we will dive into the subject of seeing yourself more clearly.

Part Two

See Yourself More Clearly

People who have a firm understanding of themselves are more effective leaders, can have great influence on others, and are often much easier to work with than those who lack personal awareness. How many times have you had a bad day, but you didn't know why you were having a bad day? How many times have you projected your bad day on everyone around you? Prior to growing in my own self-awareness, this happened to me more times than I would like to admit.

Ironically, we may think that we know ourselves well. However, according to authors Travis Bradberry and Jean Greaves in *Emotional Intelligence 2.0*, there's no finish line to understanding yourself. It's very similar to peeling back the layers of the onion.[25] They go on to say that the more we understand about ourselves and become comfortable with those findings, the more effective we will be as a leader. Without self-awareness, we're severely limiting our

---

25 Travis Bradberry and Jean Greaves, *Emotional Intelligence 2.0* (San Diego: TalentSmart, 2009), 61.

capabilities as a leader.

There are multiple ways to gain greater self-awareness. Tools include a variety of assessments, solicited feedback from team members or the people closest to you, and interaction with an executive coach. When evaluating your own self-awareness, consider the following questions:

- How can you challenge the personal assumptions you have about yourself?

- How can you develop a greater curiosity about your strengths and weaknesses?

- Ask others, what are some things about your personality that are obvious to everyone else but hidden to you?

In order to see yourself more clearly, there are four important topics to give attention to in your life. You must first achieve a good clarity of mind. Second, it's important to take steps to increase your emotional intelligence. Third, you want to be aware of what motivates you and gives you the energy to pursue your vision. Finally, it's critical to identify and soften those leadership derailers and risks that often erode leadership relationships. I will start by helping you understand the subject of clarity of mind.

chapter 7

Achieve Clarity of Mind

✝ 2 Timothy 1:7: *For God hath not given us the spirit of fear; but of power, and of love, and of a sound mind.*

Clarity of mind is incredibly important. Many people are affected by the events happening around them and all over our world. There is little doubt that pandemics and other world events bring significant stress. If we let it, the feeling of anxiety and fear can easily overwhelm us and lead to chaos in all aspects of our lives, disrupting our rhythm of life. Even though it can be incredibly hard, it's important that we make attempts to stay mentally healthy so that our stress does not begin to affect our relationships.

Scripture speaks to what is necessary to begin to achieve this type of mental clarity and peace. 2 Corinthians 10:10 says, *"Casting down imaginations, and every high thing that exalteth itself against the knowledge of God, and bringing into captivity every thought to the obedience of Christ..."* It isn't easy to bring every thought into the obedience of Christ, but when we make attempts to align our minds with the will of God through prayer and devotion, we have a much better opportunity for a tremendous clarity.

The mind is a powerful tool. When the mind is not aligned with the will of God, it is easy for the wrong type of thoughts, fears, and other destructive emotions to lead to results that may damage relationships. However, a clear mindset will produce a better rhythm of life and more healthy fruit and relationships in our lives. In this next section, I'll share with you more about why people are struggling to find this clarity.

The #1 Reason Christian Leaders Are Struggling to Produce

When we're considering our clarity of mind, one of the easiest ways to know that our minds are aligned with the will of God is to look at the results or the fruit that is being produced. Talking to his disciples, His future church leaders, Jesus said in John 15:16: *"Ye have not chosen me, but I have chosen you, and ordained you, that ye should go and bring forth fruit..."* We are chosen and challenged in scripture to bring forth fruit. After further study, it's evident that this fruit is evangelistic and relational in nature. In this scripture, there is one thing holding these disciples back at this point from producing that good fruit. It is the very same thing that will also hold us back if we don't work to overcome it. The number one reason Christian leaders are not producing the fruit the Lord desires of us is because of the lack of clarity of mind within us.

I was recently thinking about the setbacks our world has experienced this past year while writing this—COVID issues, social injustice issues, political turmoil. All of these things have worked to erode the clarity of mind within us. There have been hurricanes in Louisiana and wildfires in the west. There have been business closures, job losses, price increases—the list could go on and on and on. The church and other organizations have been forced to make major changes in strategy and methods.

Though some of these changes were needed, many of the changes were necessary for survival. Regardless of the reason, change is amazingly tough and let's face it, most of us don't like change. Many of us have gone through some of the most difficult changes and challenges in our lives in these last few years. Some of us make these difficult challenges even harder on ourselves mentally because we don't like change. Again, change erodes the clarity of mind within us.

John Maxwell, on his podcast, was talking about change and he said something very simple, yet profound. He said, "What happens to me and what happens in me doesn't have to be the same."[26]

What happened to us in 2020 and even into the next few years was horrific. The pandemic was shocking. We could never have fathomed what we all would go through during those few years. At times it felt like it was just a bad dream. Yet, in reality, our world and our personal lives were forever changed because of the events and circumstances. I heard the phrase "going back to normal after COVID" from pastors and other organizational leaders. However, as we know now, this world was forever changed. The church and nearly every organization was forever impacted. Our personal lives are forever different. This world is not ever going back to "the way things used to be." It's only moving forward to what is to come.

Here's reality: Change is inevitable. We are always changing. There's nothing any of us could have done to control any of the pandemic circumstances. So, while we grieve the old way of life, it's important we move forward with what's to come. Each of us has to realize that what's happening *to* us as individuals is not always something we can control; what's happening *in* us *is* something we can control.

The way we move forward with bringing forth fruit in our life as Jesus commanded doesn't begin with what's happening on the outside of us. This is the number one reason Christian leaders are struggling to produce. The success

---

26 "Episode 1075: The Leader's Greatest Return - Part 2," The John Maxwell Leadership Podcast, podcast audio, March 3, 2021, https://podcasts.apple.com/us/podcast/the-john-maxwell-leadership-podcast/id1416206538?i=1000511391906.

of fulfilling the call to bring forth fruit in our life must start with what's happening on the *inside* of us—our clarity of mind. We have to be better on the inside than we are on the outside. We have to grow and improve the inside of us—the mental and spiritual aspects of our lives.

What we desperately need right now are Christian leaders who are willing to admit we don't like everything that's going on around us and that we may not have the answers that will fix what's going on around us. However, we are going to bring forth fruit with the help of the Lord. We're going to use this time as an opportunity to retool some things in our lives. We are going to use these circumstances as a chance to get rid of the cobwebs in our minds and lives. We are going to figure out how to dig deep within us, how we can grow and become better and more effective Christian leaders in the midst of very tough situations.

I'm not sure we should be asking ourselves the question of when all of this (whatever "this" is) is going to be over—or when the messes around us are going to come into order—because it really doesn't even matter! I think the more appropriate question is simple. When I get control of what's internal in me and quit allowing so many external factors to influence my internal life, then ultimately the question becomes: When am I going to give the control of my life and leadership over to Jesus Christ?

The number one reason Christian leaders are not producing the fruit the Lord desires of us is because of the lack of clarity of mind within us.

The stronger you are on the inside, the less outside circumstances are going to impact you. You have to constantly remind yourself of the wisdom of John Maxwell—that which happens to you does not have to control what happens in you. It is so important that we somehow become responders and not reactors to the things around us. As terrible as some of these major life circumstances are—and all of the other things that have arisen in our personal lives—I'm certain we all wish these things had never happened. Yet, as terrible as it is, these things have forced us to put a mirror to our hearts and faces and evaluate what is most important in our lives.

For some, the tough circumstances haven't gone so well. For others, they have been a tremendous motivator to step up their game, to get more serious about what they're doing in their lives for God, to make the needed changes to be more God-centered and to make the needed changes to improve their internal selves. I realize we don't like the pressure; yet it is forcing us to dig deep, to make the mental and spiritual changes within that will really make a difference to achieve a good clarity of mind.

Evaluate your life through the lens of these questions:

What positive things have come from the negative external circumstances in my life?

How can I use those circumstances to propel me forward in what I've been chosen to do?

Once you have evaluated the circumstances you've recently experienced and how they are impacting your mindset, I want to provide some insight on what you can expect when you are struggling with this clarity of mind or when you find yourself in a fog.

This Is What Happens When You Can't See Clearly

I've noticed some common symptoms when a leader has an unclear mindset. Let me share with you a few of the main ones I've noticed, and maybe this will help you keep an eye out for them. The first thing that happens when we can't see clearly is this:

1. It creates an unhealthy fear within us.

Fear is a very real thing. It's a strong instrument of the enemy against us all. If you've ever found yourself under the spell of fearing something, you know fear can be very difficult to overcome. It is also impossible to ignore. Yet, in the midst of these realities, we have the Word of God to sustain us: 2 Timothy 1:7 *"For God hath not given us the spirit of fear; but of power, and of love, and of a sound mind."*

If and when we find ourselves confronted with fear, we have to understand God did not give us that spirit of fear. We can overcome it by the love of God that dwells in us and works through us. Fear may well be a battlefield where the battle is hard. However, it is ultimately a place of victory when that spirit of fear retreats in the face of the power of God, which is greater than the worst that fear has to offer.

1 Corinthians 2:3–5 *"And I was with you in weakness, and in fear, and in much trembling.*[4] *And my speech and my preaching was not with enticing words of man's wisdom, but in demonstration of the Spirit and of power:*[5] *That your faith should not stand in the wisdom of men, but in the power of God."*

Because of our humanity, we will be weak and fearful at various times in our lives. It's important to glean from this scripture, though, that we'll never overcome the weakness and fear by the wisdom of men. It is only through the power of the Spirit of God and His perfect love.

1 John 4:18: *"There is no fear in love; but perfect love casteth out fear..."* God's perfect love is the antidote to fear. Where do we find perfect love? Its only source is in Jesus Christ. *"Perfect love casteth out fear..."* is His promise to us. Our love toward Him may not be perfect, but His love toward us always is. When we turn ourselves to Him in the midst of our fear, the power of His perfect love can literally cast out that fear. However, if we continue to struggle with fear, which happens to us all at times, it can potentially lead to the next symptom of an unclear mind:

2. A destructive mindset starts showing up.

We may find ourselves in a downward spiral. Relationships could be damaged. Credibility can be lost. The impact of our leadership may lessen, and our leadership ability could come into question. Proverbs 25:28 speaks to this downward spiral when it says, *"He that hath no rule over his own spirit is like a city that is broken down, and without walls."* This describes what a destructive mindset would feel like—like you are broken down and have no ability to protect yourself.

If you find yourself in this destructive mindset, what is the antidote or the solution? 1 Corinthians 9:27 gives a word that can help: *"But I keep under my body, and bring it into subjection: lest that by any means, when I have preached to others, I myself should be a castaway."* This scripture speaks of bringing ourselves into subjection. We all have to submit ourselves to something or someone.

Submission is to God, but it's also to safe people in our lives, such as pastors, mentors, and other leaders. Submission may even be to safe friends and family members. We have to submit ourselves to key safe people in our lives, those people we love and trust. It's important to allow them to speak into our lives. When we find ourselves in this destructive mindset, it's important that we learn to ask for help as we submit ourselves to others. And, of course, ultimately, we must submit ourselves to God. God designed it so that other people in our lives can bring clarity to us when we're in the fog of fear and destruction. However, if we continue to struggle with fear and destruction internally, there is usually an eventual external result.

3. Relationships are damaged.

Many times, this internal fog will eventually lead to an external, relational hurt. It's amazing how quickly and easily things like unforgiveness can begin to develop in us. Unforgiveness can lead to damage to even our most important relationships. Matthew 6:14–15 says, *"For if ye forgive men their trespasses, your heavenly Father will also forgive you:*[15] *But if ye forgive not men their trespasses, neither will your Father forgive YOUR trespasses."* There's nothing Satan would desire more than to figure out how to create some sort of hurt in your heart. He knows that eventually the pain will lead to a division between you and God.

According to Ephesians 4:32, the antidote to unforgiveness is a tender heart—a humility that can only come from God, *"And be ye kind one to another, tenderhearted, forgiving one another, even as God for Christ's sake hath forgiven you."*

Now, I realize many other things can happen when we are struggling with a lack of clarity in our minds. These three seem to be the ones I routinely see and that seem to be most prevalent. They also may have the most destructive effects.

Give some thought to these two questions and take the appropriate courageous actions:

Am I seeing any of these three things in my life?

And if so, what can I do differently to get a different result?

If you are experiencing any of these results and need even more clarity on how to move into a healthy mindset, I want to share with you some important insights as we continue along.

Four Keys to a Better Leadership Mindset

I shared with you some common symptoms that show up when a Christian leader has an unclear mindset. In this section, I want to share with you a few things that will lead to an overall better and clearer leadership mindset. A clear leadership mindset will give a healthier rhythm of life and ultimately produce greater fruit. The first key to bring overall clarity to our minds is simple:

1. Take on the mindset of Jesus.

Philippians 2:5 gives me hope that we can actually take on the mindset of Jesus: *"Let this mind be in you, which was also in Christ Jesus…"* The same mind that was in Christ Jesus can be in me. Even though we can see that it is possible, what does that look like? The next few verses of Philippians 2 contain a pretty good list of what His mindset is like. I encourage you to go and read those verses carefully and prayerfully. The scripture uses words like servant, humbled, and obedient, which will give you a true glimpse of the mindset of Christ.

The entire book of Philippians has great insight into Jesus's mindset. I love Philippians 4:8: *"Finally, brethren, whatsoever things are true, whatsoever things are honest, whatsoever things are just, whatsoever things are pure, whatsoever things are lovely, whatsoever things are of good report; if there be any virtue, and if there be any praise, think on these things."* The things that are true, honest, just, pure, lovely, and of good report are the things that we should be thinking on. These are the things that Jesus would think on—this is His mindset and we, too, need to think on these things. If we do take on this mindset, Philippians 4:9 promises the God of peace will be with us. When we've made steps to learn and develop the mindset of Christ, He will lead us to the second key to a better mindset:

2. Develop a growth mindset.

Romans 12:2 shows a principle of a growth mindset: *"And be not conformed to this world: but be ye transformed by the renewing of your mind, that ye may prove what is that good, and acceptable, and perfect, will of God."* It's important to see from this verse the fact that we must continually renew our minds. We must continually refresh and grow our minds...and therefore, our mindset. If we are intent on pursuing the will of God in our lives, we must develop a growth mindset.

Dr. Carol Dweck, one of the leading psychologists on mindset, wrote: "This growth mindset is based on the belief that your basic qualities are things you can cultivate through your efforts, your strategies, and help from others. Although people may differ in every which way—in their initial talents and aptitudes, interests, or temperaments—everyone can change and grow through application and experience."[27]

To me, this is psychology at its best, and it is incredibly true because it is absolutely biblical. The fact of the matter is, if you can cultivate a mindset of growth, there is no doubt that you can and will grow. The person you were yesterday doesn't have to be the same person you'll be tomorrow. The Lord gives us the opportunity to develop ourselves—to develop and grow our

---

27 Carol Dweck, *Mindset: The New Psychology of Success* (New York: Random House, 2016), 6.

minds. That is my personal aim. What are some things you've done or ideas you could start working on to take on a growth mindset? It may help to write them down and keep them in front of you for a few days. The third key to a better mindset requires diligence:

3. Wash your mind with prayer and word.

Ephesians 5:26: *"That he might sanctify and cleanse it with the washing of water by the word..."* There's something about the Word of God that washes us. It cleanses our hearts and our minds. What an incredible concept and promise that we can be washed *"of water by the Word."* There are so many examples in the Bible of people cleansing themselves with prayer. Psalms 51 is a powerful and primary example of this. (Sometime soon, look up that passage and in addition to reading it, pray it. That's what the practice of washing your mind by prayer and His Word actually is.)

As a Christian leader, if you don't have a daily dose of prayer and the Word in your life you cannot expect to automatically have the mind of Christ. Nor will you have a clear Christian leadership mindset. Prayer and the Word are critical aspects of having a clear mindset. It must start today! The fourth and final thing that will bring clarity to your mind is this:

4. Use key relationships to filter your thoughts.

1 Thessalonians 5:11 gives a directive for us to use relationships to help the internal of our being: *"Wherefore comfort yourselves together, and edify one another, even as also ye do."* I must have other people in my life and I must give them significance. The people I draw into my circle of family and friends are there to help me filter my thoughts. They comfort me, edify me, and provide relational nutrients needed to bring growth to my life. They will help bring clarity to my mind when things might be just a little bit foggy. I need others in my life—as I know you do as well.

John Townsend uses a concept called "relational nutrients" that explains what emotional needs actually look like.[28] Relational nutrients are similar to food nutrients in that they feed us relationally. Relational nutrients include things like acceptance, encouragement, validation, comfort, respect, and more. These are all things that we must have in life in order to feel relationally connected and fulfilled. Even if a person has never heard of relational nutrients, he or she will accidentally give and receive a portion of these nutrients all throughout life. However, the more we are aware of our needs and understand how to get them, the more we are able to have a thriving relational diet.

By nature, I'm very introverted. You may be as well, yet we still need people in our lives to provide relational nutrients. The Lord designed you and me that way. In fact, I actually have built a team of people I call my life team—and they are my source of that kind of comfort and edification Paul spoke of to the Thessalonians. The only way those relationships in my life work is to make myself vulnerable and available to them and, also on my part, to provide those same relational nutrients to them. I must be able and willing to offer comfort and provide edification to them. Those same people I give to are the very ones who will bring light and clarity of mind to me when I truly need it.

Ask yourself this probing question: Do I have someone, outside my immediate family, who provides relational nutrients that help me think more clearly? Identify one additional person and take time to write down a step you can take to begin building greater and stronger relationships.

In the last few years, I've been on a personal journey to find a greater rhythm of life. I want to have a greater clarity of mind. I want to know the vision the Lord has set before me. I've studied books and content. I have worked to develop a growth mindset. I pray. I study the Word. I have key people gathered around me to provide clarity and accountability. I am, personally, a testament to what these principles can do in a person's life. They have made all the

---

28 John Townsend, "Relational Nutrients," Townsend, accessed January 6, 2022, https://drtownsend.com/relational-nutrients/.

difference in the world in my life—and I know they will make a significant different in your life.

Isaiah 26:3: "*Thou wilt keep him in perfect peace, whose mind is stayed on thee...*" When the mind is in alignment and is balanced with the will of God, then everything else in life can follow. Identify your "people," develop those relationships, set your mind and heart on Him, work hard to grow yourself. It will make all the difference in your pursuit of a good clarity of mind. When you begin to achieve a sense of clarity, it's much easier to become more emotionally aware and regulated. Let's dive into emotional intelligence next.

chapter 8

Increase Your Emotional Intelligence

† Proverbs 16:32: *He that is slow to anger is better than the mighty; and he that ruleth his spirit than he that taketh a city.*

The way we communicate with and relate to others is often a product of a different type of mental clarity called emotional intelligence. Emotions are signals that tell us what's going on internally; therefore, it's beneficial to know how our feelings impact the people around us. Emotional intelligence is important because it increases relational effectiveness and satisfaction with our family, friends, coworkers, and anyone we interact with. In an organizational context like a church or business, it can greatly improve our leadership success and productivity. Psychologist Daniel Goleman outlines many benefits of emotional intelligence, including self-awareness, self-regulation, empathy, mental clarity, motivation, social skills, and improved leadership ability.[29]

---

29 Daniel Goleman, *Emotional Intelligence: Why It Can Matter More Than IQ* (New York: Bantam), 1995.

What Is Emotional Intelligence?

You probably know people who are extremely talented but can't seem to succeed in leadership roles. I've seen excellent preachers who struggle to pastor a church. Do you know someone who has a phenomenal ability to organize and structure things but can't get along with people? Other people may have some of the greatest ideas but just can't seem to succeed in leading people forward to grow their organization. It's possible you also know people who are not quite as gifted but thrive in leadership roles. What makes the difference in leaders who are effective and leaders who are ineffective? Aside from spiritual reasons, I would insist that the greatest difference is a higher level of emotional intelligence.

At some point in the last few years, you've probably heard of emotional intelligence, which is also referred to as EI or EQ (sort of like IQ) for short. This topic has taken the business world by storm, and many people are beginning to realize its impact on leadership and life in general. I want to begin to unpack this topic by sharing a few definitions of emotional intelligence from the experts.

Drs. John D. Mayer and James Salovey were two of the first people to develop the emotional intelligence concept. According to Mayer and Salovey, "Emotional intelligence is the ability to perceive emotions, to access and generate emotions so as to assist thought, to understand emotions and emotional knowledge, and to reflectively regulate emotions so as to promote emotional and intellectual growth."[30]

Daniel Goleman was the man who, in the mid-1990s, did a ton of work to put emotional intelligence on the map. His definition reads: "Emotional intelligence is the capacity for recognizing our own feelings and those of others, for motivating ourselves, and for managing emotions well in ourselves

---

30 Peter Salovey and John Mayer, "Emotional Intelligence," *Imagination, Cognition, and Personality* 9, no. 3 (1990): 185-211, https://journals.sagepub.com/doi/10.2190/DUGG-P24E-52WK-6CDG.

and others."[31]

As you can see, there are a range of thoughts on what emotional intelligence really is. I like to take a more encompassing approach to the concept. Here's my definition for emotional intelligence: From an emotional standpoint, emotional intelligence is about being able to understand yourself, manage yourself, understand others, and manage your behavior toward others. Let's briefly walk through each of these components.

1. Understand yourself.

Understanding yourself is truly one of the most important areas of EQ. This is the foundational piece of beginning to increase emotional intelligence. I also refer to this concept as self-awareness, which is being able to understand your emotions, strengths, weaknesses, needs, and drivers. The deeper your understanding of yourself, the greater ability you will have to manage the reactions and feelings within you. There's no way you can manage something that you're not aware of.

We all have different combinations of strengths, weaknesses, and needs; and although EQ is not specifically about strengths and weaknesses, EQ allows us to recognize how these characteristics impact our emotions. Consequently, we are able to more effectively manage our strengths, weaknesses, and needs and more successfully control the emotions and the energy that are associated with them. If you are self-aware, you will have an increased ability to understand how your actions and emotions are going impact others and ultimately impact the organization in which you serve.

Let me give you an example: If you are aware that you are a perfectionist (and I do have those tendencies), you would understand the emotions and triggers associated with this part of you. With this awareness, you could push against your natural instincts and temper your emotions so that you don't drive people crazy with your perfectionist tendencies. I personally do this by not expecting perfectionism from others while pulling back on what I expect

31 Daniel Goleman, *Working with Emotional Intelligence* (New York: Bantam, 2000), 312.

from myself. This means I understand myself and am able to manage how my tendencies impact the environment around me.

Here's another example: If you know that your compassion level is really high, you recognize that, as one of your strengths, you may have to be more intentional about emotions that are associated with this part of your personality. You may struggle with telling people hard things because you have so much love, compassion, and emotion toward others. You will have to be purposeful about telling people things they don't want to hear. If you're aware of this part of your personality, you can push against your natural instincts and equip yourself to give truth in healthy ways. You can use your compassion to tactfully tell people hard things. Being able to successfully handle your strengths and weaknesses means that you understand yourself and are able to manage how your emotions impact the world around you.

Another characteristic of self-aware people is that they love to hear feedback or constructive criticism from safe people, and they know how to take this feedback in a healthy way. Emotionally intelligent people realize that constructive feedback simply helps them to become even more self-aware. People with low self-awareness, however, view feedback and constructive criticism as a threat or maybe even a sign of failure, and they often let this negatively impact their emotions.

One more characteristic of self-aware people is that they know their limits, and they will usually not take on things they know they can't handle. They understand what this does to their emotional and physical energy. They'll weigh the risks before they take on certain things, and they'll make better decisions based on their internal makeup and how it's going to impact their emotions and energy.

2. Manage yourself.

Being able to manage yourself is also called self-regulation. People who can self-regulate can control their bad moods or other emotional impulses. For example, instead of letting their anger dictate their actions, a person who can self-regulate does not overreact when they are angry. Ephesians 4:26 tells us that we can be angry and sin not. In other words, a person who can self-regulate is able control their reactions in a way that's not destructive to their relationships in spite of their anger.

People who can manage themselves don't deal with things in a passive way either. They understand the communication that needs to happen, and they actually fight through the desire to be passive-aggressive. Communication can happen in a healthy way while still managing the urges within.

A person with high EQ doesn't tell everyone everything that's going on inside of them. Instead, they carefully manage their feelings. Those feelings get expressed and worked through, but it's done in an appropriate manner with the safe people in their lives.

It's important that you pay attention to what motivates you when you are trying to manage yourself. What brings energy to your day-to-day life? What do you truly desire? What are you passionate about? If you know your motivations (more about that in the next chapter), you can make better choices, work longer and harder when needed, and fight through the tough circumstances in your life. This is the fuel that will motivate you to manage yourself and drive you forward.

3. Understand others.

When I talk about understanding others, I'm talking about the internal characteristics of a person. Our understanding of others is determined by our ability to get a glimpse of the emotional makeup of other people as well as what they may be going through in the moment. The best word I can use to describe this concept is empathy.

Empathy is not something that comes naturally to me, but I've worked hard to increase my understanding and application of it. It has become one of the most useful tools for relationships in general, but especially in my role as a leader. Empathy and making the effort to understand others are vital to building healthy relationships. I'll share more on empathy in a later chapter.

Understanding people also requires us to know what motivates the team members we work with. What do they want in life? What brings energy to their personal and work lives? What do they perceive to be their strengths and weaknesses? Tuning into these personal qualities can make a great difference in your ability to lead those people effectively.

4. Manage your behavior toward others.

The topic of managing your behavior toward others overlaps quite a bit with understanding yourself and managing yourself. It takes self-awareness and self-regulation to be able to effectively manage your behavior toward others. This idea is also called social intelligence, which we cover more in a later chapter. Social intelligence is what really helps a leader build effective and productive relationships. Social intelligence helps a person understand his or her emotion without being inappropriately offended or triggered to respond in an unhealthy way.

Paying attention to what's going on in a person and managing how you respond to the person in the moment are good social skills. A person with good social skills is adept at managing relationships and building rapport with people. It's easy for them to find common ground and build rapport with others. I want to point out that this is different than simply being friendly. Managing your behavior with others is friendliness with a purpose. It's being intentional in leading people in the direction that you feel you need to go with them. Sometimes managing your behavior with others may include having to go against your natural inclinations or even to confront a person when the situation calls for it. Sometimes we have to tell people things they don't want to hear, but if we have high EQ, we can do it in a graceful, productive, and constructive way.

These are the four components of emotional intelligence. The good thing for you and me is that emotional intelligence is mostly learned, so it develops as we go through life. We can definitely learn from our experiences, but we can also do specific things to educate ourselves even more about what's going on inside of us. Studies have shown that our level of emotional intelligence increases as we grow more proficient at handling our emotions and impulses, learning how we're motivated, and sharpening our empathy and social skills. In the next section, I'll share why emotional intelligence is critical for leaders.

Why Emotional Intelligence?

Some people are just naturally good at leading. They have a knack for influencing people, and they've led for many years in their respective careers. How do they do it so well? Charisma may seem like the primary factor in what makes these people so influential, and charisma does help. I've learned, however, that those who are influential for long periods of time have powerful interpersonal skills. Aside from spiritual reasons, emotional intelligence is without a doubt the greatest determining factor in a person's level of influence. I want to share with you how this subject impacts leadership and give you a few tips that will help increase your emotional intelligence.

The biggest reason emotional intelligence is so important in leadership is that the person with the most influence in the room is usually the one who passes along their emotions to everyone else. This helps create the culture within that organization. If you're a leader, you probably set the tempo of your work environment. When a leader is able to self-regulate and calm their emotions, there are fewer negative emotional issues throughout their team. Today, organizations are always changing, and people with good self-regulation and emotional intelligence can usually adapt to the stress of those regular changes much more quickly than those without emotional intelligence. People with high emotional intelligence don't panic in stressful situations; they're able to remain stable, gather information, and make logical decisions. Leaders can actually create a positive emotional culture within their organizations, churches, and ministries just by learning to manage their emotions.

In my earlier years of ministry, I was considered by certain important people in my life to be very good at taking care of issues and conflict. Notice

I said "taking care of" conflict. I was not necessarily good at engaging in healthy conflict resolution. If there was a problem in a ministry, I was quick to approach the ministry leader and resolve the issue, but I would usually have my own ideas for resolution. I would persuade the leader with crafty words or sometimes even dictate to them how I wanted the issue resolved. I would often leave the conversation with a false sense of success, but the other person would feel unheard and relationally empty. Ultimately, the person felt unaccepted and discontented in their position. I quickly learned that a leader's influence doesn't last too long with this type of disconnected interaction.

Thankfully, I've learned to tune-in to what other people are experiencing, and I've discovered how to develop buy-in, strong communication, and healthy conflict resolution. I'm not perfect with emotional intelligence, but I believe that it has absolutely made the difference in my ability to do these things. Though you may not be proficient with emotional intelligence, I encourage you to—like me—just start somewhere with the process of growth.

I love the quote by Daniel Goleman, "If your emotional abilities aren't in hand, if you don't have self-awareness, if you're not able to manage your distressing emotions, if you can't have empathy and have effective relationships, then no matter how smart you are, you're not going to get very far."[32] A leader must be able to understand and lead themselves before they can ever think about effectively understanding and leading others.

Another example of how emotional intelligence impacts leadership is demonstrated when a leader really understands the underlying emotions of others and learns how to give effective and healthy feedback. The leader who leads with this kind of empathy will cultivate trust and fulfillment within their organization in a much greater way than if they didn't.

Emotional intelligence also helps leaders objectively view their environments. They don't view the world through a black and white lens. They know

---

32 Daniel Goleman, *Emotional Intelligence: Why It Can Matter More Than IQ* (New York: Bantam Books, 1995), 16.

that their ideas aren't always the best ideas, and they realize that they are fallible human beings. The most effective leaders don't let their emotions, or their interpretation of a situation, cloud their vision of what is needed most for their organization to be effective. These are just a few of the reasons why the best leaders spend a great amount of time, energy, and money on developing emotional intelligence within themselves and those on their teams. As we move forward, I want to share with you some of the more practical things you can do to increase your emotional intelligence.

How to Increase Your Emotional Intelligence

If emotional intelligence is so important and will make such a difference in leadership, how can a person increase it in themselves? Of course, you can educate yourself by reading books and articles. There are also many YouTube videos that discuss the subject as well as several good assessments that can help you gain more internal awareness. But one of the quickest and most effective ways to gain emotional intelligence is to hire an executive coach or to join a coaching group. If the coach is trained properly, they can use effective, comprehensive tools as well as personal interaction to help you develop your emotional intelligence. This was the route I took. I hired an executive coach for the first year that I started working on emotional intelligence. Then I later joined a coaching group.

Both of those last two options create a unique opportunity to accelerate growth in emotional intelligence. However, to utilize them you must have the time and financial resources, and it can be quite a significant investment. I want to give you a few no cost, practical methods that you can use to begin your journey toward increasing your emotional intelligence.

1. Ask this question: "When I'm tired or stressed, what does it feel like to interact with me?"

I know that self-awareness is half the battle, and you can't even begin to learn to self-regulate and tune into what others are experiencing until you become self-aware and understand what is going on inside of you. This first method of becoming more emotionally intelligent is simple and won't cost you any money, but it's a very powerful experience if you approach it with humility and the true desire to learn about yourself.

This is a question you will need to ask people in at least three different areas of your life. Consider talking to family members, people who lead you, coworkers, and friends. Sit down with them, and ask, "When I'm tired or stressed, what does it feel like to interact with me?" I preface the question with "when I'm tired or stressed" because that's when the worst parts of us usually surface. If someone is going to be abrasive, that is usually when it will happen.

Before you ask that question, let me give you a few tips. Don't get defensive, and don't immediately respond to their answer. Simply ask them to be as truthful as possible and listen to their response. I'm warning you not to get defensive because there's no doubt that you will get your feelings hurt if these people are honest with you. We all do things that others wish they could talk to us about but don't because they know their words will hurt. You are giving them permission, without judgment, to tell you these extremely hard things. If they do it correctly, you will begin to understand your emotional and relational blind spots in life and leadership. I challenge you today to humbly ask that question to a few people.

2. Use "The Facial Feedback Hypothesis."

This next method to increase your emotional intelligence will particularly influence the way you present yourself to others. Altering your facial expressions, even when you're not in the presence of other people, can greatly benefit your emotional intelligence. Changing your facial expressions may not seem like it will work to help your emotional intelligence, but I assure you it does. Researchers Sven Söderkvist, Kajsa Ohlén, and Ulf Dimberg call this the "The Facial Feedback Hypothesis."[33] This theory says that our facial expressions impact our emotions; therefore, intentional smiling helps produce positive emotions. When we can achieve more positive emotions, over time it can greatly impact the way we interact with the people we lead. Why don't you go ahead and give it a try now? Seriously, go ahead and smile. You did it, didn't you?

3. Practice empathy.

Another suggestion to increase your emotional intelligence is to practice empathy. You may see the word empathy a lot throughout *The Christian Leader Blueprint* because of how important it is to leadership. You can show empathy by briefly expressing your thoughts about what you're seeing or experiencing and letting the person you're communicating with know that you understand what they're feeling. It may be as simple as naming the emotion that you see.

Empathy is powerful, and the great thing is that empathy can be learned, especially for someone like me who is not naturally empathetic. There are even training programs available to teach you how to express empathy and compassion more effectively. Attunement, empathy, and compassion create better and more productive environments to accomplish organizational and personal goals.

There's so much more to growing your emotional intelligence, and though I've introduced you to this topic, I encourage you to study this subject for yourself. There are books, assessments, and many other resources that can help you grow in your knowledge of emotional intelligence. I believe the primary influence killer or limiter for any leader is the inability to understand the emotional and relational needs of yourself and others. Emotional intelligence strongly impacts the environment in which you're leading.

---

33 Sven Söderkvist, Kajsa Ohlén, and Ulf Dimberg, "How the Experience of Emotion is Modulated by Facial Feedback," *Journal of Nonverbal Behavior* 42, no. 1 (2018): 129-151, https://www.ncbi.nlm.nih.gov/pmc/articles/PMC5816132.

It doesn't matter how smart you are or how well you can preach or teach, if you can't understand the emotional and relational components of your environment, there's no doubt that you'll have limited influence in your organization. Relationships are the greatest asset that you have in life. The primary theme of the entire Bible is relationships. In fact, Jesus taught us that we must love the Lord our God with all of our hearts, souls, minds, and strength, and love others as ourselves. If you value relationships as much as Jesus does, I encourage you to work hard to grow and develop your emotional intelligence.

Another big aspect of seeing yourself more clearly is understanding what motivates you. Motivation might actually be considered a continuation of the topic of emotional intelligence. In this next chapter, I want to help deepen the clarity you have of yourself by giving you a greater understanding of your motivation.

chapter 9

Understand Your Motivation

✝ Romans 15:13: *Now the God of hope fill you with all joy and peace in believing, that ye may abound in hope, through the power of the Holy Ghost.*

As previously mentioned, motivation is a subtopic of emotional intelligence. If you work to increase your emotional intelligence, there's no way you can avoid an exploration of your motivation. It helps you to see the things in your life that are going to give you the most energy to accomplish great things not only in your life but in the Kingdom of God.

In John 1:38, Jesus turned to two disciples and asked, "What seek ye?" What are you looking for in life? What is it that you really want? What do you truly desire? What are you most passionate about? The answers to these questions will ultimately determine how you live your life. Jesus knew that if His disciples didn't have a clear understanding of their motivation, they would struggle to keep their attention on what was most important.

Understanding your motivation is a critical part of *The Christian Leader Blueprint*. Without a strong and driving force, you won't have the drive to accomplish difficult tasks. If you can identify your core motivations and work toward making them healthy, you'll be able to accomplish much greater things in your life and leadership. In fact, it'll bring a fulfillment that gives life to your day like almost nothing else can.

An accurate awareness of what motivates you can help you make better choices about your future. It can also help you work longer and harder when necessary. Motivation can help you go safely through the challenges of leadership more easily. Let's face it—success is not always easy. Without motivation, success can even feel impossible. However, with a proper understanding of what motivates you, you can maintain the needed fuel and energy for long-term, continued success. On the flip side, maintaining your physical energy can also have a great impact on your motivation. I want to share with you some tips on how to increase your personal energy.

Three Tips to Increase Your Personal Energy

It's amazing to me that some people seem to have no problems with energy or motivation while I wrestle with these issues often. I have personally struggled with my energy levels for most of my life. Sometimes, I run out of fuel and can't push ahead; you may be able to relate. After experiencing a severe case of COVID in July of 2021, I had more low-energy days than not for about a year. Thankfully, though, I seem to be back to my old self again. Because I struggle with energy levels, I've had to experiment with activities that increase my personal energy, such as my diet, sleep, exercise, and others, so that I can maintain the needed motivation to do hard work.

One thing I've learned over the past few years is that my emotional energy probably has the greatest impact on my overall motivation. Amazingly, motivation for life and work improves drastically when your emotional energy is in check. I want you to learn how to increase your personal energy so that you will feel motivated to move forward in life and accomplish big things.

We can't expect to be motivated to take action in life without personal energy. Again, there are many factors that influence a person's personal energy. I've already mentioned that eating habits, sleep, and exercise can play a part in a person's motivation and energy levels. These are the primary factors that impact your physical body. Regarding your mind, your mental clarity can heavily impact your ability to focus, process things, create a game plan, process stress and anxiety, and even execute tasks properly. All of these things and more will heavily impact your personal energy for the good or the bad.

The main reason I think emotional energy has the greatest impact on overall motivation compared to other things is because I believe that all of the other topics impact our emotional energy. I know that if I'm eating well, sleeping well, exercising, and taking care of my physical body, I will feel emotionally better about myself. If I'm mentally processing things in a healthy way and taking care of the spiritual side of my life, again, I will feel emotionally better. Doing these things well just fuels me and gives me the emotional energy that I need to push through difficult situations that may normally deplete my energy. This is why *The Christian Leader Blueprint* model, especially "Establish a Better Rhythm of Life," is such a vital concept to an effective leader.

There are other things that keep my emotional energy up. I will share with you several actions that I've personally taken to drastically improve my emotional energy and keep me motivated and continually moving forward these last few years:

1. Create good routines.

I cover how to create good routines for life in Part 1 of this book, so I will only share how that affects emotional energy here. Regardless of whether you are a naturally structured person or not, having good weekly and daily routines that keep you focused on getting things done will give you a sense of fulfillment and help your emotional energy. I have good, rigid routines in the spring and fall. These routines help me stay focused and on the right track for most of the year. During this time, I know that by 9:00 in the morning on most days I'll have done the necessary things to keep me grounded before I start my workday. This is important to me emotionally. When I accomplish my personal devotion, writing, and other important tasks first, my day feels significant. The rest of my day could drastically change because of having to help someone through an unexpected crisis or other important interruptions, but I will still feel grounded because I have already accomplished my important routines for the day.

During the summer, I usually give myself a chance to take a break from my routines for a short time. I still have my daily prayer and devotion, but I'm not as rigid with the rest of my morning routine as I am during the spring and fall. To be transparent and to emphasize my point, though, I sometimes have to work through emotional energy struggles during this time because I don't accomplish as much as I normally do while practicing my normal routines. My routines make a significant difference in my emotional energy and, ultimately, my motivation to deal with the difficult things that I may have to encounter in the future. This is primarily because using energy also helps produce emotional energy. When I'm accomplishing a large number of tasks with my routines, I produce and use more energy for the other responsibilities I need to accomplish. I know that when I become focused on my routines, I have energy and motivation to move ahead in life.

2. Develop a personal vision.

I also discussed vision in Part 1, but I want to share how very important it is to your emotional energy levels. Solomon, the wisest man in history, outside of Jesus, spoke to what vision does for a person. Solomon said in Proverbs 29:18, *"Where there is no vision, the people perish: but he that keepeth the law, happy is he."* I don't think King Solomon was saying that the people would literally die if they had no vision. I believe he meant that having no vision can take the life or the energy out of a person. Where there is no vision, the people perish. You can't sustain a flourishing, prosperous life that's full of energy and motivation without a sense of vision.

When I'm not doing well with my personal vision, it's interesting how quickly I can be emotionally drained and even cynical. I start viewing situations as problems and excuses. However, when I know where I'm headed, I start viewing issues as opportunities rather than problems. Obstacles actually begin to motivate me to figure out a way to accomplish my God-given, personal vision.

3. Engage in the key relationships.

When I'm emotionally depleted, I can count on someone in my structured inner circle or my personal support team to refuel me. This happens as key relationships give me the relational nutrients I need to maintain my emotional energy. Relational nutrients are like the wood in a fireplace. If you have no wood, you have no fire. If you are not receiving from key relationships, your emotional energy will quickly burn out, including your motivation for life. We must resource from people who leave us feeling relationally full, excited, energetic, and motivated to achieve what the Lord wants us to accomplish.

I can also use my emotional energy to give others relational nutrients. Doing this can create a flow of emotional energy instead of stagnating my emotional energy. Emotional energy is like water; if we only receive and never give, there is not a constant flow, and we can become stagnant and stale. Just like stagnant water, we will eventually begin to harbor the growth of unwanted things that create relational imbalances. Our emotional energy will decrease and our motivation for doing significant things will begin to diminish as well.

When it comes to emotional energy, these are the three things that make the biggest difference: creating good routines, developing personal visions, and engaging in key relationships will help us maintain a healthy sense of emotional energy. These, ultimately, will keep us motivated to move forward in our lives and ministries with bigger and better things.

Along with these three things, there is one specific emotional factor that I see more than any other in leaders; it deserves some special attention in this chapter. A fear of failure greatly impacts the motivation of the leader. It has the power to literally stop a person in their tracks or to help fuel a person to greater things. I want you to be fueled by it, and so I'll share with you how to find balance in your fear of failure.

How to Find Balance in Your Fear of Failure

It doesn't matter how competitive or self-confident a leader is, fear of failure can still be debilitating. When the fear of failure is overwhelming, people can lack the motivation to move forward. In fact, the fear of failure can cause a leader to give up their entire career or ministry. It can also become one of your greatest motivators when you learn to balance it correctly.

Failure is part of life, especially a motivated leader's life. The only way to avoid failure is to never try anything significant. When we give in to the fear of failure, we easily lose motivation and energy. Unfortunately, a true fear of failure is usually difficult for people to recognize on their own. We are usually blinded or desensitized to the effects of it in our own personal lives. I don't want you to be blind to it, so I will give you a few questions to ask yourself to more easily recognize the fear of failure in your life.

First of all, do you consider yourself a realist? In other words, do you accept things as they are, or do you to try to put a positive spin on everything? If you're more of a realist and you tend to focus on the actual problems you are facing, you probably have a fear of failure.

Second, do you look for what can go wrong in a situation, or are you occasionally blindsided by problems while working on something? If you generally look for what can go wrong in a situation, you probably have a fear of failure.

Third, when you make a mistake, fail on your first attempt, or you don't do things exactly as you would have liked, do you become anxious and nervous, believing you will never succeed? If so, you may regularly experience the fear of failure.

Fourth, and last, do you often find yourself stalled in decision-making, especially when you're tired and stressed or when you have to make a big decision? Do you often worry too much about making the wrong decision? If so, then you might have a fear of failure.

Most people who want to be the best version of themselves often struggle with some sense of fear of failure. These people often ask themselves, "What if I fail? What if I can't make it? What if I don't have what it takes to last? What if I make the wrong decisions?" The fear of failure is an awareness of the possibility that you may not finish well. If you struggle with the fear of failure, welcome to the world of doing something great with your life. You have no reason to fear failure if you're not doing anything significant with your life. It's normal to fear failure from time to time.

If you fear failure too much, you can easily become stalled in your progress, feel scared to dream big, lack motivation and energy to move forward, and even put limits on what God can do through your leadership and ministry. It's also possible to not fear failure enough. I realize that scripture says, *"God hath not given us the spirit of fear"* (2 Timothy 1:7), but not having an appropriate fear of failure can leave you feeling unmotivated to work hard. It can prevent you from establishing and maintaining the good routines that are required to get big things done. It can also cause you to avoid important tasks like anticipating and preparing for problems; you won't be able to finish strong or accomplish the God-given vision that you see in your future.

The key to making the fear of failure a positive thing is to find a sense of balance in your mind. Having an adequate balance of the fear of failure is important to maintaining the motivation that's necessary to keep moving forward with the significant things in your life. To find balance, it's important to understand the promises in the Bible that relate to failure. Jeremiah 29:11–13 says, *"For I know the thoughts that I think toward you, saith the LORD, thoughts of peace, and not of evil, to give you an expected end.*[12] *Then shall ye call upon me, and ye shall go and pray unto me, and I will hearken unto you.*[13] *And ye shall seek me, and find me, when ye shall search for me with all your heart."* God's thoughts toward us pertain to peace. They are not evil thoughts; He does not want to cause us unnecessary failure and humiliation. God has an expected end for us. He listens to us when we pray, and He desires that we succeed in accomplishing the work we do for Him.

You must truly seek God with your whole heart and abide in Him if you want to work through your fear of failure and create a sense of balance in your mind. This is hard, but give all the results of your leadership to God. He will direct you; you can trust Him with your life. If you do fail at something, and we all do from time to time, trust that God is with you. He will use your failure for good in your future. He can use your failures to ultimately accomplish your God-given vision and bring you an expected end in whatever leadership ambition is before you.

I want you to consider the possibility that something you are completely convinced you can accomplish is probably not a vision God has given you. A vision you are 100 percent positive you can succeed at is too easy. However, a vision that you are only 70 percent convinced you can accomplish is a big, God-sized vision. Ask yourself this question, "Does it seem a little scary to accomplish the vision that I feel the Lord has given me? Does it feel like a 70/30 vision?" In other words, "Is there a 30 percent chance that I will fail at this?" If so, then let that motivate you to step out in faith and get it done.

We can't let the fear of failure prevent us from taking action, and we also can't let the lack of fear cause us to become lackadaisical or deplete our energy and motivation to do something big. Somehow, we need to create a 70/30 mindset and prayerfully trust God and His involvement in our lives. Don't get hung up on the exact numbers. The intent is for it to feel a little risky. If we do this, we will begin to accomplish big things for Jesus. Learn to let the fear of failure motivate your faith to move forward rather than harm your progress.

An unhealthy, debilitating fear of failure is often rooted in a selfish motivation to succeed. If we get our intent right, it usually helps overcome fear and it improves our overall motivation to work through the hard things of leadership and life. In this next section, I want to help you evaluate what you're looking for in life.

What Are You Looking for in Life?

What are you looking for? As mentioned, that is the question Jesus asked His disciples in John chapter 1. In other words, He asked, "What are you looking for in life? What is motivating you to do what you do?" This is a tough question, but it's one that we should ask ourselves periodically. I want to examine this question and discuss why it is so important to our leadership.

In John 1:38–39, the disciples asked Jesus, *"Rabbi (which means Teacher), where are you staying?"* And he said to them, [39] *"Come and see."* The disciples came to see where He was staying and spent time with Jesus that day. Jesus then asked them what they were seeking. This is an important question Jesus asked. What is it that we really want? What do our hearts really desire in this life? What brings us passion and joy? These questions will determine how we live our lives as well as influence the motivation we have to accomplish significant things for the Kingdom of God.

We all have personal ambitions, desires, likes, and dislikes, but when the answers to the questions above are mostly rooted in selfish motivation, we can greatly struggle as Christians. Our world is crazy; there are all kinds of stresses and strains. Everything is constantly changing. We deal with issues involving the pandemic, the economy, social injustices, job losses, and even disruptions to normal life. These problems not only create stress and cause feelings of discouragement but also sometimes make us want to quit and escape our circumstances. These difficulties are not only in the secular world, they are also prevalent in the church.

Attempting to escape these circumstances seems like the quick way out of the issues. We often believe that the grass is greener on the other side; if we can change jobs, leadership positions, churches, or physical locations, those tough things will just go away. It seems easy to make a change, but it seems very difficult to conquer our problems, push through the difficulties, and finish strong.

It's important to realize that the grass is rarely greener on the other side. In fact, the same issues that we struggle with on one side of the fence often follow us to the other side. I'm not saying that transitions and changes in life are not necessary at times; we need to make changes occasionally, but if the issues are rooted within us and we're discontent within our own minds and hearts, the problems won't go away simply because we change our circumstances. The issues within us will stay with us.

One of the biggest issues I see in people who want to continually chase something better than their current circumstances is the absence of understanding why they want to initiate the change. They don't know why they are exhausted from their current situation or why they don't have any energy or motivation to persist in the routines or struggles of life. They have a hard time figuring out what motivates them to get up every morning and do the things they normally do. They have no idea what can help them in difficult circumstances or what they are truly looking for in life.

It's important to recognize that we all have different passions, desires, and callings; our leadership lives are not all the same. Some people love art while others love business and finance. Some love to have fun and bring joy and laughter everywhere they go. Some people love to analyze and figure things out while others like organization and structure. I want to help you understand the motivation behind what people have passion for. I want to help uncover the underlying motivation that gives a person the energy to do the things they love to do when life gets hard.

The question to ask is whether your motivation is self-serving or rooted in the desire to serve God and others. This is what I'm really asking when I say, "What are you looking for in life?" If you want to be a great leader and disciple of Christ, you must go beyond your personal incentives and discover what will sustain your motivation for years to come. For a Christian, that motivation should come from loving Christ and serving others. 1 Peter 4:2 says, "*That he no longer should live the rest of his time in the flesh to the lusts of men, but to the will of God.*" Even if you work in a secular job and spend most of your time serving a secular business, you must be motivated by the will of

God so that you can dedicate your time to pursuing the mission of Christ and serving others. You can do this in whatever setting you are in.

I want to ask you again, "What are you looking for in life?" Your motivation as a Christian leader shouldn't be about money, position, power, or influence. Your motivation must be about the mission of Christ and serving others. This is the only way to sustain your motivation as a Christian leader. As a Christian, you may have a position of involvement of some sort in your local church. However, if you don't have the mission of Christ as your motivation, you will not last in your ministry. In this day and age, you likely will burn out at some point, or another opportunity will distract you, or a hardship will derail your ability to serve.

It is important to determine what you are looking for in life and the reason for your motivation. Honestly, the answer to this question is never really complete. We must learn to settle this answer regularly in our hearts. That's why Paul said in 1 Corinthians 15:31, *"I die daily."* Paul understood the need to stay grounded to Christ and His mission on a daily basis. Doing this kept Paul's motivation in the right place and helped him look for the right purpose in life.

In conclusion, I want you to evaluate yourself with a couple of questions that will hopefully inspire you to stay motivated and grounded to the mission of Christ:

1. How is your emotional energy? A lack of emotional energy can literally kill your desire to do big things. If emotional energy impacts motivation in such a great way, what's one thing you can do this week to work toward increasing your emotional energy?

2. Do you have balance in your fear of failure? Not having enough fear of failure means that you may not be doing all you can do for the Kingdom of God. An inadequate fear of failure can leave you unmotivated to work hard. Having too much fear of failure can easily stall your progress and leave you feeling scared to do big things

145

for Jesus. It's important to work on finding a balance in your fear of failure in order to stay motivated and grounded to the mission of Christ.

3. If your motivation isn't grounded in Christ, you will prioritize getting what you want at the expense of others. If you're truly focused on the mission of Christ and serving others, however, you'll use your influence to help develop others as you accomplish your God-given vision. Helping others is a large part of the mission of Christ. Knowing what you are looking for in life is something you must regularly evaluate in order to properly assess your motivations in life. It's important that we all stay grounded to the mindset of pursuing the mission of Christ and serving others.

Once a leader has found a greater clarity of mind, it makes it much easier to achieve growth in emotional intelligence. The increase in emotional intelligence will hopefully lead to a more thorough understanding of your motivation. From here, it's important for the leader to learn to manage the things that have the potential to disrupt or derail his or her leadership. In this next chapter, I want to help you identify and soften your leadership derailers.

chapter 10

Identify and Soften Your Leadership Derailers

✝ Jeremiah 29:11: *For I know the thoughts that I think toward you, saith the LORD, thoughts of peace, and not of evil, to give you an expected end.*

With more understanding of clarity of mind, emotional intelligence, and motivation, you should be well on your way to knowing what's important for a clear picture of yourself. I think of this next concept—leadership derailers—as "next level." Only the most invested leaders know themselves well enough to identify and soften their leadership derailers. I think you can be "next level!"

How do you behave when you are hurt, frustrated, or embarrassed? What comes to the surface when you are exhausted or stressed? Do you lash out, shut down, or smile through the difficulties? Most everyone has internal leadership derailers that can activate when life gets tough.

A leadership derailer is a behavior that gets in the way of our progress with relationships and team cohesiveness. A derailer isn't just a weakness in our personality that can be bypassed. It's something that requires improvement if we truly want to reach our greatest potential as a leader. These behaviors are much like a fingerprint because no two people's risks and challenges are exactly alike. We all have our own distinct ways of responding to the circumstances and events that happen to us. When our negative reactions go unchecked, they become detrimental to our interactions as leaders. If you want to be a healthy leader, it is important to identify your derailers and the things that may trigger these negative reactions. Often times, the wounds and pains of your past, your successes and failures, and your key emotional moments have a major impact on your current state of mind and regulate your defense mechanisms and triggers.

These leadership derailers can significantly undermine our leadership effectiveness. Failure to recognize these risks can often cause a leader to make decisions that are not best for his or her organization, resulting in a loss of credibility and trust for their team. By examining the weak points of your leadership, as well as the factors that cause you the most stress, you'll discover the primary issues that impair your leadership.

The greatest influence occurs in making the necessary adjustments to soften and possibly remove these derailers and strengthen these key weak areas in our lives. Yet, the awareness alone will usually help to lessen the impact of these negative points. We'll start bringing light to this subject for you by talking about some of the weaknesses that can and will kill your influence if these things are not considered.

Ten Weaknesses That Can Kill Your Influence

I don't recommend that people focus too much energy on their weaknesses. If we always focus on our weaknesses instead of our strengths, we greatly limit what we're capable of accomplishing. Focusing on improving your strengths allows you to maximize your God-given abilities; however, there are exceptions to this rule. There are a set of particular weaknesses that can derail your ministry and hinder your influence with others if you don't give them adequate attention.

Let me give you an example. I naturally struggle with showing compassion. Even though I'm a pastor and do a great deal of counseling and coaching, I struggle to lead in a warm, caring, and sensitive way if I'm not intentional with how I present myself. This is especially true when I'm tired or overly stressed. If I don't work to improve this area in my life at least a little, I am likely to come across as harsh to people. I can easily hurt someone's feelings while struggling to empathize with those I lead. Obviously, this could negatively impact my influence with the people I serve.

Lacking compassion is a weakness that can derail my leadership if I let it. Therefore, it's imperative that I work hard to exhibit Christ-generated compassion when I meet and interact with people. To help me maintain this Christ-generated compassion, I first try to start every day with prayer and devotion. This gets my mind and heart in the right place and hopefully exhibiting Christlike characteristics. Second, I make sure that I have enough energy through my good rhythm of life to push past my natural lack of compassion and show the love and care that is necessary throughout my day.

Lacking compassion is just one personal example; there are actually quite a few weaknesses that can derail a person's leadership if they are extreme enough. There's no way to name all the various things a person may exhibit, but I want to share with you 10 of the more common weaknesses:

1. Lacking compassion

In the story I just shared, I showed how this weakness can affect successful leadership. Having compassion is important to leading effectively. It's not possible to have sustaining influence with people who do not feel some sense of warmth and care from you. As you will see a little further ahead, acceptance is a critical need of any effective relationship. Your compassion is one of the methods of communicating a sense of acceptance and connection.

2. Having low emotional intelligence

This is an important weakness to address because the less you're aware of yourself, the less you can regulate how you interact with others. The less control you have over your actions, the less influence you will have with the people you lead.

As I mentioned in Chapter 8, in today's world emotional intelligence is not optional if you want to lead well and grow an organization. Lack of emotional intelligence is not easy to overcome; it takes time and much personal growth to increase this area of your life. I encourage you to revisit Chapter 8—Increase Your Emotional Intelligence if this continues to be a weakness for you. In addition, good counselors and executive coaches can also help you grow in a much quicker way than trying to do it on your own.

3. Having no vision or direction

Vision is also something that I address in detail in Chapter 4. I'm sharing it here again in brief form to accentuate how it relates to derailers in your leadership. You must understand that not everyone is gifted in creating vision. If you do not excel in this area, it's okay and you are not alone. Many good leaders struggle deeply with creating vision. To compensate, it's important to your organization that you recruit others on your team to help. There are likely individuals around you who can help you brainstorm a positive vision and establish direction for your organization. It's a false belief that all vision has to be created by the leader. I encourage you to gather people around you who can help you create productive vision; then, as the leader you can work hard to communicate that vision and move the organization toward it.

4. Settling for mediocrity

You don't have to be perfect in everything you do; perfectionism is a killer of progress. However, if the product or the service that your organization produces is not excellent, I challenge you to raise your level of expectation. People want to follow leaders who love excellence. If details are not your strength, gather around you those who love to consider the things that you may find taxing. This will bring value to them and bring a different perspective that is needed to create an excellent environment.

5. Not regularly developing yourself and others

As we established in Chapter 1, part of the big picture of leadership is to help others grow and develop to be all that the Lord has called them to be. This book is about development, but there's no way you can effectively lead others to growth if you are not pursuing growth for yourself. When we work hard to develop ourselves in a healthy, biblical way, this helps to create a much more effective leadership environment and it helps us lead others to growth and greater influence as well. When you and others on your team are growing, the entire organization is impacted in a positive way. It fuels forward movement and the ability to accomplish big things.

6. Neglecting to delegate to people's strengths

The only way to be an effective leader is to release tasks, jobs, and responsibility to other team members. Without effective delegation, it's not possible to have a complete team. We must realize that there's no way for one person to be good at everything. Consider the strengths of the people on your team and delegate accordingly. This will bring fulfillment to the team member and free you up to focus on different, maybe more important things. Again, when you learn to pull others in to help you, the entire team is impacted in a positive way.

7. Distrusting people who have proven to be trustworthy

I realize that it is becoming more and more difficult to trust people with so much uncertainty in the world today. However, when you withhold trust from a person who has worked to gain your trust and has proven to be trustworthy, it often devalues the person. It's discouraging and may have detrimental effects on the relationship. Though it can be difficult, I try my best to keep the policy of trusting others unless they prove that I can't trust them. We must realize that if we can't learn to trust our team members, it's not likely that they will trust us. Trust is the glue that's needed for a healthy team.

8. Remaining unsociable at important times—even if you're an introvert

As I've mentioned previously, I'm an extremely introverted person. It would be so easy for me to not engage in social settings like parties, large group meetings, and other group settings. Do you feel this way occasionally? If we choose to withdraw from people because of these feelings too often, it will eventually erode some of the relationships that we desperately need to be effective in leadership. This means that even if you're an introvert, you've got to push yourself to become an extrovert at times.

You can't avoid the limelight when it's necessary as the leader. You need to be able to float around a room and talk to people occasionally. The key for you and me being able to do these things is to make sure we are well rested prior to attending important social settings and then to make sure that we rest after we leave them. It's vital that we push ourselves to step out of our shell with people. I'll usually leave those settings drained of energy, but it'll be worth it as I've invested in relationships that are important for the success of the organization.

9. Being too impulsive and regularly breaking the rules

It's amazing how common it is for leaders to be impulsive in nature and for them to step outside of the rules set by an organization. Many times this is rooted in an entitlement mentality. The rules set by an organization are necessary guardrails to keep order, a healthy culture, and forward momentum. They cut down on chaos, especially as an organization grows. When leaders do not respect the plans and rules of the organization, it makes it difficult for others to fully trust them. This also communicates a lack of respect and damages the influence of the leader. Though there may be some special perks and flexibility that come with the role of leader, it's important that he or she respects the overall parameters for the good of the organization.

10. Refusing to create a culture of acceptance on your team

I believe that acceptance is the number one relational need of any person. This makes it vital for a leader to create a culture of acceptance on a team. Acceptance is connection without judgment. When team members don't feel connection without judgment by the leader, it's not likely that the team member will be with the leader very long. People gravitate to where they feel most accepted. If the team member happens to stay around and fight through those feelings, it will usually be with a halfhearted mindset and unnecessary disfunction at its best. A culture of acceptance is not optional for effective leadership.

These are 10 of the greatest weaknesses that can derail your influence. Having these issues can easily frustrate your success as a leader if you don't seek to improve the areas in which you struggle.

Perhaps you are now starting to identify with some of these weaknesses. Most of the work in overcoming these issues involves going against your natural instincts as well as allowing the people who are gifted in the areas that you are not to help you. You do not have to be perfect in the areas that you struggle in. You simply need to make sure those areas aren't so weak that they harm your influence with the people you lead. I often tell people to just "Get them out of the ditch…you don't have to walk the center line of the road… just get them out of the ditch and onto the road."

I encourage you to go back and review these 10 weaknesses and evaluate your own limitations. I want you to reflect on these two questions:

1. Which one of these weaknesses do you struggle with the most?

2. What's one thing you can do this week to help you improve as you work to develop your influence and overcome your weaknesses?

Don't try to do too much. Start by doing one thing that develops an area of your life where you feel you lack. It's incredibly important to not make excuses with your personal areas of weaknesses. Work to shift your perspective and give attention to your natural inclinations, use other people in your life to help you improve, and work to develop yourself in the area where you are the weakest. Doing these things will help you avoid derailing or damaging your influence with the people you lead. It's not always these weaknesses that will derail us. Sometimes our deepest insecurities can rise up at the most inopportune time and cause major issues. I want to share with you why these things will sometimes arise in your life.

Why Do I Feel so Insecure?

Honestly, I've probably felt insecure more days of my life than I've felt secure. That's the reality for most of us. Anyone who is truly authentic and transparent will admit to having insecurities. It's easy for insecurities to drain the emotional energy of a leader and even stifle the progress of a team. Insecurities can derail a leader's potential quicker than most things. I want to share with you where these insecurities come from and give you the first step toward overcoming them.

One Sunday morning at my church, The Pentecostals of Alexandria, I preached a message called "He Makes Beautiful Things." In that message, I testified to the emotional healing that was taking place in my life. I began the message like this: "My name is Ryan. I'm a grateful believer in Jesus Christ, and I'm in recovery from self-reliance and approval addiction." In the past, I would have been scared to death to say those words. I wouldn't have wanted to admit those truths to anyone, much less announce them to a room full of hundreds of people. For many years of my life I woke up every morning and put on a mask in order to protect my image.

Shakespeare once wrote, "Away and mock the time with fairest show; False face must hide what the false heart doth know."[34] That quote explains what I did most days, I covered up who I really was in order to hide from the world.

---

34 *Macbeth*, 1.7. 81-82.

154

I desperately wanted to run from who the Lord was calling me to be and what He was calling me to do.

Because of my personal and leadership insecurities, I had to convince myself that God does indeed make beautiful things. To do this, I had to go to scripture often to remind myself that I wasn't a mistake and that He'd formed me perfectly. Verses like Genesis 1:31 helped as I read, *"And God saw every thing that he had made, and, behold, it was very good."* God's creation isn't just good. According to this scripture, it is very good. Even when He made *me*, He made a very good thing.

Ecclesiastes 3:11 says, *"He hath made every thing beautiful in his time."* It was important for me to know that everything God made was beautiful. There really wasn't anything about me that I needed to hide. He'd made me very good, and He'd made me beautiful. This scripture reminds me of the chorus to a song written by Michael and Lisa Gungor, "You make beautiful things. You make beautiful things out of the dust. You make beautiful things. You make beautiful things out of us."[35] As a Christian leader who seeks to positively influence people, I encourage you to take some time to reflect on this verse and how he made *you* beautiful as well.

I want to declare to you today that God makes beautiful things. On the last day of creation, God created man in His own image. He finished His work of creation by adding a personal touch. God formed man from the dust of the ground and gave man life by breathing His own breath into him. No matter how old, young, broken, tired, confused, or scared you may be, God still has a ticket of destiny with your name written all over it; and it really is a beautiful thing.

Many of you are hearing my words of hope today, but you may be thinking, "Ryan, you have no idea how much I want believe your words, but every attempt to step into the dreams that I feel God has given me has been a repeat-

---

35 Michael and Lisa Gungor, "Beautiful Things," Brash Music, track 2 on *Beautiful Things*, released February 16, 2010, CD.

ed scene of failure." I was there at one point in my life as well. If you're like me, after each of your repeated failures, you have even less confidence that anything will ever change. You are constantly left with doubt, fear, and deep insecurities. I want to encourage you today to believe that there is a solution to your problem. I know that the Bible is true, and I know that God does make beautiful things. He provided the answers for me, and He continues to provide those answers as I move through my life.

There is some fine print in this disclaimer—most every contract has fine print, right? God's dreams for us are really not about us because ultimately this life isn't about us. God's plan will definitely bring fulfillment to us, but it's not about what we want. This life is about helping others, loving others, bringing the Gospel to others, guiding, serving, leading, influencing, and imparting to others hopes and dreams.

Unfortunately, pride often slips into our hearts. The Bible portrays pride as an unholy preoccupation with self. There's nothing wrong with being occupied with ourselves to a certain degree. That's normal. There's nothing wrong with taking care of our own needs, interests, and ambitions. There's nothing evil about wanting to protect ourselves. That's completely natural and expected. The problem is that pride influences us to become occupied with ourselves first. We become preoccupied with putting our needs and our interests ahead of others' needs and interests. We sometimes leave God out of the equation all together, and we forget that God is the source of everything that we have and all that we enjoy. We forget that He is the only one worthy of worship.

James 4:6 tells us, *"Wherefore he saith, God resisteth the proud, but giveth grace unto the humble."* Through this scripture, we understand that pride doesn't settle too well with God. My problem was that no matter how hard I tried, I could never get my pride to work for me. No matter how hard I struggled, Ryan-plus-pride would never equal abundant life. That equation will never work.

The enemy wants you to believe the lie that abundant life comes from the pride of life. John

Several years ago, I read the book *TrueFaced: Trusting God and Others with Who You Really Are* (rewritten as *The Cure*). I was deeply moved by a particular passage, and tears began streaming down my face as I read these words on the page:

> "God couldn't help us until we trusted him with who we really were. That was perhaps our first taste of a TrueFaced life. It was stunning. Incredible. It painted our world in colors we hardly knew existed. But, something happened to many of us in the intervening years. We lost confidence that His delight of us and new life in us would be a strong enough (force) for a growth that would glorify God and fix our junk. So, we gradually bought the slick sales pitch that told us we would need to find something more, something others seemed to have that we could never quite get our hands around. Something magical and mystical that we would receive if we tried hard enough and proved good enough, often enough. And so we began learning to prop things up. We went back to trying to impress God and others—back to posturing, positioning, manipulating, trying to appear better than who we were. Our two-faced life has severely stunted our growth. And broken our hearts. And left us gasping. Although we may have accumulated titles, status, and accomplishments, we personally remain wounded and immature—long on "success," but short on dreams. We admire people who live the TrueFaced life, but our loss of hope has forced us into desperately trying to discover safety from behind our masks. In a very real sense, we are all performers. Because of sin we've lost confidence that we will always please our audience, and so we put on a mask. As an unintended result, no one, not even the people we love, ever get to see our true face."[36]

---

36 Bill Thrall, Bruce McNicol, and John Lynch, *TrueFaced: Trust God and Others with Who You Really Are* (Colorado Springs: NavPress, 2004), 87.

As I read those words, I felt convicted of my deep-rooted insecurities and pride. I'd worn a mask for most of my life, and I had been living two-faced before God and people.

The problem with pride, from a biblical perspective, is that it leaves God out of the picture. Pride can quickly make us believe that whatever good things we've attained or received in life are purely the result of our own achievements. We start to view our accomplishments possessively—my hard work, my good looks, my intelligence, my talent, my persistence. We make ourselves the source of all good things instead of God. We end up exalting ourselves, serving ourselves, and trusting ourselves instead of exalting, serving, and trusting Christ.

Romans 12:3 says, *"For I say, through the grace given unto me, to every man that is among you, not to think of himself more highly than he ought to think; but to think soberly, according as God hath dealt to every man the measure of faith."* We're not supposed to think too highly of ourselves; that's pride. But we're not supposed to think too lowly of ourselves either. We're to think of ourselves with sober and sound judgment. In other words, we have to honestly evaluate ourselves. Our honest, sober evaluations should not be based on what others think of us or what we think of ourselves but should instead be based on what God thinks of us.

In order to overcome deep-rooted insecurities, you must understand how God thinks of you. Scripture says that God loves you in spite of your sinfulness. It says that you're fearfully and wonderfully made and that you're of incredible value to Him. Scripture also tells us that when we turn to Christ in repentance and faith, we can be forgiven of our sins and be made new from the inside out. When you are in Christ, you are destined for glory.

The Lord really does make beautiful things; He made a beautiful thing even when He made you. When you know exactly who you are in Christ, you are free. You can remove your mask, admit you're a sinner, and say, "I'm sorry." You're free from having to manage other people's impressions of you so that your insecurities can diminish. You don't have to compete with everyone else's looks, status, accomplishments, or spirituality. You can do tremendous things for God without needing people to notice you. It's possible to let others have their way, lose graciously, and rejoice in someone else's success because you know exactly who you are. You understand that there's no one else like you in the universe.

Think about how good it feels when you're being your true self, when you're engaged and energized by what you're doing. When you attempt to hide things about yourself—the good parts, the quirky parts, the awkward parts—you are missing out on becoming the person you were born to be.

You are a special person! I know this because I know that God makes beautiful things. I encourage you today to allow the Lord to search your heart. Let Him reveal things to you and allow Him to make you into the beautiful person you were meant to be. Remove the mask and realize that the Lord made a beautiful thing when He made you. Realizing what God says about you is true is the first and most important step to overcoming your insecurities. This alone will greatly impact your effectiveness as a leader, but there's more. Let's take a look at a few ways you can conquer your insecurities.

Four Steps to Help Overcome Your Insecurities

I've had to work hard to minimize the deep-rooted insecurities in my life and leadership. Insecurities are a reality for most of us. In fact, as previously mentioned, I don't know of any truly authentic and transparent person who hasn't admitted to having insecurities. It's easy for these insecurities to drain the emotional energy of a leader and even stifle the progress of an entire team. Insecurities can derail a leader more quickly than anything else. I want to dig a little deeper now and discuss the four steps of how to overcome those insecurities.

Because of my deep-rooted insecurities and pride, I wore a mask for most of my life. I hid behind my achievements, hard work, gifts, and persistence. So many leaders look like they have it all together on the outside, but many struggle with issues no one can see. Our pride is what keeps us from admitting that we have these struggles. It also prevents us from receiving the healing needed to overcome our insecurities.

Jesus came to save us from our broken, sinful lives, but He also desires to deeply heal and restore us over time. It is important that we overcome our insecurities so that we can do the work that Christ has designed us to do. There are several steps that I've taken to help me overcome the insecurities in my life. These steps can help you navigate your own insecurities and embrace God's purpose for your life.

Step 1: Embrace all that scripture says about you through the lens of prayer.

This is the very first and most important step to overcoming your insecurities. Scripture is the foundation of understanding our identities in Christ. The only way to embrace what scripture says about you is to read and study it regularly. I study scripture on a daily basis and there are not many days that go by when something in scripture doesn't speak to my identity in Christ. One thing you could do to help deepen your learning is to journal any scripture that speaks to your identity as you're reading and then reflect on it while you are in your prayer time.

Step 2: Admit that you have insecurities and determine how those insecurities have impacted your life.

As I've mentioned, we all have insecurities, and I can guarantee that yours have negatively impacted your life in some way. Increasing your awareness to what these insecurities are and where they come from is important in being able to make positive changes in your life, such as eliminating negative or destructive self-talk.

We can overcome some of this negativity on our own through prayer and self-reflection, but you will likely require help from an outside source such as a counselor or an executive coach to thoroughly conquer these issues. If the source of the insecurity is complex, a licensed counselor would be the best person to turn to in order to start getting help. Receiving help to understand why that insecurity is there will help you minimize the effects of it.

Step 3: Develop reasonable expectations for yourself.

This includes working on your rhythm of life, learning to see yourself more clearly, and leveraging your strengths—all fundamental pillars covered in detail in *The Christian Leader Blueprint*. A better rhythm of life allows you to manage stress and anxiety so that you can better recognize your limits and manage your energy levels. Seeing yourself more clearly allows you to manage the mental and emotional factors that play an important role in your insecurities. A self-aware person is able to better control a downward spiral of their emotions and recognize the circumstances that trigger their insecurities. Leveraging your strengths helps you understand what you were designed by God to do and allows you to fully accept and embrace your weaknesses. It is possible for us to be validated by the things we do well, celebrate our accomplishments, and leverage our strengths while tolerating the things that we don't do so well.

Step 4: Build a personal support team.

Although all four of these steps are important, the fourth step is the one that is most frequently left out. I have an entire chapter in the last section of the book that covers this subject in detail, but I want to share with you here how it helps you overcome your insecurities. Humans need important relational nutrients in order to feel fulfilled and satisfied. In *People Fuel*, John Townsend said, "God designed needs in order to foster relationships."[37] We need things like acceptance, affirmation, and encouragement from safe people for our relational survival. When we understand this about ourselves, we can work to build a support team that gives us these key relational nutrients so that we don't seek these things in unhealthy ways due to our insecurities.

---

37 John Townsend, *People Fuel: Fill Your Tank for Life, Love, and Leadership* (Grand Rapids: Zondervan, 2019), 18.

We can focus on being liked by the safe people in our lives and avoid seeking approval or acceptance from the wrong people. I cover this topic in more detail in Part 4 of this book.

In review, Step 1 to overcoming your insecurities is to embrace what scripture says about you, Step 2 is to admit that you have insecurities and seek to understand them, Step 3 is to develop reasonable expectations of yourself, and Step 4 is to build a personal support team. I encourage you to reflect on your insecurities and identify the best next step that can help you begin to overcome them. These are the things that have changed my life as I've worked to overcome my deep-rooted insecurities, and I hope these steps will give you direction as you seek to overcome your insecurities as well.

This next type of derailer is likely heavily connected to your insecurities but seems to be much more difficult for leaders to identify and overcome. Our leadership risks are best described as the fruit of our insecurities. Everyone around the leader can see and feel the risks, but the individual can easily be blinded to the truth of how it's coming across to people.

Understanding and Minimizing Your Leadership Risks

How do you act when you're hurt, frustrated, or embarrassed? How do you respond to people when you're exhausted or stressed? Do you lash out in anger? Do you shut down and detach from people, or do you smile through the difficulties and try to act like nothing's wrong?

Most people have internal, relational risks that manifest when life gets tough or certain triggers are released. Leadership risks are behaviors that, when left unchecked, damage the influence we have with others. They can even derail or undermine a person's leadership all together. Though these risks may or may not have immediate impact, they can slowly decrease any influence you have and greatly limit the overall progress of a church or organization.

Although these leadership risks look a little different for each of us, we all have them. Unfortunately, every one of us has experienced hurt at some point in our lives. These risks develop from the relational injuries that we experience throughout life, especially in childhood. There isn't anyone alive who hasn't experienced pain in their past or assumed a defensive posture in retaliation to perceived threats to the heart.

We must understand that these defenses are not *always* negative. Our defenses can help keep us alive and prevent us from experiencing hurt from unsafe people. Defenses can be very important to our health and our ability to thrive. Paul tells us in Ephesians 6:10-11, *"Finally, my brethren, be strong in the Lord, and in the power of his might. 11Put on the whole armour of God, that ye may be able to stand against the wiles of the devil."* We must armor up and protect ourselves from the wiles of the devil. Of course, this implication is spiritual, but it's just as applicable and important from a human relational standpoint as well.

King Solomon tells us in Proverbs, *"Keep thy heart with all diligence; for out of it are the issues of life"* (Proverbs 4:23). There are many spiritual and practical reasons why we should protect our hearts, including:

1. Your heart has immense value. Your heart is the essence of who you are. It is the core of your being, connecting you to God and people. Solomon says we must protect it "above all else," which means we must make it the highest priority.

2. The vitality of your life depends on your heart. Solomon says that the heart is a "wellspring of life." Everything good that comes out of you flows from your heart.

3. Your heart is always under attack. There is a war going on in each of our lives, and there are people seeking to devour others. Solomon knew how important it was for us to guard our hearts.

Because of its value, necessity to the vitality of life, and the fact that it's always under attack, it's important that we learn to protect our hearts. Healthy defenses are needed in leadership and in life, but there are times when the good defenses we've put in place can get in the way of our healthy, life-giving relationships. When this happens, our defenses can become an issue, and they become leadership risks.

Unfortunately, we use the same defenses that protect us from unhealthy attacks on our healthy relationships and we usually aren't even aware of it. Perhaps you have experienced these defenses from others, or you have been responsible for this type of behavior yourself. When our defenses go unchecked, they can begin to damage our leadership influence. Therefore, it is important to become aware of risks and the things that trigger unhealthy reactions if you want to be a healthy leader.

I want to reiterate that these risks are sometimes hard to recognize, and they're often referred to as blind spots. Let me give you an example of what I'm talking about. I have a coaching client who has the amazing ability to show compassion toward others; it's one of his greatest gifts. The people he leads feel loved and cared for and accepted by him, but when he's tired or experiences a buildup of stress from all that he is responsible for, he can feel overwhelmed. When he has to tell someone something that they don't want to hear, confront a situation, or tell someone "no," his compassion can get the best of him. He doesn't want to hurt anyone's feelings, so he gets a little passive-aggressive. He avoids the real issue and handles the problem in a passive way.

Instead of the leader being straightforward with the truth and using his amazing gift of compassion to mercifully confront the situation, he strains the relationship with his passive-aggressive behavior. This behavior may not hurt the relationship the first time; but over time, if this type of behavior continues, the relationship will deteriorate.

Passive-aggressive behavior is just one of many types of risks in leadership, there are many others. Some leaders become selfish when they're stressed and tired. Some act out in mood swings or emotional tirades. Some leaders withdraw and tune people out. Others worry and have trouble making decisions, frustrating the people they lead. Some leaders want to unhealthily please everyone. Others struggle with perfectionism so badly that they drive everyone around them crazy. There are a host of negative behaviors that can create risks and reduce the effectiveness of successful leadership. Two of the things that I've personally worked to overcome and I'm still working to overcome are perfectionism and mood swings. These issues usually come to the surface when I'm tired and stressed.

If these things are so detrimental to leadership influence, what can we do about them? What can we do to overcome these passive-aggressive and perfectionist tendencies as well as our emotional imbalances? There are three concepts that I want to remind you of from *The Christian Leader Blueprint* model that can help you successfully navigate these risks. If you haven't adequately addressed these subjects, I would encourage you to revisit them again in earlier chapters. The three concepts are:

1. Establish a better rhythm of life.

The leader's first defense is to create a healthy rhythm of life, minimize unnecessary stress, get adequate rest, and learn to function with a good work-life balance. Considerable time was given to this topic in Part 1 of this book because it is critical to softening our risks. When our lives are healthy and we experience a good rhythm, the tough, stressful times are not as frequent and the risks to our leadership don't affect us as often. When we're healthy in rhythm, we can respond to people in a much better way.

2. See yourself more clearly.

Awareness alone is very powerful. This chapter and the entirety of Part 2 of this book is focused on helping you see yourself more clearly. We can also increase our awareness with the help of a counselor or executive coach or even just by having good, honest conversations with the people we lead. When a leader becomes more aware of his or her leadership derailers and risks, that awareness alone will help him or her push against their natural inclinations and respond in a healthier manner.

3. Grow your character.

The last and most effective way to minimize negative risks is to grow your character. When I say, "grow your character," I don't mean for you to develop your morals. I mean that you need to cultivate the things that increase your maturity and your ability to face the realities of life.

Unfortunately, doing this is not easy. It takes hard work to create and maintain boundaries, engage in need-based relationships, regulate emotions in a healthy way, experience loss, failure, and weakness properly, and expand and maintain your emotional capacity. Growing your character takes time and usually requires help from coaches and counselors as well as from healthy peer relationships.

If you truly want to minimize the effects of your risks on your life and leadership and improve your influence with people, you must be willing to work hard to establish a healthy rhythm of life, see yourself clearly, and grow your character. Effective leadership is possible when we make the necessary adjustments to soften and even remove leadership risks from our lives.

Most of the time our leadership risks are going to surface when we are most tired and stressed. However, there are times when we may see some of these things from an event or circumstance that triggers us relationally. I want to give you some thoughts to help you stop those triggers.

How to Stop Your Relational Triggers in the Moment

Even though I've worked hard to minimize my leadership risks, there are events or circumstances that cause me to feel triggered at times. Have you ever felt triggered? Of course, you have; we've all felt provoked at some point in our lives. We can easily become frustrated, angry, or defensive by something someone says or does. Our greatest leadership risks can come to the surface during these times. These actions trigger us to say and do things in the moment that we later regret. Our responses can be very harmful to our relationships, even to those relationships that mean the most to us, such as those with our spouses, kids, or the important team members who are vital to the success of our organizations. I want to share with you a few steps you can take to help you stop your relational triggers and avoid doing or saying things that will damage your influence.

Relational triggers can surface in any leader's normal relationships. A common example of a relational trigger is an anger outburst prompted by the anger problems of your parents and their responses to you as a child. If you've dealt with these issues in your past, someone becoming visibly angry *with* you now could trigger a retaliation of anger *in* you.

Another example of a relational trigger is your reaction to someone's response to your boundaries in work and leadership. If there is an emotional breakdown by someone you are working with, it can cause you to become overly nervous, prompting you to give in to what they want in order to appease and calm them, even though that reaction is not in your best interest or the best interest of the organization.

There are many other ways that triggers occur. Perhaps someone on your leadership team doesn't respond to your repeated attempts to reach out to them and that reminds you of the times you felt extreme loneliness as a child; lack of attention can trigger a negative response in you. These situations are uncomfortable, and they can leave us feeling vulnerable and embarrassed as we retaliate inappropriately.

Take a minute and reflect on times when you have felt "triggered" emotionally. What were the preceding events that caused this? How did you respond after it happened? Sometimes it helps to just talk through the circumstances with a friend to deepen the reflection. It's important that you learn to identify what leads to this response and how your body responds in the moment so that you know exactly what to do when you find yourself in that situation.

I usually feel triggered when I experience a lack of approval or acceptance from others. Most of the time, I respond by becoming rigid and serious. I can feel myself getting defensive in those situations even if I don't say anything. Many times, I'll become irritable and avoid people in order to try to gain my composure. Although these are common responses for me, it's important that I find a way to respond differently so that I can avoid being triggered.

When someone does or says something that triggers you and makes you feel angry, defensive, or frustrated, you don't need to retaliate negatively in anger or frustration. It's important that you have a plan and that you understand what to do in these situations. In elementary school, you are taught that if your clothes catch on fire, you are supposed to stop, drop, and roll, right? You must have a series of steps to go through that are easy and actionable without giving them much thought. Likewise, your response needs to be automatic when you recognize that you are being triggered by someone else's actions or words. When you feel yourself being triggered, there is a way that you can calm yourself and respond in a positive manner without outburst or other negative responses. I encourage you to try these steps:

1. Recognize the emotion.

First, it is important to recognize the emotion that comes to the surface for you when you feel yourself being triggered. The neuroscience behind why it's important to know what emotions you're experiencing says that everything you see, smell, hear, taste, or touch travels through your body by an electrical signal. These electrical signals travel from cell to cell until they reach your brain. When these signals hit your brain, they must go through the frontal lobe before they reach the rational, logical-thinking place of your brain. The signals hit the emotional part of your brain before they hit the rational, more logical part of your brain.

Unfortunately, this means that you'll experience sensations emotionally before you can think about them logically. Therefore, if we recognize and even name the emotion we experience in our minds, we will allow ourselves time to think much more clearly and quickly about the situation. For instance, if I slow down enough to recognize and tell myself that I'm angry, that will usually give me just enough time to calm myself enough to respond in a more logical way. I've heard it said quite often, "If you can name it, you can tame it." If you can name the emotion you're experiencing, you can usually tame that emotion.

2. Listen to the other person.

It is important to use active listening and give people the benefit of the doubt. It is also important to validate what the other person says and to let them know that you hear them. Either repeat what they've said to you or paraphrase their words. You don't have to agree with what they say, but you do need to let them know that you've heard them.

If the circumstances are such that you don't feel you can repeat their words back to them, you can say something like, "Wow, that's really hard to hear." By saying these words, you can still be authentic and truthful without assuming a defensive posture toward the other person.

3. Gain perspective.

Ask the other person questions to gain perspective about the situation. Avoid being abrasive when trying to figure out what they're thinking and where they're coming from. Instead of defending yourself or making sarcastic remarks, try to find out why that person is saying those words or responding in that way. There's usually a deeper reason for their response and gaining that perspective can open your mind to a whole new understanding.

4. Own your part.

Own your part of the problem by practicing compassion and acceptance. Think about why you are feeling the emotions you are feeling and try your best to take responsibility for your part in the situation. Apologize if you need to. Maybe the issue isn't about what you did, but more about something you didn't do. Perhaps you could have communicated better or been less passive in your approach. Think about what part of the situation *you* can own. When you own some part of the problem, it helps the other person feel less judged and defensive. With their guard down, you can then work on what is necessary to move the conversation forward.

5. Move forward.

Finally, turn your attention toward moving forward. Instead of focusing on the past, look to the future. Keep the conversation focused on what is ahead. Concentrate on what will best help you and the other person move forward. For instance, think about the problem and focus on what it would take to get a different and better outcome in the future that feels good to everyone involved. You must remember to take the high road in this situation. I know it's not easy, but it's the best thing for you and the organization.

There's a saying that I like to quote, "Never wrestle with a pig. You both get dirty, and the pig will like it." Even if the other person is completely wrong and the problem comes from their insecurities or past hurts, try your best not to wrestle with them. It's usually better to look to the future and focus on what will help you both move forward than to concentrate on past issues.

After following these steps, you should feel calmer and more level-headed. You should be able to think more clearly without retaliating or damaging the relationship. The goal of this process is for you to come out of the situation with a win-win result. You don't want to ignore the issue that caused you to feel triggered, but you also don't want to get so defensive that you damage the relationship. The goal is for you to walk away with an effective resolution that leaves everyone involved in a good state of mind.

Triggers are a natural part of our human experience, but they do not have to ruin our leadership relationships or disturb our peace. It's important when having hard conversations and dealing with triggers to recognize the emotions you are feeling, listen to what the other person is saying, stay curious and gain perspective on the situation, own your part of the problem, and focus on moving forward in the relationship. Doing these things will help you find a resolution that benefits you and the other person, and ultimately foster a situation that doesn't damage your influence and leadership.

In Part 2, I trust that I have given you enough information on achieving clarity of mind, increasing your emotional intelligence, understanding your motivation, and softening your leadership derailers to begin the process of seeing yourself more clearly. My hope is that you can identify what might have the greatest potential to impact your leadership and create some growth around those things. When we generate growth around understanding ourselves more, it usually puts us in a much better place for being able to leverage our strengths. There's nothing I desire more than to see you use your God-given abilities to accomplish big things in the Kingdom of God. Continue on to Part 3 to learn key insights on how to leverage your strengths.

Part Three

Leverage Your Strengths

There's something amazingly fulfilling about knowing with certainty what God has designed you to do. Ironically, many learning programs help leaders become more aware of who they are NOT rather than who they are. Many end up spending time and energy trying to improve weaknesses instead of focusing on their unique strengths. This can have a crippling leadership effect.

As a Christian leader, the key to success in your church or any organization you lead is to concentrate on what you are uniquely designed to do and to recruit a team of people whose strengths make up for your weaknesses. Create a team in which each member utilizes his or her talents so that your organization can achieve exponential success. The primary goal is for everyone to maximize their unique giftings. Do not strive to do many things satisfactorily, but instead, strive to do a few things excellently. Make it your goal to invest in the development of your team while delegating tasks. Aim to lead well, not just manage.

I was recently reading in Acts and a few of the scriptures jumped out at me.

They reinforced the need for developing a team and leveraging your strengths:

Acts 6:3, 4, 7 says, *"Wherefore, brethren, look ye out among you seven men of honest report, full of the Holy Ghost and wisdom, whom we may appoint over this business.⁴ But we will give ourselves continually to prayer, and to the ministry of the word.⁷ And the word of God increased; and the number of the disciples multiplied in Jerusalem greatly; and a great company of the priests were obedient to the faith."*

Because of their honest report—and the fact that they were full of the Holy Ghost, wisdom, and faith—and because they continued in prayer and ministering the Word of God—in verse 7 they increased in number. In other words, they had great success. However, I want you to pay close attention; it was also because they recruited seven people among whom they could distribute the workload.

Here's what I want you to get: Success would not have happened without having a team of people tending to the business of the church. They were a team that undoubtedly utilized one another's strengths. Because of this efficiency, everyday people were transformed through a relationship with Jesus Christ. Their ability to leverage their strengths and work as a team helped them accomplish the mission that was set before them. In this third part, I want to give you a variety of insights that will help you leverage your strengths. We'll start with the topic of your calling.

chapter 11

Discover Your Calling

✝ 1 Corinthians 7:17: *But as God hath distributed to every man, as the Lord hath called every one, so let him walk. And so ordain I in all churches.*

One of the fundamental aspects of a person leveraging strengths to complement a team is to know what the Lord has called him or her to do. A calling is what will give long-term fulfillment and motivation. What has the Lord called you to do? There is something in everyone that drives them to pursue certain areas of ministry or life. God created each of us with a special purpose in mind. He wants nothing more than to see you fulfill your God-given assignment. Discovering God's vision for your life is not easy, but there's no doubt that it will help bring fulfillment to you in a way that nothing else will. Having no understanding or knowledge of your calling leads to a life of unnecessary frustration and increased anxiety.

A person's gifting, which we'll discuss more in the next chapter, is what the Lord has equipped you to naturally and effectively do. It's similar to a calling, which is an internal mission that's been shaped with a purpose by the Lord. However, the calling of God always overrides a person's natural giftings.

The Lord will equip those whom He calls, even if that calling is outside of a person's natural giftings. God wants you to rely on Him, not solely on your own strength or abilities. God's grace is sufficient for all things (2 Corinthians 12:9).

Romans 8:28 promises us that *"all things work together for good to them who love God, to them who are the called according to his purpose."* So, what has God called you to do? What burning desire has the Lord placed within you to accomplish with your life? It's amazing to me how the fulfillment of an individual's life so heavily depends on the answer to these questions. In this chapter, I'll share more about this fulfillment, including thoughts on how to develop the right mindset and discover your calling. I also want to give you some important things I've learned about my calling in 26 years of ministry.

Prayer is the first step in finding your calling. It is vitally important that you pray and fast to clearly hear God's voice when He speaks to you. God wants nothing more than to communicate with us, but oftentimes we get in God's way by allowing the wrong people or thoughts to influence our decisions. I encourage you to pause for a few minutes now and pray that the Lord would focus your mind on what's needed to dive into this subject of calling.

This Is Why You Feel Unfulfilled

Talking to the disciples, His future church leaders, Jesus said in John 15:16: *"Ye have not chosen me, but I have chosen you, and ordained you…"* The lives of these disciples perfectly intersected with the Master. Jesus called these future church leaders. Jesus Himself chose them. Yet not all of them found lasting fulfillment. I think there are Christian leaders today struggling to find that as well. I want to share with you why I think most people, possibly even you, can't find that sense of long-term fulfillment.

When I was growing up, nearly every Sunday afternoon between church services, a bunch of us guys would go to Alexandria Senior High School to play football. I had a little personal dilemma. At that time, I was usually one of the younger guys in the group. In addition to that, I was small in stature. However, I was a fast little guy. That's about the only thing I had going for me in those days. Here's where the problem was though: Before we started playing, two team captains were chosen, then they chose their team members. The team captains took turns picking the players they wanted, and obviously, when you're playing football, no one really wants the young, little guy.

Inside, I was thinking, "Look, if you don't choose me first, you're making a BIG mistake! I'm really, really fast. Those boys may be bigger, but if you'll just choose me, I'll show you dynamite comes in small packages!" At least that's what my dad used to tell me to try to make me feel better about my size. Of course, I would never be picked first. In the end, what would make me feel a little better was just not to be the last person chosen. If I wasn't the last person, I was at least better than whoever was the last person.

It really feels good when you're chosen. Even today, it really feels good when I'm chosen for something. Here's the deal, though. If I'm chosen for something, even for a Sunday afternoon football game, it then becomes super important to actually show up. It becomes super important to produce, to be fruitful within the position I've been given or the task for which I was chosen.

In John 15:16, we're given a sacred task. We have been called. You and I have been chosen for this special sacred task. The last part of that scripture says we were chosen to go unto the world and add to the Kingdom of God— to make disciples—to be fruitful in the Kingdom of God. It's not enough to be called. It's not even enough to be chosen. The scripture says that we must go and bring forth fruit.

In this verse, it is evident the disciples were selected by Jesus. These future church leaders had a choice at this point. They were absolutely called. Yet, the fact that they were called and chosen had to collide with their decision to go and bring forth fruit. Jesus specifically said, *"You haven't chosen me, but I chose you... to go and bring forth fruit."*

They were chosen. They were given a really important task to go and build a habitation for the Spirit of God. This going and building would prepare them for the purpose set before them. It didn't matter what life brought them. It didn't matter the internal turmoil they may have felt at the time. It didn't matter that they were arguing with one another about strategies or tactics or who would be in charge. None of that mattered at all.

They were chosen for a task. That was it. No excuses, Simon Peter. No excuses, James. No excuses, John. Work through your issues. Overcome your self-doubt. Overcome the restrictions humanity puts on you. Overcome the mental struggles you are experiencing right now with stepping out of your comfort zone. Overcome the selfishness and self-ambition within you. Go and bring forth fruit! "You haven't chosen me, but I chose you… to go and bring forth fruit."

As I got a little older and probably a little more athletic and competitive, I eventually quit playing football with all of the guys on Sunday afternoon. At the time when I probably could have competed the best, I stopped playing because I was too busy working and doing other things.

It's interesting, looking back, to realize that in this and other instances, when it might have been time for me to do something great in my life, I somehow found all sorts of reasons to play it safe or sometimes to not play at all. Sometimes that's still true. I find myself retreating under the pressures this world brings to the table. It's easier just to "be," to be doing something else or even just be on the sidelines watching others… rather than risking failure. Can you relate to my sense of risk aversion? Sometimes it's easier just to "be" rather than to push forward and do the work required to fulfill the calling and the mission, to produce the fruit the Lord desires of us. If this description resonates with you, I would encourage you to review the previous chapter on motivation, particularly the section on fear of failure, to gain a better understanding of how you can use fear as a motivation rather than something that stalls you.

This is the reason many leaders don't feel the fulfillment in their life that they should. Yet, this is when we have to rise up from our self-doubt, insecurities, or whatever other things may have us bound at times. Whatever is holding us back, we have to do what's necessary to work through those things on the inside of us. We have to rise up from it. We have to realize, just like His chosen disciples, this simple fact: We did not choose Him first, He called and chose us. He chose us to go and bring forth fruit, and not just any fruit, but He chose us to bring forth holy and divine fruit unlike any other fruit—supernatural and God-given productivity.

I can just hear Him saying, "Ryan, you haven't chosen me. I—chose—you! I chose you to go and bring forth fruit." I can hear Him calling your name as well. "You haven't chosen me. I chose you... to go and bring forth fruit." If we truly want to find fulfillment in this life, we must embrace our calling and bring forth fruit in our lives. I want you to evaluate your life through the lens of these two questions:

1. What do you feel the Lord has chosen you to do?

2. What is something you can do this week to begin producing fruit in that calling?

It's not easy to move into your calling and produce fruit in leadership. It takes introspection. It takes increased emotional intelligence. It takes leaning into key relationships in your life. It takes doing the hard work to eliminate the barriers. I believe you can do it. I know the Lord will lead and guide you just as He has in my life. It all starts with allowing the Lord to begin to prepare your mindset for the specific purpose and calling He has placed on your life.

Be an Ambassador of Christ First

Since you are reading this book, you are likely feeling a call to something that involves leadership. I want you to know that you were created on purpose with a purpose. You have a calling that can bring such fulfillment and fruit to your life. Even though we are each called by God, this is a subject that many people wrestle with. Most Christians feel a strong desire to do something great for the Lord, yet they struggle in their minds to know what that is exactly. You may feel this same struggle at times, so I want to bring some clarity to the mindset that is needed to embrace the calling God has on your life.

At 16 years of age, I began examining and searching the Bible so that I could work out my own salvation. I had been told what to believe about salvation most of my life, but I wanted to discover the Gospel for myself. As a result, I published a Bible study called *Salvation Made Simple*. This Bible study has been translated into seven languages and distributed to many thousands of people. It has become such a pillar in my life that I printed a large version of the cover, framed it, and hung it in my office years ago so that I'm constantly reminded of what I'm called to do. This Bible study reminds me of who called me. It has been sort of a burning bush type experience.

During the time I spent searching out my personal salvation, I felt a call to the ministry. I knew, even at 16, that I wanted to spend my life helping people to understand and obey the Gospel. It didn't matter how my occupation changed over the years. I tried to keep the mindset of helping people move from spiritual death to abundant life. This is why I do what I do even today. My calling gives me the energy to work hard and produce good things for the Kingdom of God. I have a great ministry as a pastor and an executive coach, but ultimately, it doesn't matter where my paycheck comes from. I work for Jesus and His Kingdom, and my calling comes from Him.

The mindset that we must pursue is found in 2 Corinthians 5:20, *"Now then we are ambassadors for Christ..."* It really doesn't matter what your job is, if you are a Christian, you must make up in your mind that you are called as an ambassador for Christ. You may work at a bank, but you are in full-time ministry. You may run a contracting crew for a construction company, but you too are in full-time ministry. We're living with a purpose and are called to be ambassadors of God; our motives must be spiritual.

According to writer and entrepreneur Regi Campbell, Ron Blue, an author and speaker on personal finance, once shared his purpose statement, "I, Ron

Blue, exist to glorify God by loving and serving others and by using my financial skills and experience to help people become better stewards of what God has given them and, as a byproduct of that, to bring more resources into the Kingdom of God."[38] That's a powerful mission; Ron Blue has his mind fixed on exactly what he's called to do. He's an ambassador of God through his professional life, and this helps him produce fruit and fulfill his calling.

Though Ron's work may be made up of non-spiritual tasks, he approaches his job with a spiritual mindset, and that is what makes his assignment spiritual. If we tune into the Spirit of God as we go throughout our day, we can live on purpose whether we are working in our secular jobs, buying food in the grocery store, or supporting our kids at their ball games. We can live on purpose as ambassadors of God.

We can't discuss the mindset of calling without talking about the fivefold ministry as well. Paul writes in Ephesians, *"There is one body, and one Spirit, even as ye are called in one hope of your calling"* (Ephesians 4:4). Paul goes on to say, *"Wherefore he saith, when he ascended up on high, he led captivity captive, and gave gifts unto men"* (Ephesians 4:8). Finally, Paul explains, *"And he gave some, apostles; and some, prophets; and some, evangelists; and some, pastors and teachers"* (Ephesians 4:11).

This particular verse clarifies that the fivefold ministry is made up of apostles, prophets, evangelists, pastors, and teachers. These are special offices of leadership. Paul goes on to explain that these callings are *"For the perfecting of the saints, for the work of the ministry, and for the edifying of the body of Christ…"* (Ephesians 4:12). The fivefold ministry also creates a unity of purpose and balance in the church so that, according to Paul, "…We henceforth be no more children…" (Ephesians 4:14).

The fivefold ministry is present to help bring the church to spiritual and relational maturity. Although the fivefold ministry is a gift from God, I think

---

38 Regi Campbell, "Living on Purpose," RadicalMentoring, August 29, 2019, https://radicalmentoring.com/living-on-purpose/.

it's much more than a gift. It is a calling. If you feel called to one of the five-fold ministries, I believe your giftings will reveal that. Your giftings will align with your calling, and the important, trustworthy people in your life will confirm it.

If you truly feel called to one of the fivefold ministries, I want to give you some important advice. Be comfortable giving to people out of the abundance of the giftings within you. I know many people who feel called but only seek position. It's important to be patient in the process of growth that the Lord has for you. Don't seek a position or a specific opportunity and then get frustrated because that opportunity doesn't present itself within your timeframe. Let the position find you. Focus on letting the fruit of your gifting go before you and speak for you to confirm your calling to the fivefold ministry.

I think it's important to talk about the fivefold ministry when discussing the topic of calling because sometimes people solely delegate the "call of God" to the fivefold ministry. Though you may not be called specifically to the five-fold ministry, every believer has a part in the work of the ministry. We are all ambassadors of God. Jesus told us that we would do greater works than He. He has given us the power to do the miraculous.

As Christians, it's important for us to understand the purpose of our callings. This is not a self-serving or self-promoting purpose that we can bypass or ignore. Our callings are all about fulfilling the Lord's will in our lives and in this world. Our callings will bring us energy to get up every day. They will drive us to do things that are uncomfortable and beyond our own natural talents and abilities.

We're called by God for a purpose. We're ambassadors of the Kingdom of God. I want to encourage you to evaluate your mindset on your motive today by asking yourself these questions: "Why am I doing what I'm doing? Am I focused only on getting the job done or am I intentionally loving, serving, and helping people find and follow Jesus?" When your motive is right and your mind is focused on being an ambassador of Christ, I believe it's then okay to begin wrestling with the profession you will pursue to fulfill your calling.

Who Do You Want to Be When You Grow Up?

When you are settled that you're an ambassador of Christ no matter what you spend your time on, then you can begin to further develop what it looks like to fulfill your calling. Have you ever grappled with the question, "What do you want to be when you grow up?" I know that there are probably many of you who have struggled with that question even though your mind is focused on fulfilling the will of God in your life. In fact, some of you are still struggling to determine what exactly you want to do, and there are many people who are halfway through their careers or even nearing retirement who have never found the answer to that question.

The question is innocent when you're a child and there is time ahead of you, but the older you get, the more serious and important that question becomes. If you're struggling in this area, I want to suggest that you make a small shift in the way you approach the idea of what you want to be. Instead of thinking about *what* you want to be, think about *who* you want to be. Thinking about who you want to be is much more impactful. When you decide who you want to be, you can begin to understand the calling of God on your life a little better.

Our callings are not simply about what we do for a living, and they are not about the tasks we perform on a daily basis. Our callings are not about whether we work for a church or a secular job, which is usually driven by our spiritual and natural talents. Calling is more about who we are. Who we are emanates from deep within us. Knowing who you are is about having an awareness of what you value and what is truly most important to you. Your calling could be broad or specific, but it's an internal leadership mission that's been shaped by the Lord and all of the learning experiences of your life. The Lord makes those good and bad experiences work together for the good.

As we discussed earlier, this concept of calling is fully demonstrated in John 15:16: *"Ye have not chosen me, but I have chosen you, and ordained you, that ye should go and bring forth fruit, and [that] your fruit should remain: that whatsoever ye shall ask of the Father in my name, he may give it you."* Christ chose you so that you can go and bring forth fruit. When you start to answer the question of who you are called to be, your life will begin to produce this positive fruit.

Discovering the things that bring you energy and joy, determining what you truly value, and deciding on what you want to be known for increases your productivity and success. Whatever setting you find yourself in, you will be able to see the fruit of your labor if you are dialed in to who you want to be.

That is where I want to be in life. I can accomplish amazing things when I learn who I am supposed to be. When I build on that knowledge with my talents and God-given vision, all things in my life will work together for the good.

Leadership is tough. Therefore, it's important that we don't waste our time and energy doing things that don't fit us well. With leadership being so broad, you will want to narrow your focus so you maximize your limited time and efforts. There are a few things you can do to help you process who you want to be when you grow up and what you want to be known for:

1. Commit to prayer and fasting.

Make your calling a spiritual matter before you give it too much intellectual thought. It's really not a calling if it's not a spiritual matter. I would recommend spending significant time in prayer and fasting to help you develop in your mind what you want to be known for. Scripture speaks of the effect that prayer and fasting can have on our sensitivity to the Spirit of God. This will help you lessen the impact of your fleshly desires and increase your ability to tune-in to the desires of the Lord.

2. Consider your history.

What significant successes have you had in your past? Think also about some of the challenging experiences you've had in life—challenges you've had the resolve to overcome. Even negative failures can help you learn more about yourself. Knowing and understanding your personal history will help you further develop your calling and who you want to become in your future.

3. Concentrate on your spiritual and natural gifts.

Unless you have specific direction from the Lord, it's not advantageous to do something that doesn't naturally align with who you are as a person. People will usually quickly see your incompetence if you attempt to do something outside of your giftings. There's a reason the Lord has made you and equipped you with certain gifts. Therefore, it's important to pay close attention to what those are. The next chapter will dive much deeper into helping you understand and determine your giftings.

4. Determine what you value the most and why.

You value certain things in your life for a specific, possibly even unknown, reason. For instance, you may value the community and structure a church provides for your family. You may value the safety and security of a "nine to five" job. You may value the adventurous feeling that you get from doing something risky. Think about the things that you value the most and ask yourself why. This will help bring additional clarity to your calling and the things that you are motivated to do.

5. Decide on what you want to be known for at the end of your life.

Imagine yourself in the casket at the end of your life. What do you want said about you that mattered to others? Specifically regarding leadership, what do you want said that *you* accomplished? Unless your desires come from purely selfish ambition and gain, the Lord has likely placed those desires in you. Begin to cultivate your calling and your leadership around those desires.

6. Reflect on the traits you admire in other people.

When I was a teenager, I remember consuming the writings and teachings of the leadership guru, John Maxwell. There were certain traits about him that I wanted to study and emulate. I can remember longing to be able to exude the passion that Anthony Mangun had while preaching and teaching. I always admired the organizational structure that Terry Shock provided. Romans 8:28 says, *"And we know that all things work together for good to them that love God, to them who are the called according to his purpose."* I believe the Lord placed these people in my life to shape my mindset on my calling. Pay attention to the qualities in others you admire and want to emulate. Study those qualities. Then let those things shape your mindset on your calling.

7. Ponder the advice, thoughts, and suggestions of the trustworthy people in your life.

Sometimes people we trust can see things within us that we can't see ourselves. The Lord has designed it that way so that we may take advantage of those key relational insights that others can give us. Give ear to those insights as you're trying to determine your calling and who you want to be when you grow up. There's usually valuable gold in the advice of others around us.

The Lord has called you to His service in His Kingdom in some way. Though you may grow and develop your talents and gifts, your calling is sure. You lack nothing. Therefore, I encourage you focus your time and energy on your calling now. I promise the fruit of your investment will come; and when the fruit comes, you will truly enjoy the journey of life. I've lived out my calling through 26 years of ministry, and I've learned a few things about calling. I'd like to continue sharing with you as we discuss what I've learned throughout the years.

Six Things I've Learned About Calling in 26 Years of Ministry

Honestly, I've never really struggled with my calling. I knew at 16 who I wanted to be when I grew up. I knew I wanted to serve the Kingdom of God in a leadership role with my time, energy, talents, finances, and every fiber of my being. I even had a clear idea of where I wanted to work. Though I've never really struggled in these areas, there are some important lessons I've learned over the last 26 years of ministry.

Earlier in this chapter, I mentioned that searching out my own salvation created a deep desire within me to serve God. I knew at 16 that I wanted to spend my life helping people understand and obey the Gospel. I wanted to help people move from spiritual death to abundant life. This is why I do what I do even today. It's why I have a passion for Bible studies and small groups and teaching people about leadership. This calling gives me the energy to work hard and produce good things for the Kingdom of God.

Though I've never struggled with this calling doesn't mean I've never struggled. In fact, this calling has actually caused me to wrestle with certain things and I've learned a ton along the way. I want to share a few of the things I've learned over the years that have helped me successfully navigate my calling.

1. Devotion to the Lord must increase.

I realize that I frequently refer to devotion in this book, but it needs to be repeated often if we want to succeed in leadership. There was a time in my ministry that I got "too busy" to give adequate time to devotion, and that was a big mistake. I learned quickly that if I want to be successful with a spiritual calling, I must pray, fast, and study the Word of God routinely. The only way you and I can keep the busyness of life from distracting us is to make devotion our first priority. Above all else we must have devotion with the Lord. If we are going to embrace our callings, we need the power that comes from these sources. If I want to become who the Lord wants me to be, I have to remain humble and hungry for more of God in my life.

2. Desire for the approval of man must decrease.

Over the course of my childhood, I developed a deep desire to please people in my life. This is called an approval addiction. My motivation would come from the desire to get a pat on the back or an accolade from my leaders. So, I would do things I wasn't gifted in and didn't feel were in line with my calling just to get that acknowledgment. I think it's healthy to be a team player and do things you don't want to do, but when this happens over and over at the expense of your own personal calling it moves to an unhealthy state. I now have a much healthier aspiration to please the pastors, leaders, and other important people in my life. I have to be very careful, though, that my desires don't gravitate back to that unhealthy state. I can't live seeking to please man. There's no way I can please everyone all of the time, and still pursue my ministry and leadership calling.

I also have to understand that the Lord moves on me at times to do things for His Kingdom that don't always make complete sense and definitely aren't popular with the people around me. It's important that I don't allow the approval of man to stop my God-led progress. However, I do have a very short list of people who I submit to who have the authority to overrule any decision I make in my life if I step out of what is reasonable—though it's rare that they would ever have to do that.

3. Do not overly value your image.

This point is an important one for me and is closely related to that of seeking approval. The difference here is that this doesn't necessarily involve a leader in my life (the other does). This is relative to people in general. Even the best of us can fall into the trap of comparison and protecting our images. If I allow my image to motivate what I do, the job I take, or the leadership opportunities I pursue, it's very possible I will miss God's will for my life and derail my calling.

4. Enjoy the process of development.

A calling is not an event in your life; it's not a leadership role or job that you accept and suddenly your calling is fulfilled. Your calling is a lifelong journey. Consider Moses. He had a calling to write the first five books of the Bible, but he had to grow up and receive an education in Pharaoh's house. He then spent 40 years in the wilderness, but it was that same wilderness through which he would later lead the Israelites.

There are many things in life that I don't understand, but I do know that God works all things together for good. I once heard Pentecostal leader Thetus Tenney say, "If you're still struggling, God hasn't finished working all things together." Calling is fulfilled over the course of a lifetime. A person's calling is usually less defined at the beginning of their life and becomes clearer as time passes. Calling can take a while to completely manifest, so focus on enjoying the process of developing your calling. I believe the Lord wants us to have fun and enjoy our spouses, kids, and friends. He desires that we have margin in our lives so that there's balance and fulfillment as we live out our callings.

5. Your calling is to God but through people.

You must learn to build productive relationships, which I discuss in detail in the last part of this book. As an introvert, there are times when I'd love nothing better than to go live on an island for the rest of my life, but the Lord designed us to need people. He designed us to be insufficient in ourselves so that we need others to accomplish our purposes and fulfill the callings He's placed within us. Work to fulfill your calling to God, but love people, cultivate relationships, and use the people around you to achieve that calling. In doing this, you will help others fulfill their callings as well.

6. Start fulfilling your calling now.

As I look back over the last 26 years of my life, I realize that the process of living in my calling has helped me develop into the man and leader that I am today. If I had waited until I was qualified to engage in my calling, I'd probably still be waiting. Wherever you are on the journey of life, live out your calling and your mission. You can't read enough books or obtain enough resources to be qualified. Know that God develops the people He calls. Embrace your calling and engage in the developmental process. I promise He'll make it happen.

These are the things that have helped me navigate my calling and engage in leadership over the years. As you went through these six tips, which of them stood out to you the most? Which do you feel is needed to help you successfully navigate your calling? Take some time to reflect on those things in prayer. It's critical that you do whatever is necessary to move forward with your calling. There's a ton at stake if you choose to sit on the sidelines and not get involved in what the Lord has called you to do.

What's at Stake If You Choose to "Sit the Bench?"

Consumer Christianity, where the church is all about giving to you, just doesn't seem to be fitting in the picture anymore. Sitting on the sidelines and watching others live out their callings is just not an option anymore. I believe the Lord is calling us to do more. The Lord has chosen us as Christian leaders…for more. 1 Peter 2:9 tells us, *"But ye are a chosen generation, a royal priesthood, an holy nation, a peculiar people; that ye should shew forth the praises of him who hath called you out of darkness into his marvellous light."* You have been called out of darkness. You have been chosen for a purpose. Now, the question becomes a little more difficult. How are you going to react to what you've been chosen for?

It is obvious from this verse that the Lord is not going to allow you to be satisfied with just being out of darkness. He didn't call you out just to get you out but so that you would "…shew forth the praises…" He chose you for something greater, something high and holy. There is a reason He chose you. Are you going to just come out of the darkness… or are you going to move into the light… into more… into the fullness of what He has for you? Because if you choose to "sit the bench" and not pursue the calling the Lord has for you, there's no doubt that you will miss a huge portion of satisfaction and joy in your life. Life just won't be quite as sweet along the journey or when you reach the end.

Read this passage from Revelation carefully. Revelation 17:14 says, *"These shall make war with the Lamb, and the Lamb shall overcome them: for he is Lord of lords, and King of kings: and they that are with him are called, and chosen, and faithful."* As a Christian leader, I really hope you can grasp that it's not enough to be called. It's not even enough to be chosen. That's not the ultimate destination for you. When you get to the end of the Book—when you read Revelation 17:14—there's another word there, *"...called, and chosen, and faithful."* Those who are with Him at the end are the ones who were called and chosen and faithful. There will be some who were called and chosen who were not faithful. For these individuals, it seems that they missed out on a significant part of the ending.

Let's revisit the verse we used earlier in this chapter and explore more of what is at stake if we choose not to be fruitful and faithful. John 15:16 reads, *"Ye have not chosen me, but I have chosen you, and ordained you, that ye should go and bring forth fruit."* Judas was in the group of 12 that Jesus was speaking to at this time. Judas was literally handpicked by Jesus Himself. Judas was chosen. He was told in this verse the same thing the others heard: "I have chosen you and I want you to go and bring forth fruit..." Yet, as you may know, Judas not only made the decision to not be fruitful, in the end he wasn't faithful. Sometime after Jesus called him and chose him, something went terribly wrong. Judas lost out before he could be proven faithful.

I am by no means putting you in the category of Judas. I realize Judas is an extreme example. Yet, at the same time, I wonder how many Christian leaders over the last few thousand years were called and chosen but refused to be faithful? How many did not take it a step further and ultimately refused to be fruitful? I have to imagine that these individuals missed out on so much joy and fulfillment throughout the journey and especially at the end of their lives.

He has called us out of darkness into his marvelous light. He chose me and He chose you to go and bring forth fruit. God called the children of Israel out of darkness when He called them out of Egypt. His desire was for them to reach the Promised Land. He knew they would have to go through the wilderness. He knew they would have to endure some major things. Yet, He still wanted them to possess the Promised Land.

To get to that Promised Land, they had to go through the wilderness. Every single Israelite was called and chosen. However, there was a whole generation of Israelites who died in the wilderness and never reached the promise because they refused to remain faithful. They went to the grave in the wilderness because being chosen is just not enough. Somewhere in the wilderness they came upon a well of water that was bitter; they resisted against their leader, Moses, and ultimately against God. The result was that they never actually reached the Promised Land. They missed the ultimate fulfillment at the end of their lives. Just because a person is called and chosen doesn't mean that person is in God's will and is bearing fruit.

I hope you understand I'm not trying to speak of negative things here, but I feel an urge to stir some things for you today. I know there are many Christian leaders out there who are excited to be in ministry, excited to be in a great organization and a part of a great team. The point of being on a team is to get on the field and play ball. It's no fun to sit on the bench when we really need to be in the game producing big results, producing fruit for the Kingdom of God—fulfilling the calling that He has placed in our lives. The purpose of being chosen in the football game is to take the ball across the goal line, not just to sit the bench. When we fulfill this purpose completely, it's amazing how good it feels when the game is over.

I know you have it within you to do great things. You have a special God-given calling on your life that only you can fulfill. Rather than allowing the pressures of this world to derail you, let them motivate you to go and bring forth positive fruit for the Kingdom of God. It's not sitting on the bench but getting in the game that will bring long-lasting fulfillment to your life. Then at the end, you'll look back and reflect on a life well lived.

Once we begin to identify what we have been called to do, there's usually a wide range of ways to fulfill that calling. This is why it's vital to learn to maximize your unique gifts. Identifying, understanding, and using the gifts within us will help us begin to narrow down a practical way to fulfill the calling within us. In this next chapter, we'll get into the details of gifts.

chapter 12

Maximize Your Unique Gifts

✝ 1 Peter 4:10: *As every man hath received the gift, even so minister the same one to another, as good stewards of the manifold grace of God.*

What practical gifts do you have that will help you significantly impact your church or organization? Just pause for a moment and give that question some thought.

God gave those gifts to you for a particular reason. Paul challenges us not to neglect our gifts, failing to use them for the benefit of others. Romans 12:6 says, *"Having then gifts differing according to the grace that is given to us..."* The word "differing" in this scripture means "different" or "excellent." We all have unique gifts that we excel at, gifts that are needed for the Kingdom of God. Learning to maximize these giftings is what helps people and organizations thrive.

In this chapter, I've got a huge surprise gift I want to give you. Actually, it's no surprise, but it is big. I want to help you discover and maximize your unique gifts. We'll start with an introduction of what gifts are all about. Let's jump in!

Gifts Explained

Have you ever been charged with a task or duty that felt awkward and energy draining for you? Perhaps other tasks you've been assigned felt easy to accomplish. You know that if you could practice the doable tasks and separate them from the awkward responsibilities, life would be so much easier, right? Absolutely, life would definitely be easier! When the people in your church or organization are doing things they enjoy, things that are easy for them to accomplish, they become much more fruitful, and your organization thrives.

The subject of gifts can be a little confusing and difficult to understand; it's often confused with other topics such as vision, motivation, and calling. I want to begin by clarifying the difference between vision, calling, and gifts and discuss how they relate to one another. I shared this information earlier, in Chapter 4—Vision's Role in a Leader's Rhythm, and I think it's worth repeating. I believe the Lord, along with a few people in my life, helped me work through these terms and come to this realization.

God created you with a special purpose in mind—a calling. Your calling is the purpose or reason you exist. It's what will bring fulfillment and happiness to you. A person's gifting is the lens through which that calling is projected into the world. The Lord provides these gifts as His way of equipping you to fulfill your calling. A vision is having the ability to imagine a future that doesn't yet exist. With a clear vision, you can get a glimpse of what your life may look like a little further down the road. When your calling and giftings align, it's much easier for you to develop and work toward a vision that's true to you. Therefore, understanding and discovering your gifts are vitally important to your future fulfillment in life.

Let's start by discussing the word "gift." I had to wade through a ton of craziness online to find a simple definition. It seems everyone has a different idea of what the word "gift" means. The best online definition I found is "a natural ability or talent." I like this definition because I know that everyone has natural abilities or strengths. However, in the Christian world, we also have spiritual gifts. These two topics, natural gifts and spiritual gifts, are often confused, so I want to bring clarity to the differences between them.

As Christians, we receive both types of gifts from God. We may be born with some amazing natural abilities—like athleticism, the ability to sing well, an incredible memory—but you may notice someone who has recently been filled with the Spirit of God develop an uncanny ability to teach or preach. People may turn to this person for advice because they have developed wisdom that's helpful in the Kingdom of God. This is a supernatural, spiritual gift or ability that's only given after a person is filled with the Holy Spirit. Some people have also described the fivefold ministry as a type of gift, and they're very closely related, but I believe the fivefold ministry should be classified as a calling rather than a gift. For the sake of this discussion, we will focus on natural and spiritual gifts here. As I worked years ago to identify and leverage my natural and spiritual gifts, I first went to the Bible for clarity. What sources have you used to understand and discover your gifts?

Scripture speaks of gifts in a few places. 1 Corinthians 12:4–11 says, *"Now there are diversities of gifts, but the same Spirit.[5] And there are differences of administrations, but the same Lord. [6]And there are diversities of operations, but it is the same God which worketh all in all. [7]But the manifestation of the Spirit is given to every man to profit withal.[8] For to one is given by the Spirit the word of wisdom; to another the word of knowledge by the same Spirit; [9]To another faith by the same Spirit; to another the gifts of healing by the same Spirit; [10]To another the working of miracles; to another prophecy; to another discerning of spirits; to another divers kinds of tongues; to another the interpretation of tongues: [11]But all these worketh that one and the selfsame Spirit, dividing to every man severally as he will."*

Paul speaks of spiritual gifts here; these are gifts from God, and they operate through the power of God in the church even today. Some may argue that these types of gifts are no longer present in the church in the 21st century, and I would argue that they are alive and well even today. The Lord's power is just as real today as it was during the book of Acts. The word of wisdom, the word of knowledge, faith, healing, and so on are all working through Christians even today.

I stand as a witness that spiritual gifts are very much alive today. Spiritual gifts empower us to reach this world with the Gospel. When a non-Christian receives a healing in his or her body for instance, it's amazing how open the individual can become to receiving and obeying the Gospel message. In the ever-changing world that we live in, we need these gifts for spiritual protection, provision, and empowerment to help convince others that they need Jesus to survive.

Many times, it takes a supernatural manifestation to convince someone that they need the Gospel in their lives. Jesus was clear that we would do greater works than He, and He raised people from the dead. I need and want the spiritual gifts in my church and in my life and in the lives of the people around me. It gives me such peace of mind and rest to know that spiritual gifts are present and at work in me and around me. Just days before writing this passage, I felt the Spirit prompt me to give a simple word of encouragement to someone while he was praying after a Sunday church service. As soon as I gave the word, the young man started weeping under the power of the Holy Ghost confirming that it was exactly the encouragement that he needed that day.

Though we may see spiritual gifts routinely in operation, we may not see them manifested all of the time. I think if we did, we might not even think of them as supernatural. They would become commonplace to us and could even be inappropriate at times. If I walked around giving tongue interpretations in the grocery store and the gym, it could quickly become quite humorous. Instead of attracting people to the Gospel, they would be running from me and anything I represent.

These gifts are extended to everyone; they aren't just for people involved in ministry. Not everyone will experience every gift, but every Spirit-filled person will be empowered with at least one spiritual gift. We are a vessel for those spiritual gifts. The Lord does His greatest work through us, and it is our responsibility to be tuned in through prayer and the Word of God. The purpose of these spiritual gifts is ultimately to build up the church; they're not for our personal benefit.

We must understand that God is the source of both of these types of gifts. He gave us our spiritual gifts, and He also gave us our natural gifts. As we move on to discuss natural gifts, I want to say that man's natural abilities are so deficient compared to the supernatural abilities of God, yet our natural gifts are still extremely important in our everyday Christian lives and leadership as well as the Kingdom of God.

Think about people who have a long history of talented family members. We're all familiar with those families who are known for their musical abilities—perhaps almost everyone in the family is an amazing singer. There are also families like the Mannings who have amazing athletic abilities and a history of producing phenomenal NFL quarterbacks. These natural gifts were given to us at birth by God, and they shape the picture of our natural personalities and abilities. These natural gifts are inherited from our parents, and they're developed in our childhood as we grow. We receive our natural gifts from our DNA and our families of origin.

For most of my life, I have been considered to be "the structure guy" to others around me. Organization, structure, and processes come easy to me. In fact, structure is so intense in me that I can easily drive people crazy with it if I'm not careful. To some degree, everyone has some kind of natural talent. I know there's a possibility that you think you do not have a natural ability or maybe you simply have no idea what it could be, but I'd argue that you have some ability that is greater than that of those around you.

Another aspect of natural gifts that sets them apart from spiritual gifts is that natural gifts can be used for personal interest, whereas spiritual gifts are used for the glory of God and the building of His Kingdom. Though it's okay to use our natural gifts for personal desires and interests, I do believe, as Christians, it's very important for us to look for ways to use those same natural gifts to serve the Kingdom of God. Natural gifts are meant for the benefit of the church just as spiritual gifts are. Next, I'll give you some tips on how to discover those natural gifts.

Discover Your Gifts

As I mentioned earlier, one of my greatest natural gifts is prudence. I have a natural inclination for structure and organization as well as an ability to get things done. My wife will tell you that I can easily drive her crazy with structure if I don't hold it back to some degree. My other greatest natural gift is leadership energy which is manifested in my competitive nature, ability to take charge, and expectation for success. I've known these things about myself for most of my life, but it wasn't until a few years ago that I began using these strengths to bring growth to certain areas of my life, helping me thrive in the environment and role the Lord has placed me in. It feels great to know what the Lord has designed me for.

What practical and natural gifts do you have that can significantly impact your church or organization? Take a moment to think about it. The gifts we possess make up a large part of our personality. My giftings are the things that come naturally to me. I've received my giftings partially from my DNA, but they were also developed during my early years of childhood as I learned to interact with the world around me. Even if you're not sure about your own natural gifts, there is still probably a part of you that wants to thrive in this same manner. I believe the Lord puts the desire to understand our own natural abilities within us so we'll work to maximize the talents that He's given us.

As I previously mentioned, Paul challenges us not to neglect our gifts; or, in other words, he tells us not to fail to use our gifts for the benefit of others. In Romans chapter 12, Paul appeals to the members of the congregation in Rome to use their abilities to benefit those around them. Our gifts are available to use in administrating, teaching, serving, encouraging, exhorting, ministering, helping, leading, as well as many other areas.

What natural gifts and abilities do you have and how can those gifts be used in a way that will bring honor and glory to God? You must also consider how your gifts can produce life-giving fulfillment as well as positive results in the church or the organization in which you serve. Think about the things that you naturally do well. Just as importantly, what do you struggle to do and find yourself spending unnecessary time and energy on? In other words, what are your strengths and what are your weaknesses?

It takes a tremendous amount of humility to focus on your unique giftings because you must acknowledge the things that you don't do well. I had to come to grips with the fact that I'm not a creative person with a high volume of ideas. If you ask me to throw a party, it's probably not going to be the most exciting party you've ever been to. You must be able to recognize your deficiencies and imperfections. No one likes to admit to their weaknesses, but we all have them. It's important that you become aware of the things you do well and the things you struggle with in order to increase your authenticity and effectiveness as a leader. When you recognize your strengths and weaknesses and admit to them, you become true to yourself as well as others. Recognizing your own abilities also creates opportunities for other people to openly acknowledge their strengths and weaknesses and operate in their giftings.

Think about what the Lord has equipped you to do. I encourage you to be honest and ask yourself the following questions. Make sure you write down your answers to get the full benefit of this exercise.

1. What do you enjoy doing that doesn't leave you drained at the end?

Your answer to this question should come easily. Do you enjoy leading? Do you enjoy serving, encouraging people, assisting other leaders, exhorting, counseling, brainstorming? Do you enjoy figuring out why something isn't working so that you can make it better? Think about the tasks that bring you joy at work or in ministry and don't leave you drained at the end.

When I say drained, I don't mean just tired. I mean empty. Some things I do may be tiring, but they leave me feeling emotionally full when I'm done. With other things, I may even be able to do them well, but they leave me feeling tired, drained, and it may take a few days to recover. Those are not my natural gifts. The things you enjoy and—though you may be tired—leave you feeling complete when you're done, those are most likely within your natural gifts.

2. Of all the things you do in your life, what has a significant impact on others?

When you listen to people's problems, do you help calm their anxiety? When you have the opportunity to manage money, are you and others blessed financially? When you organize events for your church or organization, does life seem less chaotic? When you get the opportunity to speak in front of groups of people, are you eloquent? Are people moved to change their lives when they hear you speak? Of all the things you do in your life now, what has a significant impact on others? Why don't you pause here and consider these questions before moving on.

Most people usually know deep within themselves what they're good at and what they aren't good at, but sometimes it can be quite difficult to bring this knowledge to the surface of a person's mind. I don't want to overwhelm you with this question but think about your weaknesses as well. What do you secretly wish you could give up in your life that's not making an impact? You may do something well, but it may drain your energy and leave you feeling empty when you're finished with the task. I realize that we all have to do things we don't enjoy for the sake of our jobs. That's life, but there are tasks that you probably want to try to move away from if you're able to.

Also, think about whether you are an introvert, extrovert, or ambivert. An ambivert is someone who possesses a mixture of both introverted and extroverted qualities. Knowing this about yourself is important when considering your natural gifts.

How do you hold up in social situations? Are you able to be with people for long periods of time without feeling tired and drained or do you need routine alone-time to re-energize? Do you have a high volume of ideas? Are you a visionary? There are many questions you could ask to help determine what your natural abilities are. All of these questions lead back to the primary question, "What do you do that has a significant impact on others?" I realize I've given you a ton of questions in this portion, but my hope is the questions will help you begin to organically bring your natural talents to the surface. Again, I encourage you to take some time to process through these questions before moving on.

3. What do you secretly believe you can achieve but you've never attempted?

I encourage you to be honest and ambitious with this question. Think about the idea that there's a possibility you've never used one of the natural gifts that the Lord has given you.

One of my recent coaching clients spent most of his life as a music minister in various churches. He spent nine years in full-time music ministry and was very successful. His interpersonal sensitivity and leadership energy allowed him to thrive in those roles, yet he wasn't maximizing some of his greatest gifts. After spending some time with this client, it didn't take long to realize that he was made to pastor a church.

Just a few months after this realization, the Lord opened the door for a pastoring opportunity, and this man and his family relocated and took on the role of senior pastor at a local church. Now, four months into his new role, he's excited and thriving in a way that he had never previously experienced.

What do you secretly believe you can achieve but have never attempted? Of course, there are all kinds of assessments available that can help you realize your natural giftings—some much more impactful and even more expensive than others—but hopefully, as you wrestle with some of these questions that I've given you, you will start to recognize your strengths and weaknesses.

There's a sweet spot of things that you enjoy that don't leave you drained, things that make a significant impact on others, and what you secretly believe you can achieve but haven't attempted. When you find that sweet spot, you will likely have a much better idea of your unique gifts. Once you've identified your unique gifts, it's time to make steps to maximize those gifts.

Maximize Your Gifts

One of the reasons I need to discover my strengths is because I want to pour my time, energy, and growth opportunities into my strengths and the tasks that I naturally do well. Doing these things will help me get the most out of my limited resources and maximize my efforts for the Kingdom of God. It will also help me to be a good steward of what God has given me. I imagine that you feel the same way, and I have some great advice to help you maximize your unique giftings.

The Bible tells us in 1 Peter 4:10–11: *"As every man hath received the gift, even so minister the same one to another, as good stewards of the manifold grace of God. 11If any man speak, let him speak as the oracles of God; if any man minister, let him do it as of the ability which God giveth: that God in all things may be glorified through Jesus Christ, to whom be praise and dominion for ever and ever."*

This scripture speaks of being good stewards of the grace of God, speaking as the oracle of God, and glorifying God through our abilities. Therefore, the first and most important part of maximizing our gifts is:

1. Keep a God-centered mindset.

If we're focused on selfish things in ministry or work—such as money, position, or power—we greatly limit what we can accomplish for God. When we don't have a God-centered mindset, we limit what God is willing to do through us supernaturally. Though we may see our natural and even spiritual gifts manifested to some degree, we will not reach our full potential.

It's important that we understand that everything we do is for the glory of God. If you find yourself gravitating toward selfish ambition, which is so easy for any of us to do, you must find a place of prayer and even consider fasting to get your flesh under subjection and recapture the right frame of mind. If we align our natural giftings with the Lord, He will add the super to our natural.

Great things happen when we are motivated to work for the benefit of others. We can comfortably pursue excellence and even maximize our giftings when we use our gifts to help those around us. This is actually considered good spiritual stewardship.

2. Discover what your top gifts are not.

Part of maximizing your strengths is understanding your weaknesses. What are you doing that you're not good at? I believe that most people would admit that they don't need to pursue things they aren't good at. It's important that we delegate the tasks we struggle with to those who are better equipped to handle them. But what about the things that you do decently yet don't excel at? Many times, these are the things that can drain your energy. You may have enough skill to get the job done but not enough talent that the work comes easily for you.

Let me give you an example. I'm an introvert, therefore, being the center of attention does not naturally energize me. I don't enjoy it, and it drains energy from me. However, because of the nature of my calling, I have to be the center of attention occasionally. I'm fine with that; I can handle it, but I try to spend most of my time and energy behind the scenes of the organization I work for, working with people one-on-one or doing work alone in my office.

I know that tasks that make me the center of attention are not aligned with my top gifts, so I don't seek out those extroverted opportunities. I simply do those things when I need to. Thankfully, I have a ministry that allows me to maintain a good balance between the opportunities I excel at and situations I'm a little less comfortable with, but it's important that I don't seek to do things that I'm not especially gifted at doing. There are other tasks that I struggle with, and in those situations, I need to say "no" to those things as much as I possibly can.

3. Work hard to improve your gifts.

Let me start this point off by saying I do not recommend you work so intensely that you negatively impact your family or your health. I always recommend that you consider your health and family in whatever you are doing.

When it comes to developing your gifts, it's important that you put time and effort into your work. If you work hard, persist, study, practice, and receive coaching and mentoring, you can develop your natural gifts and even excel above those who have the same natural talents.

For example, I have high leadership energy as well as a highly competitive nature. I love to take charge and get things done, and I can easily envision a future and work toward it. I love working in this area, and I love leadership. It's one of my gifts. Because of this, I've studied leadership since I was 15 years old. My youth pastor bought me my first subscription to the Maxwell Leadership tape club (funnily enough, some of you reading this may not even know what a tape is). I've read hundreds of leadership books. I've gone to school and studied leadership. I've hired an executive coach to extract the best qualities from me. I've submitted myself to great leaders in my life, and I've learned from their leadership. I could list many other things I've done to develop my natural gifts. I believe these things have made a tremendous difference in my leadership life. I'm not perfect by any means; I'm far from it. I don't do everything right, but I will say that my desire to develop my gifting has absolutely paid off and has given me the ability to do what I do.

Learn from your experiences, listen to corrections from experienced people, and never stop learning and improving your natural gifts. Think about the tasks you are really good at. What can people around you confirm that you're really good at? Find those things and work hard to develop them. Keep a God-centered mindset, avoid those things that you're not good at as much as possible, and work hard to develop your best gifts. Doing these three things will maximize your giftings.

When you're able to maximize your unique gifts, it's amazing how others around you begin to flourish as well. Maximizing your gifts makes leading others well so much more important. In this next section, we will dive into the topic of leading others well.

chapter 13

Lead Others Well

† Philippians 2:3–4:*Let nothing be done through strife or vainglory; but in lowliness of mind let each esteem other better than themselves. 4Look not every man on his own things, but every man also on the things of others."*

W hen we are able to truly understand our unique gifts and maximize them, it allows us to recognize the big picture of the team as a whole. Strong leaders are not only competent at their own tasks but are also strong members of the team or organization for which they are responsible. When a leader directs others effectively, he or she helps the people working together unite as a team. The team mentality will facilitate an atmosphere of encouragement and support, increasing the potential of the team collectively. This is done with effective communication while being sensitive to one another's needs.

Leading others well requires making decisions that collectively help the team solve problems, work through challenges, and achieve goals. It means encouraging individual team members to use their talents to benefit the organization as a whole. Strong leaders build a sense of confidence and momentum within their group. There are many topics to explore that will help a person lead well, but there are a few topics that are not talked about as often. Topics such as effective delegation, being able to safely say no, having tough conversations, and the value of acceptance aren't taught as often, but they can make a big difference in your effectiveness in leading others well. Let's dive into these topics.

Improve Your Ability to Delegate

If we want to lead others well, we must learn to release tasks, jobs, responsibility, and more to other team members. Most of us think of delegation almost in a selfish way. We think of it almost as a relief from our own pressure. Sure, it is a relief to us, but we also need to consider the fact that delegation is just as important for the other members of our team.

If we don't release things into the care of others, then we, as leaders, don't give those individuals the opportunity to be strategically involved in the vision of the organization. In addition, when we unnecessarily hold onto things, we run the risk having an unhealthy work-life balance and possibly even burnout. In a complex organization, there's no way that we can do everything on our own. We don't need to do everything. The health of our organizations depends on us to be good delegators.

1 Corinthians 12:17–18: *"If the whole body were an eye, where were the hearing? If the whole were hearing, where were the smelling?*[18] *But now hath God set the members every one of them in the body, as it hath pleased him."*

Paul speaks of how there is one body, but many parts to that body. Then, Paul goes on for the rest of 1 Corinthians chapter 12 talking about the various gifts and contributions of the body of Christ. As human beings, we are all a little different, but we each bring a contribution to a team. In fact, our contribution can be as unique to each one of us as our fingerprints. We have different motivations, desires, temperaments, strengths, and weaknesses. We were uniquely and perfectly put together by the hand of God.

For instance, I thoroughly enjoy getting into the details of an organization, but another leader may dread the fine details. Some individuals may pull their hair out if they are tasked with things that require specific structure or following a process exactly. When we're considering delegation, it's important to remember that all people are wired differently. It actually raises the importance of delegation. If I don't delegate, first I'm going to fail in accomplishing everything that I need to accomplish because I can't do it all. Second, someone is going to miss out on making the personal contribution that they are designed to do.

There are tons of things that we can potentially delegate, from small tasks to projects to leadership roles within an organization to management of entire areas of an organization. When we consider these various opportunities of delegation, it's important that we ensure that the opportunity matches the level of a person's maturity and competence. Obviously, the more that's at stake the more competent and trustworthy the person we're delegating to must be. Matching the right opportunity with the right person is a significant aspect of leadership.

Once we understand the vision of delegation and give something away to someone, the process doesn't stop there. It's just the beginning. There's so much more to delegation. The biggest key to successful delegation is within the accountability process. If accountability is created and maintained in a healthy way, delegation can thrive. However, when a person delegates and then micromanages, it can literally kill morale and can greatly impact the outcome. As the delegator, we must resist the urge to jump in and do it for them. We can't rescue them when it gets tough. Ultimately, the culture of the organization can be damaged if this is the norm.

When a person delegates, it's important that they focus on the desired goal and release control of the process. It's amazing the difference that it can make in achieving a great outcome. It also has the potential to bring great fulfillment to those who are involved. The people you're delegating to need the ability to make decisions on how to accomplish the goal or task that needs to be done.

We do need to make sure that we engage with them along the way. It is important to create routine touch points and opportunities to interact. When those times come, ask them how their progress is going and look for opportunities to provide relational nutrients. For instance, if they're experiencing difficult obstacles, they may need empathy. If they're making good progress, it could be a good opportunity to give affirmation. If they are falling behind, it may be important to give encouragement. The goal is to let them know we're there with them. It could just be as simple as a text message or phone call. We want to let them know they're not on an island and isolated from us. We need to convey the good to them. On a rare occasion—and only if they ask for it—we can offer some insight or perspective. On an even rarer occasion—and only if they ask for it—we may even give them advice. The best delegators provide good vision for what's ahead and then give only the necessary relational nutrients to support the relationship as the individuals walk down the road to accomplishing that vision.

Delegation has been vital to my life and ministry; I know it's what will make or break the success I have in the future. If I delegate well, I have no doubt that I'll accomplish significant things. At the same time and most importantly, I'll see people around me accomplish big things as well.

Here are a few questions to consider:

1. What's one thing you're hanging onto in your organizational role that you know you should delegate?

2. What's one step you can take this week to move toward delegating that one thing?

3. When I take that step of delegation, what do I need to do to release control while, at the same time, providing relational nutrients of support?

Empower people through delegation. It will make a significant difference in your ability to lead others. Delegation is a tough aspect in leading others, but this next subject can be even tougher at times. Many leaders struggle to tell their team members "no" because it feels like it will hurt the relationship. However, in some cases, it's important to just be able to tell people "no" in order to maintain healthy boundaries. In this next part, I'll share with you how to say "no" without damaging your influence.

How to Say "No" Without Damaging Your Influence

Noooo… I *said* no… no, no, no!

No is *not* a bad word, but it surely does feel that way sometimes when you have to use it. In fact, the word "no" can sometimes have a uniquely overwhelming effect on the person saying it. But it doesn't have to be that way, especially if you know how to say it well. There's an art to saying no without losing influence.

In many organizations, the teams that support the mission are small. If one person decides to leave the team, it can drastically affect the team's productivity. Because of this, we're tempted as leaders *not* to say no to a request even when we really want or need to say it. When we say yes, even when the answer should be no, we usually end up working ourselves longer and harder in order to figure out a way to accomplish the task. That's okay occasionally when it's REALLY needed, but if saying yes when we really should say no happens regularly, it can negatively impact our leadership or even lead to burnout. In my earlier years of ministry, I would often take on way too much because I struggled to say no to certain authority figures. This would cause me to start showing signs of high stress and a negative state of mind.

Before we move forward, I want you to admit something. I need you to really do this. Turn on your phone camera and turn on the front camera so you can see yourself on the screen. Now, I want you to talk to your yourself, and

I want you to admit, "(insert your name), you can't do it all." Say that with me again in the first person, "I can't do it all." Doesn't that feel good? Just to admit that you're not superhuman?

There's no way that you and I can do everything that is asked or needed of us. We just can't. It's not humanly possible. So, we have to do what we can, delegate some things and then say no to other things. But how do you say no without losing your influence with those you're leading, especially if it's a volunteer organization like a church? I'm going to give you a few things that have worked for me.

Step 1. Gather information.

Leaders can sometimes say no to a person asking for help or asking for direction without understanding the full scope of a situation. It's important to be inquisitive and not let your biases override logic and reason. The way to do this is to stay curious, ask questions, and gather as much information as possible before moving on to step 2.

Step 2. Acknowledge that you understand the other person's need.

Acknowledging and understanding another person's need is a form of empathy, which means you "get" them. You understand that they have a need or a deficiency, and that the need is leaving a gap that's a little uncomfortable. Tuning in to what people are feeling on the inside is often all they need. Empathy is a key relational component that is extremely powerful in connecting with others and making them feel loved and accepted in the moment. Don't overlook the power of empathy when you need to say no. After you have shown empathy, move on to step 3.

Step 3. Deliver the truth.

Sometimes we can approach the task of saying no by being passive. It's important that we not try to skirt around the issues. If we can't or don't want to do something, we must deliver the truth. However, we can deliver that truth with a little strategy as well. In other words, you don't always have to give a reason if it's personal to you. You can deliver the truth by saying something like, "I would love to meet with you, but I am unavailable now," or, "I would love to be able to do that (whatever) for you, but it's just not possible for me right now." Then give them the real reason that you are having to say no. You don't have to share all of the details, but if you're schedule is too full, it's just too full.

Sometimes I have to tell people, "I'm so sorry, but my schedule is literally full for the next two weeks. I will be glad to schedule you in a few weeks, or I can try to refer you to someone who may be able to get to you sooner." I don't like doing that. I want to help everyone. This is *so* hard for me, but I have to keep reminding myself that I can't do it all. Why don't you say that with me again? "I can't do it all." After delivering the truth, move on to the step 4.

Step 4. Stick to your "no."

If the individual does not respect your limits and they continue to persist with some story of overwhelm, it's going to be tempting to cave to the desire to help them. If you cave to that desire, your margin—maybe even your health if you do it too much—will suffer. As hard as it may be, it's so important to stick to your "no." You may have to reiterate the same truth that you told them in the last step: "I would love to be able to do that for you, but it's just not possible right now." If that feels too robotic to you, then say the same thing but say it in different words. If possible and if needed, to ease the person's disappointment, try to refer them to another individual who can help. Then move on to the final step, step 5. This final step, "give affirmation," is what will help you stick to your "no" and not harm the relationship.

Step 5. Give affirmation.

When you go the extra mile to affirm the person you are saying no to, they'll see that you aren't just being mean to them, trying to avoid or reject them. Affirmation will actually speak to the judge within them while perhaps making it a little easier for them to accept your limits.

An example of affirmation could sound something like, "I want you to know that I love and appreciate you. You're a tremendous asset to this team. Thank you for understanding that I can't take on any more this week."

In the end, there will definitely be some individuals who still don't respond well to your no. At this point, you have to be willing to accept the consequences of the no. You have to face the fact that a relationship without limits is no relationship at all. The healthy people in your life will learn to respect your no, and you will all become a better team because of it.

I would like for you consider the following questions:

1. What relationships in your life seem to be invading your limits?

2. What's one step you can take this week to say no without damaging your influence?

When you learn to say no well, you'll have more time and energy to do the important things that will move the organization forward. Learn to lead well by embracing your limits and exercising the word "no" when it's needed.

Sometimes when people do not respect your boundaries or react inappropriately to the guidelines you have set, it's necessary to have a tough conversation. Tough conversations can be challenging for the best of leaders.

How to Have Tough Conversations

As leaders leading others well, we're often required to tell people difficult things. The only way to avoid having tough conversations is to live in seclusion, which is not really healthy or possible. We may not want to have difficult conversations because our natural inclination is to avoid conflict; we know the news we're delivering is hard to hear, or we want to escape delegating a difficult task.

I don't know about you, but I find it really difficult to tell people hard things. It's stressful. It drains my energy. Truthfully, it's one of the things I hate most about leadership. I want to share with you a simple formula that has helped me make tough conversations a little bit easier. Perhaps not all of the time, but most of the time you can successfully deliver negative news by using a simple formula that I will outline in this section.

Before sharing the formula, I'll share with you my old mindset on tough conversations. Ironically, I used to think I was pretty good at having tough conversations. I looked at it as a challenge to resolve issues and I would allow my competitive nature to kick in. Most of the time, having those conversations would benefit me. Notice I said, "benefit me." I hate to admit it now, but I was really taking on the role of a bully. I had to win, and I often left a bad impression on the person I'd had the tough conversation with. Now, after several years of doing hard work on myself—including coaching, counseling, and personal growth—I try to keep the perspective of a win-win situation with whomever I'm working.

I want to be successful in tough conversations, but now I want the other person involved to be successful as well. I want to have resolution and influence in these situations. It's not always possible, but I try to give it my best effort. Before I give you the simple formula for successfully getting through tough conversations, I want to talk briefly about one of the main barriers that keep us from properly approaching these situations.

One of the main obstacles that we face when approaching tough conversations is that we want to avoid hurting people's feelings. I think it's good that we don't willingly want to hurt others' feelings, but there may be internal reasons for our apprehension as well. For example, if a leader is naturally compassionate, he or she can feel what other people experience even before they experience it. Sometimes empathy can cause the leader to delay those tough conversations because they imagine how the other person will take the hard news. A leader may also have self-confidence issues or a lack of motivation or vision. They may have past hurts that hinder them from having hard conversations. No matter the root cause of their apprehension, the reality is that we must all be able to speak truth to people in order to fulfill the vision that the Lord has given us.

As leaders, we cannot avoid telling people hard things. John 1:14 tells us, *"And the Word was made flesh, and dwelt among us, (and we beheld his glory, the glory as of the only begotten of the Father,) full of grace and truth."* In this scripture, we see that Jesus was full of grace, but He was also full of truth. We must first have grace and give grace, but the truth has to follow. In my own life, if I only have grace and never truth, I'll never grow, develop, or mature as a disciple of Christ or as a leader in my church or organization. If I only have truth, there's a great possibility that I'll immaturely reject the truth by rebelling or fighting against it, getting hurt or wounded in the process.

It's biblical to have a combination of grace and truth. It facilitates a healthy environment of love, care, and growth that we can't get any other way. I love what 1 Peter 5:10 says about this concept, *"But the God of all grace, who hath called us unto his eternal glory by Christ Jesus, after that ye have suffered a while, make you perfect, stablish, strengthen, settle you."* Think about those words, "The God of all grace... after ye have suffered a while... [will] make you perfect, stablish, strengthen, [and] settle you." When I read that scripture, I see grace, but I also see truth. I understand that the process may hurt a little, but it results in a perfecting, establishing, strengthening, and settling within me that can't come any other way.

There are examples throughout scripture of the Lord giving people truth to mature them, establish them, and bring them to the place that He desires. He also molds us with a great deal of grace. There's no way we'll make progress in our churches and organizations if we don't live by this principle of grace and truth when having those tough conversations. You have to speak truth; but I also need you to understand that when you speak truth, you must speak it with a significant amount of grace. This simple biblical formula will help you tell people hard things: grace, truth, and then more grace.

As an executive coach, it is often my job to present hard truths to clients. I recall having to break the news to one pastor that his team was experiencing passive-aggressive behavior from him. I knew that it would be tough news for him to take in, but it was a limiting factor for his leadership that he needed to be aware of. I started this portion of the conversation by telling him some of the positive things that his team said about him. These words of grace and affirmation prepared his mind for the tough news. Then, I quickly and directly told him the truth of how his team was experiencing him during stressful times. I followed the tough news with some of the positive things that I have experienced with him. Because of how well he received this truth, we were able to spend the next few sessions working on how to combat his passive-aggressive behavior.

There are many methods for communication and conflict resolution. Many of those methods go into a great deal of depth, and some of them are really good and needed, but if you don't remember anything else, remember this very simple formula: sandwich truth between grace. Speak truth but start with grace and end with grace.

What does grace look like in difficult situations? Grace can look like letting the person know that you respect and care for them and understand them. You can't have hard conversations with negative emotions if you want the person to receive your truth well. Giving grace while administering truth creates a level of safety with the person. It lets the person know that you're not attacking or judging them. After you have shown grace, speak the truth that needs to be said. Don't attack or condemn. Don't belabor the point or continually repeat your message. Speak the truth concisely and clearly.

I do want to caution you that when you have difficult conversations, consider that your perspective is not always the correct perspective. Understand that the other person needs to give their viewpoint as well. There are always at least two perspectives to every problem, and you may be part of the problem. I know this is tough, but remember, for the sake of your organization and for the sake of your influence with this person, you want a win-win situation. It's important that even though you want to make a needed change in this person, you also want them to feel like they're winning in the conversation as well. This is what keeps us grounded in these difficult conversations, helping us build trust and healthy relationships in our organizations.

When you are finished giving truth, remember to follow up with more grace. The person may feel like beating themselves up by this point, or maybe they feel like you have beat them up. This is where giving grace can help bring a level of positivity to the situation. Remind the person how much they mean to you; tell them how important they are to the church or the organization. This type of encouragement will go a long way in helping them know that you're still a safe person, that they can trust you, and that you're not out to get them or judge them. It may feel unnecessary to do this step but do it anyway. Let them know you still love and care for them. Showing grace after speaking truth will bring a level of safety to the situation and help the person accept the hard news and move forward successfully.

Although there may be much more involved in having hard, stressful conversations, many times we don't have time to prepare for those difficult moments. When you are faced with having to speak a hard truth, remember to sandwich that truth between grace: grace, truth, and more grace.

In this chapter, we have learned about effective delegation, how to say no effectively, and how to have hard conversations. In this last part, I want to share with you something that I feel is the most important topic if you truly want to lead others well. The most effective leaders understand the value of acceptance when leading others.

Understanding the Value of Acceptance in Leadership

The power of acceptance can easily make or break a team or organization. Many times, acceptance is at the center of the struggle for those who come to me seeking clarity in life or their role in their organization. Many people don't feel accepted or valued in the way that they believe they should be. Sometimes these feelings originate from insecurities within the individual, but many times these issues come when leaders do not understand the value of showing healthy acceptance to those they lead.

People who feel accepted will follow even the weakest of visions. People who don't feel accepted can quickly become derailed from pursuing the greatest of visions. I believe acceptance is the greatest relational need within each of us.

The word "accept" is used in the Bible over 100 times. For instance, David expresses his need for acceptance from the Lord in Psalms, *"Let the words of my mouth, and the meditation of my heart, be acceptable in thy sight, O LORD, my strength, and my redeemer"* (Psalms 19:14). Just as David spoke of it, God placed something within every one of us that craves acceptance from God.

The good news is that acceptance is easily achievable according to Romans 8:1, *"There is therefore now no condemnation to them which are in Christ Jesus, who walk not after the flesh, but after the Spirit."* There is no condemnation, or disapproval, if we truly engage in the will of God for our lives and continually keep Christ at the forefront of everything we do. The Lord is for us, and He accepts us as we are.

If we make a mistake, God will not attack us. God is for us. He accepts us with all of our flaws, and He wants us to succeed. He wants us to arrive at a place of productive gain in His Kingdom and in our lives. We all have the need to be accepted by God, and He is able to thoroughly meet that need.

Acceptance of one another is just as prominent a need, but this concept is often much harder for us to grasp. In fact, it's one of the things that makes us feel insecure and struggle to find our identities. Our need for acceptance from others can cause us to pursue the wrong things in life in order to feel accepted. Romans 8:31 says, *"What shall we then say to these things? If God be for us, who can be against us?"* This scripture is clear: If God is for us, who can be against us? Yet, many times, we still have relational issues that make us feel as if people are coming against us. I believe the reason for this problem lies within the sin issues of humanity.

Essentially, acceptance is approval, grace, and the act of saying, "I love you, I'm for you, and I value you." Scripture specifically describes how we need to accept and interact with one another. Romans 15:7 tells us, *"Wherefore receive ye one another, as Christ also received us to the glory of God."* It says, "receive each other as Christ received us." Other scriptures, such as Matthew 10:40, Matthew 25:40, and many others, also speak to our need to receive one another. It's from scriptures such as these that we can gather that the Lord has designed us so that nothing good happens in our relationships without mutual acceptance. Acceptance is the foundation of any effective relationship.

Christ designed us so that acceptance is a fundamental need in any relationship we have. It may sound easy for us to go through life accepting one another, but the problem in most relationships lies with our need to assert our opinions. I admit that I'm just a little bit opinionated. I like things the way I like them, and (just to be transparent) some people rub me the wrong way. I may not like their attitude or their personal flaws. As much as I try to ignore my instinctive opinions about other people, the fact of the matter is that my opinions still impact my views of people. After all, I'm only human, and I bet that you are just as human as I am.

I find it interesting that you really can't know the level of acceptance a person has for another until there's a flaw in their relationship or someone does something the other person doesn't like. Most everyone has ugly relational defense mechanisms that are expressed when things go wrong in a relationship. The level of acceptance in a relationship often changes when those negative issues begin to surface. If someone accepts you only when you're doing well, they really haven't accepted you at all. If you attempt to cover up the bad parts of another person's life in order to accept them, you have not truly accepted that person either. Acknowledging a person's imperfections and brokenness while still accepting them for who they are is true acceptance. Recognizing the reality of the hurt, pain, and negative issues in a relationship and continuing to move forward with love, grace, and mercy is sincere acceptance.

As I mentioned previously, acceptance is one of the most important and fundamental needs in our lives. From a leadership standpoint, acceptance is one of the most fundamental needs of any team as well. Paul tells us in 1 Corinthians 12:23–25, *"And those members of the body, which we think to be less honourable, upon these we bestow more abundant honour; and our uncomely parts have more abundant comeliness.* [24] *For our comely parts have no need: but God hath tempered the body together, having given more abundant honour to that part which lacked:* [25] *That there should be no schism in the body; but that the members should have the same care one for another.*" Paul is teaching that acceptance is important for anyone no matter what flaws they may have.

Paul not only taught this concept, but he also exampled it. Paul's relationship with Titus illustrates a great level of acceptance. The Apostle Paul was the mentor to the younger leader Titus. They worked in ministry as a team. Titus 1:4 says, *"To Titus, mine own son, after the common faith: Grace, mercy, and peace, from God the Father and the Lord Jesus Christ our Saviour."* Titus was far from perfect; he was human, but Paul accepted and loved him so much that he called him his own son. This is true acceptance.

We sometimes find this level of acceptance in marriage or parental relationships, but this kind of acceptance is rare in organizations and teams of people who are working together. If a person doesn't feel like they have a seat at the table of your church or organization, they most definitely won't be as devoted to the cause as they could be. They will not stay long in that place; or, if they do, they may only half-heartedly dedicate themselves to the mission of the organization.

One of the most difficult tasks that any leader has is to create a sense of acceptance within their organization. In its simplest form, acceptance is feeling a deep sense of love and value. Creating a sense of acceptance within an organization is difficult to achieve as a leader because many times our own internal struggles get in the way of our ability to love and interact appropriately with others. I want to give you a couple of quick tips to maximize your ability to show acceptance to your team.

1. Limit the things in your life that cause harm to relationships.

Are you tired? Are you stressed all of the time? If you are, think about how that affects your life. Perhaps stress and exhaustion lead to moodiness, detachment, or passive-aggressive behaviors as well as other negative actions. To be fully accepting of others, you must take steps to identify and work through those things about yourself that are relationally abrasive. One of the best ways to reduce those abrasions is to simply rest and ensure there is adequate margin in your life.

2. Reinsert the qualities that communicate love in your relationships.

Be intentional when walking through a group of people or through your office. Take time to connect with people. Talk to people, make eye contact, deliver words of affirmation, give a physical pat on the back or an appropriate hug. Think about what you need to do to make sure the individuals you lead feel loved and valued. These are the things that will communicate acceptance.

3. Dwell on the words of 1 Corinthians 13:13: "And now abideth faith, hope, (love), these three; but the greatest of these is (love)."

Remember that more than anything else you do, communicating love and acceptance motivates people to support you and the mission the Lord is calling you to. Acceptance is vital if you truly want to lead others well.

There are many other components that you could study in learning to lead others well, but in my life and through my coaching experiences I have found that these four are prominent and make the most impact in others' lives. When you begin to take steps toward leading others well, it will often open up more opportunities not only to lead people, but to develop them. In this next chapter, I'll share with you some tactics that can help you become more effective in developing others.

chapter 14

Invest in Developing Others

✝ Ephesians 4:11–13: *And he gave some, apostles; and some, prophets; and some, evangelists; and some, pastors and teachers;*[12] *For the perfecting of the saints, for the work of the ministry, for the edifying of the body of Christ:*[13] *Till we all come in the unity of the faith, and of the knowledge of the Son of God, unto a perfect man, unto the measure of the stature of the fulness of Christ.*

Investing in the development of others is one of the most important jobs of an effective leader. According to author John C. Maxwell, Zig Ziglar once said, "If you help people get what they want, they will help you get what you want."[39] Developing others is a process of guiding people to achieve their full potential. Effective leaders invest their time in the right people, take on responsibility for mistakes or failures, encourage and uplift their team members, give specific and constructive feedback, and provide ongoing coaching and learning opportunities in an environment where people feel valued and appreciated. In other words, these leaders connect the people to their vision

---

39 John C. Maxwell, *Developing the Leader within You 2.0* (Nashville: HarperCollins Christian Publishers, 2018), 145.

and help each team member understand how they can contribute.

Developing others is essential to the leader who wants to lead an organization with a lasting legacy. This process is not about trying to develop a team that will make you look good as a leader, but rather it's designed to help you cultivate a group of followers who go further than they ever would have without your leadership. Following Christ's admonition of the Great Commandment and the Great Commission, investing in others and developing your team is a selfless act that benefits all parties involved.

Invest in Developing Leaders

Few organizations spend the necessary time developing leaders. Developing leaders is a hard task, but organizations that put a focus on development go further with success and usually do it in less time. Development creates a culture of growth, promotion, and longevity.

A number of years ago I stepped into a pastoral role at The Pentecostals of Alexandria, a fairly large church in Louisiana. Though I had been involved in developing leaders and others all of my life, I suddenly felt the weight of this task heavy on my shoulders. I began to ask myself, "How do I take a person who I think has leadership potential and move them forward to lead in some capacity?" Everyone is different; no two people are the same. No two people have identical upbringings, education, resources, or experiences. So, how could I cohesively teach leadership to people from so many different backgrounds?

Even though I had focused on growth for myself for many years, I didn't know how to effectively develop others. I began to analyze the process (or lack thereof in some cases) that others were using to develop leaders. On this journey for others, I experienced development in myself in ways that I had never imagined before. The experience exposed certain character traits of mine that I didn't know were there: negative traits, harmful traits, traits I didn't like. For instance, one of the most impactful realizations was just how shallow my ability to love and bond with others was. I was able to take some significant steps that helped my relationships with my family, friends, and people I lead. My character grew in ways that I never expected, and through this process I started to see a vision for what it would take to develop others.

I practiced some of the techniques I learned with the people in my sphere of influence. I tried techniques with pastors and business leaders around the country through coaching. Even though each person I worked with was unique, I started noticing patterns. I began to organize a process of development, and out of this process and journey came the model that you are learning: *The Christian Leader Blueprint*. *The Christian Leader Blueprint* establishes a solid model that can help you develop, but it is perfect for investing in developing others as well.

I believe one of the biggest, most impactful components that impact the development of others is having a plan or vision for what you're working toward. With no plan, you will likely aimlessly meander around and possibly do very little to impact the person you desire to develop. The person you're working with will be frustrated with the lack of traction and you will feel a sense of failure in your efforts. *The Christian Leader Blueprint* creates that plan for you and sets you up for the possibility of greater success.

There is no way to haphazardly move into effective development. It's important to consistently and purposely help an individual see a future that doesn't yet exist. The process of visualizing a future that isn't yet established is called vision. Without vision, those you are working with won't be as motivated to do the hard things that are required to move forward in their development. When you give your future leaders a plan, you help them figure out what resources and tools they need to move toward that vision.

The second greatest resource in the development process is relationships. Relationships don't happen accidentally; intentionality is key. If you let this process organically occur, it's possible you'll wake up in a few years and realize you haven't seen any development or growth in the people you desire to help. You have to build relationships with those you're working with and make purposeful time for those individuals. You can spend this time one-on-one or in small groups, but you must make time for these relationships.

Purposeful relationships and focused development will equip, mature, and bring individuals to the fullness of what the Lord intends for them. Ephesians 4:11–16 gives us insight into the importance of purposeful development:

> *"And he gave some, apostles; and some, prophets; and some, evangelists; and some, pastors and teachers;*[12] *For the perfecting of the saints, for the work of the ministry, for the edifying of the body of Christ:*[13] *Till we all come in the unity of the faith, and of the knowledge of the Son of God, unto a perfect man, unto the measure of the stature of the fulness of Christ:*[14] *That we henceforth be no more children, tossed to and fro, and carried about with every wind of doctrine, by the sleight of men, and cunning craftiness, whereby they lie in wait to deceive;*[15] *But speaking the truth in love, may grow up into him in all things, which is the head, even Christ:*[16] *From whom the whole body fitly joined together and compacted by that which every joint supplieth, according to the effectual working in the measure of every part, maketh increase of the body unto the edifying of itself in love."*

This is speaking of how the body of Christ is fitly joined together. It's talking about our need to work with a variety of different people; and this will require perfecting and edification for the work of the ministry. We don't need to stay as children, but we must grow up and become a contributing member of the team.

Perhaps you think, "Well, I don't have the time to invest in people." I'm going to argue that you don't have time not to invest. If you desire to move out of the one-dimensional, do-it-yourself life of leadership and create an effective team, you must invest in people. You must invest your time now for the gain of what will come later.

Think about this through the eyes of the person you desire to develop.

Would you stay in a place giving all of your energy to a leader you don't have a relationship with, who is unwilling to spend time with you, who you don't feel a great level of acceptance and support from? You wouldn't! You wouldn't stay in that place, so why should they if you aren't choosing to do those things? As you think about the importance of leadership development, I want to share with you a few practical tips to get you in the mindset of developing leaders:

1. Identify prospective leaders.

If you don't already have some potential leaders in mind, identification of those people is first and foremost. To help, ask yourself the following questions: Who is showing a strong work ethic and passion for what you're doing? Who is engaged in the values that you represent as an organization? As you make this a matter of prayer, who does the Lord place on your heart? You can ask others around you to get their opinions of who they think are prospective leaders. I wouldn't get hung up on particular characteristics at this point. I would focus on those who are hard workers and have like-minded values.

2. Gather to talk.

The next practical step is simply to gather prospective leaders and talk. You can give them some insight into what you're envisioning and gauge their interest. If any of the individuals are resistant or hesitant, you likely will need to move on to someone else. In my experience in developing others, it's hard work for me and the person I'm developing. If they are not full of desire and energy to make progress, it will be a struggle to keep them motivated. Likewise, it will be a significant and unwanted energy drain for you as well. Therefore, gather to talk to further identify good candidates to invest in.

3. Develop a plan together.

Developing a plan together will give you both a vision and a strategy to keep you moving. My suggestion is to submit 70 percent of your plan for development to the potential leader or group of leaders, then develop the remaining 30 percent of the plan with them. This means that you will need some clarity on your plan of action before you meet, but you should allow the person (or people) you're working with to give some input as well if they're going to buy into the process with you.

For example, you could bring *The Christian Leader Blueprint* as the primary guide (that's your 70 percent). Then, let the individual you're working with decide how he or she will unpack the information given, how often you will come together to talk about these subjects, what subjects will you start working on first, or how best to process other topics you are working on. For the sake of buy-in and long-term motivation to press on, it is important that those you are working with have input into the process.

4. Establish a routine time to meet.

If you're going to see effective growth, consistency is important. Though you want to create an atmosphere of grace, your excuses as to why you have to cancel meetings are not a good way to gain trust and reciprocal commitment. Your excuses will kill this opportunity more quickly than anything else. Building relationships is the most important component in leadership development, and this takes time. It is also important that you hold those you're working with to a high standard of accountability as well. Exercise grace but encourage them not to make excuses. You will have to discuss this topic at the beginning and talk about it often in order to effectively communicate your expectations.

5. Talk content but also go deeper.

You want to talk about things like leading others well, gifts, calling, and more, but don't stop with those technical topics. Attempt to go deeper. Talk about things that are holding them back from progress. Don't be afraid even to talk about the emotional things that get in the way. You don't have to have all the answers; most of the time the people you're working with have the answers within them. A good rule of thumb is to explore the topics of interest with questions of curiosity and resist the urge to give advice. Let their answers to your questions drive the direction of the conversation. Then, after you have gone deeper in the conversation, it may be appropriate to give advice, your perspective, or a challenge.

6. Celebrate the growth progress.

When you see growth, don't be afraid to celebrate! Occasionally, you need to step back and look at the growth a person is experiencing, even small growth, and acknowledge it at various points in the journey. One method of celebration is to give rewards. Depending on the circumstances, rewarding a person with something like a meal or a coffee, may be appropriate. Other times, it may be helpful to reward a person with a promotion or delegating a task that they would consider important. Celebrating growth is important if you want to continue to maintain the motivation to move forward.

I hope you are encouraged to develop leaders in your organization and see that this doesn't have to be complicated. The only way your church or organization will stay healthy and thrive long into the future is by investing in the development of others, especially leaders. If you resist this aspect of leadership, it will eventually negatively impact the overall growth of your organization; but if you embrace this process, it has the potential to drastically impact the trajectory of growth of your organization in a great way. In this next section, I want to give you some thoughts more specific to using *The Christian Leader Blueprint* as you invest in developing others.

How to Use the Blueprint to Develop Others

If you're a leader in any organization and you want to use this resource to help develop others, it's important that you use it for yourself first. As you read through this book, I trust that you are gaining an in-depth understanding of what the model truly is about. Keep in mind that you don't have to be proficient in every topic the resource covers. You really don't have to be proficient in any subject, but I would highly recommend that you approach this resource with the mindset that you're learning as well. This will allow you to use the blueprint without feeling the pressure to know everything that the resource discusses.

It's not possible for you or me to "arrive" at some euphoric place where we no longer need growth in these areas of our lives. There are always greater depths you can experience. There is deeper learning and understanding that you can receive within each area of growth. I've personally studied all of these topics for years and adapted them for my own life; and yet, I still have much to learn.

I also want you to consider as you're working with people, you do not necessarily have to take a mentor/protégé approach, even if you're in a leadership position overseeing the person you're working with. I like to approach the topic of leadership development when using *The Christian Leader Blueprint* from the perspective of a guide. A guide is generally the person that points the way and comes alongside a person on the journey. When I'm working with someone, I'm a guide to provide vision and direction, and we may even grow together at some points.

As mentioned in the last section, you need to establish a routine time to meet with the person you're trying to help. We often get distracted with the busyness of life. If you don't set aside a routine time to meet, you're probably not going to interact enough with the individual to make an impact.

Before you meet for the first time or at least by your second meeting, get the person you're helping to read through the blueprint and study it. I recommend starting with the free short-guide version because it's less comprehensive and less overwhelming as an introduction to the topics. As they're reading through the resource, encourage them to underline, star, and take notes on anything that stands out to them. It's very important to identify those topics and items that resonate with the individual because these are the topics they will have more energy to work on. Most of the time, it's the pain points in a person's life or the things that bring them the most grief that they will be most eager to focus on.

Although *The Christian Leader Blueprint* will give you a basic understanding of the topics included, you'll want to try to grasp why the person chose their topics of interest to work on. Encourage him or her to start searching for ways to grow in those areas. I believe books are the best place to start—I've always been told that a leader is a reader. The person you're working with can search for books on Amazon or Google that relate to the topics they want to know more about. If a person reads two to three books on any topic, he or she will have a great deal more knowledge than most people on that particular subject. This is likely to create significant growth.

I know that reading books sounds overly simple, but let me give you the reason this practice is so effective. According to research done by WordsRated, over 50 percent of Americans haven't read a full book in the past year.[40] It's no wonder that people don't grow, but that's great news for you and me. If you read two to three books on a subject, particularly on one of the topics found in *The Christian Leader Blueprint*, you'll be considered almost an expert on that topic, at least compared to the average American.

If a person doesn't like reading, they can get an audiobook. Nearly every good book available has an audio version these days. It helps for me to buy the Kindle version and the audio version. If a book is worth my time to read, then it's worth a little extra money to buy both versions. I read and listen at the same time, and this really helps me retain the information.

You can also look for online courses or blog posts on the subjects that interest you. I've got YouTube videos and other resources on all of these subjects contained in *The Christian Leader Blueprint*. You can have conversations with others that you know study in those particular areas to see if they have any thoughts or ideas in order to learn more on the topic.

Since you are the guide in this situation, you don't need to do all the work. Get the person you're meeting with involved in the process and challenge

---

40 Nicholas Rizzo, "Over 50% of Americans Haven't Read a Book in the Past Year [2022 Study]," WordsRated, July 13, 2022, https://wordsrated.com/american-reading-habits-study/.

them to go out and find good resources on these topics. He or she can also join any of the Christian Leader Made Simple coaching and community opportunities available at the time of you reading this book. In those settings, you can ask for help and suggestions. I am continually looking for ways to expand my offering to better equip you on this journey. I truly want to help you succeed in your personal development as you help guide others in theirs.

Keep it simple as you meet routinely with the individual at the designated times. All you have to do is discuss the topics that interest or concern them; there is little to no preparation needed. Center your discussions on those learning opportunities that they have identified. These discussions are incredibly important in order to bring to the surface those impactful moments that will create change in the individual. These conversations will generate memorable experiences as you dig into these topics.

The leader should then explore the question of "why" with the person. Get curious, and ask, "Why did this particular topic grab your attention? What significant things should be considered regarding this topic? What pain points are there? What is important to learn regarding this subject?" Another really good question to ask is, "What else is a challenge for you here?" When they answer that question, respond with, "Tell me more." Many times, a person's first answer is not their best answer; therefore, it is important to prompt them to give more information.

Proverbs 20:5 says, *"Counsel in the heart of man is like deep water; but a man of understanding will draw it out."* There's usually always a more meaningful answer if you allow the conversation to go a little deeper. When you feel like you've gotten to the root of their responses, ask the individual, "How can I, as your guide, help support you during this learning process?"

Finally, wrap up the conversation by saying, "What was most useful or most valuable for you in our conversation today?" This question will deepen the learning process. Come back together in a few weeks and talk about this topic again, or move on to whatever is standing out to them in that moment. I encourage you to stay curious and move slowly through these topics.

One of the great benefits of using *The Christian Leader Blueprint* is that it helps you explore sensitive topics that you may not have had the opportunity to explore in the past. It gives you an excuse to talk to others about things like work-life balance, routines, character growth, empathy, or personal support teams as well as a host of other important subjects. It allows you an opportunity to examine these areas and continue to invest in developing others as you work to grow and develop your organization.

To develop others effectively, you must have the ability to relate well to the people you lead. In fact, rhythm of life, seeing yourself more clearly, and leveraging your strengths all contribute to effective relationships. This makes Part 4: Building More Productive Relationships, a critical part of the blueprint. The first three parts lead to more effective relationships, but in a reciprocal way, effective relationships, discussed in Part 4, will help growth in the other three parts as well. Let's explore this final, yet vital, part of the blueprint.

Part Four

Build More Productive Relationships

As mentioned, the first three parts of the *The Christian Leader Blueprint* lead to more effective relationships, but productive relationships in turn help growth in the other three parts. They work hand in hand. You really can't have one without the other. This makes building more productive relationships a critical area of growth for effective leadership.

Connection absolutely counts. Effective leaders clearly recognize the importance of relationships and making connections. Leaders who value relationships are those who accomplish the most in their leadership. As leaders, we must learn how to properly add value at the right time to those who need it. If you tend to be more task-oriented, a perspective shift may be needed for you to become a relationship-focused leader.

Sometimes it's difficult to move past the biases or misconceptions we have about certain individuals. We can jeopardize or even lose critical connections as a result of our unfair opinions, leading to a lack of sensitivity to the needs of those with whom we work. There are useful tools that can help bring clarity to the needs of the people we lead. Social intelligence, for example, is a needed tool that gives leaders insight into the wants and needs of others. Other skills, such as self-regulation, empathy, and relationship management, can also help leaders obtain the competitive advantage to achieve organizational success through relationships. In Part 4 of the blueprint, we will explore these things and more as we work to achieve more productive relationships in leadership.

Throughout this fourth part, I encourage you to expand your thinking to a level that allows for the growth of new and innovative connections in your life so that you can experience amazing relational growth and success as a leader and within your organization. Next, we'll explore the topic of social intelligence, which is necessary to consider when pursuing more productive relationships. I invite you to break away from your preconceptions regarding your friends, team members, and other important relationships around you.

chapter 15

Increase Your Social Intelligence

† Colossians 4:5–6: *Walk in wisdom toward them that are without, redeeming the time.*[6] *Let your speech be always with grace, seasoned with salt, that ye may know how ye ought to answer every man.*

S ocial intelligence is one of the most basic aspects of building more productive relationships. Are you healthily aware of how other people see you? Are they intimidated by you? Do they enjoy being around you? Can you relate to people in a deep, emotional way without feeling overwhelmed? Answering these questions can help you recognize your level of social intelligence.

Social intelligence can be defined as your capacity to understand and manage your interactions with the feelings, thoughts, and behaviors of others. Social intelligence is simply about understanding social dynamics in order to function well in relationships; it helps us learn how to manage and build effective networks. Qualities of a socially intelligent leader include the ability to negotiate within his or her team in a way that produces win-win situations, manage difficult conversations with grace, empathize with other team members, and recognize different perspectives.

Even though some people may naturally function better than others in social intelligence, this is a skill that can definitely be developed over time. Therefore, it's important that we look for ways to grow our social intelligence and practice it in our day-to-day interactions with others. As we dive into this subject a little more, I want to start the conversation by talking about learning to manage relationships.

Learning to Manage Relationships

When the world shut down due to the COVID-19 pandemic in 2020, it initially strengthened many of our relationships. Suddenly, we all had more time for each other, but it wasn't long before many people started to realize that the extra time created new and unusual stress in their relationships. After all, we weren't accustomed to spending that much time together. My wife and I both work busy full-time jobs, so my family had never before spent weeks in the house together with very few breaks. It turned out to be an enjoyable thing for us after we made some small adjustments, but I remember some of our neighboring families admitting to high stress situations.

Many struggled to manage the closeness of their relationships. Why did this happen? What was the problem? I suspect that many people were trying to exercise a social intelligence, something they had created very little time for previously. Many lacked understanding of social intelligence and competency in knowing how to navigate their relationships. I want to give you some insight into social intelligence so that you can avoid this issue in the future. I want to help you improve any relationship in your life.

Social intelligence is a subtopic of emotional intelligence. As I mentioned previously, social intelligence is the ability to understand and manage one's interactions with the feelings, thoughts, and behaviors of others. It is the art of knowing when and how to talk or listen to people as well as understanding the importance of body language and timing in your interactions.

Jesus exampled social intelligence in a masterful way with the Samaritan woman at the well in John chapter 4. He knew everything about this woman, yet He didn't immediately expose what He knew. He didn't even allow Himself to be offended by this woman's lack of knowledge of who He was. He first expressed empathy by focusing on the hurt and pain in her life. Instead of creating an uncomfortable wall between them, Jesus approached the woman in a way that encouraged her to open up her heart to Him. He understood her first, then He effectively managed His own reactions to her feelings, thoughts, and behaviors. Finally, He responded appropriately to her pain. This is the supreme example of social intelligence.

Social intelligence allows you to build more productive relationships with those most important to you. As a leader, you must form relationships and inspire people to become involved in the vision that the Lord has given you. That is the essence of leadership.

When you have increased social intelligence, you have a greater understanding of people; you are able to attune better to their needs. You are more empathetic and discerning and have a much greater ability to motivate people to cooperate with you and others. You can understand a person's awkwardness in social settings and help them relax. You can provide acceptance, affirmation, and encouragement in ways that are healing and life-giving to relationships. This is the power of social intelligence.

I want to help you understand a few important elements of social intelligence. These are things that I've had to learn mostly by trial and error:

1. You must become a student of people.

We must attempt to understand what makes people act the way that they do. When you're in conversation, think about what the other person is saying and what they are not saying. Tune into how they're behaving, what emotions they are displaying and why, and what is motivating them to do the things they are doing. Try not to be defensive if they seem abrasive, and instead seek to understand why they are reacting in that way. If they are having a negative reaction, they may not feel accepted by you or they may have a mis-understanding of what is going on. If you don't become a student of people, it is unlikely you'll ever know what's really happening inside of others. Our next element, learning to listen, is very closely related to becoming a student of people.

2. Learn to listen effectively.

Now, you may say, "Ryan, really? I know how to listen to people." I'm go-ing to push back on you a little here and say that most people are not great listeners. A good listener is an active listener. If you think you already know what the person will say before they even fully say it, two things are true: first, there's a good chance you're wrong, second, the other person will likely realize you've tuned them out. They will more than likely do the same to you. Trust me, it happens. Tuning someone out feels like the equivalent of getting slapped by someone. It feels disrespectful, and that person isn't going to listen to someone who has tuned them out and disrespected them.

When developing your social intelligence, strongly resist the urge to jump to conclusions. Relax, listen, and focus on hearing the person out completely. This will make them feel heard and comfortable, and it will encourage them to hear what you have to say. It is also important that you listen and reflect. Don't just say, "I understand" in response to someone. Reflection means lis-tening to what the person says to you and repeating it back to them in your own words. When you do this, the other person knows that you truly listened to what they said. There's no doubt that they will know you understand. This practice removes the barriers most people have when they enter con-versations. People will feel like you "get" them, and that's a good feeling for everyone. This leads me to the third important aspect of social intelligence:

3. Know how to manage your body language.

People can see through a lack of authenticity, so, do you present yourself in an authentic way when someone is talking to you? Does your body language show that the other person truly matters to you? When you look bored or disinterested in the other person, it communicates a lack of empathy and acceptance. It's important to lean into the conversation, give eye contact, and visually show your interest. As a leader, you want to be sure to communicate positive things when interacting with others through your body language.

There are times at home when I'm distracted with a book or an electronic device and my kids come to talk to me. I may acknowledge them briefly but still not hear a word they say. As they have gotten older, they know by my body language whether or not I'm really listening. They know how to pick up on it in an instant and they call me out on it. If kids can read the image you are portraying, think about how much more an adult can tune-in to your body language. This will have a heavy impact on your influence with others as you navigate social settings in leadership. When your posture is right, it will then be easier to engage in the next recommendation:

4. Stay curious.

It is also important to stay inquisitive in your conversations. Before giving a person advice or a "piece of your mind," remain interested and explore the topic they have presented. When you are interested in them, what they're doing, and what they're experiencing, they will feel validated and understood. Like the woman at the well, they'll feel connected and energized by your conversation. I strongly encourage you to stay curious when you're talking to people.

5. Be a student of your social situations.

My final thought on social intelligence is simply to be a student of your social situations. Think back to the tough or important conversations you've had earlier in the day while they're still fresh on your mind. Consider the things you've done well socially, and think of ways that you could have better interacted with those individuals. Learn from your successes and mistakes.

While exploring some of those situations you've recently encountered, pay special attention to the things that seem to come from insecure places. Most of us have insecurities related to tough conversations or high stakes conversations. In this next section, I want to help you work to overcome this social insecurity.

How to Overcome Social Insecurity

I am naturally and deeply introverted. On a personality assessment I took a few years ago, I scored a 7 out of 100 in the area of sociability. I'd like to say that I was surprised by that result, but I actually wasn't. I can remember the first time I had to stand in front of a crowd and speak. One of my youth leaders, Wes Whitehead, brought me and a group of others to a women's prison service. In the van on the way, he told me he was going to call on me to testify. I quickly told him that if he chose to do something ignorant like that, he would deeply regret it. Well, he did, and it was about the roughest thing I've ever experienced in my life. I didn't seek revenge on my friend Wes, but I'm pretty sure I wrestled him to the ground later.

The rest of my assessment scores in the area of sociability only further revealed how introverted I am. I scored a 15 out of 100 for social events; I sometimes struggle at social events. I scored a 40 out of 100 for crowds; the only reason my score was that high in this area is because I can blend into crowds without being noticed as much. I scored a 19 for exhibitionist, which means I try to avoid the limelight; and I scored a 36 for entertaining, which means I'm usually direct. If I'm going to use humor, I will probably use dry humor.

I'm curious; when you read the title of this section, did you wonder why I'd talk about social security? You can be honest. Of course, I'm kidding. See? I do have a sense of humor; it may be dry and corny, but it's there.

I tell you all of this so that you know how stressful social settings usually are for me. Yet, I help lead many people. I'm a pastor and I speak in pulpits regularly. It's not that I can't engage in social settings. I even enjoy them occasionally. It simply means that they are usually stressful and energy draining for me. When I come home from church on a Sunday morning, it's common for me to crash for an hour or two before I can do anything else.

I used to struggle with social intelligence. Imagine my introversion coupled with a lack of social intelligence; it created the perfect internal storm. I didn't know how to manage social settings, and I found myself feeling very insecure in groups of people, even early in my life. Many people struggle with managing social situations, and I assume you've struggled with insecurities related to social settings in your life as well. I want to share with you how I've worked to overcome this struggle.

When we're socially insecure about ourselves, we turn our thoughts inward and over-analyze who we are. Have you ever walked into a room full of people and thought that everyone was staring at you, but no one really was? You were concerned about making sure your clothes were fixed and every strand of hair was perfect, yet no one even noticed those details. Your thoughts may be turned so far inward that when someone speaks to you it sometimes catches you off guard and you respond in an awkward way. Extroverts don't struggle with this quite as much as introverts do, though they can definitely experience social insecurity as well.

When we're inwardly focused, we can exhibit fear, insecurity, and anxiety. When those issues are on the inside of us, people around us can sense our inner turmoil. Unfortunately, even with the best of intentions, those social insecurities can negatively impact our interactions with others. Overcoming or improving these insecurities is important if you truly want healthy and impactful relationships, especially if you're in a leadership role. Leadership often requires a person to portray an external confidence that is difficult to maintain if the social insecurities are too visible to others.

Thankfully, there are several things that you can do to help overcome your social insecurities. Here are some practices I've personally used to help me overcome my aversion to social situations.

1. Work on your own emotional health.

Everyone who's breathing has either worked in the past to overcome emotional barriers in their life or they are currently working to overcome them. We all face emotional obstacles. There are problems in our childhoods, families of origin, or even innate to our DNA that have shaped the way we see the world and respond to people. We really can't avoid these issues. We don't come out of our mothers' wombs with a clear understanding of how to navigate through difficulties or process loss and grief.

1 Peter 5:10 tells us, *"But the God of all grace, who hath called us unto his eternal glory by Christ Jesus, after that ye have suffered a while, make you perfect, stablish, strengthen, settle you."* After you have suffered a while, He will make you perfect, establish, strengthen, and settle you. You may suffer a while with the things of life, but through His grace and mercy, you have the opportunity to receive emotional healing. This healing is usually not immediate but a journey. At some point, if we truly want to build and nurture healthy relationships in our lives, we have to put some intentional time and work into our own emotional health. I've learned to incorporate this work into my daily routines. I process problems through prayer and journaling, but I also resource regularly from my personal support team and counselor. I spend time, money, and resources to do this, and it drastically helps me feel more secure and confident as I'm interacting with others.

2. Push yourself out of your social comfort zone.

It's so easy for me to withdraw to the safety of my own little circle, especially when I'm tired. As an introvert, sometimes I just want to be alone; and I think that's perfectly fine and definitely needed at times, even for extroverts. It is, however, the Lord's will that we engage ourselves in relationships. John 13:34-35 tells us, *"A new commandment I give unto you, That ye love one another; as I have loved you, that ye also love one another.³⁵ By this shall all men know that ye are my disciples, if ye have love one to another."* It is obvious from this scripture that we are commanded to love one another. Isolation is not acceptable in the Kingdom of God. Therefore, we must push ourselves out of our social insecurities and form healthy relationships with people around us. We must purposely fight through the awkwardness and insert ourselves into others' lives.

3. Don't avoid critical feedback (and don't seek it in an unhealthy way either).

I used to ask for constructive criticism from people because I felt that only those who were critical of me could be trusted. I believed that their criticism was a form of authenticity. It was definitely an insecurity of mine. I sought their criticism, but when I heard their disapproval, I responded negatively. Even though I was seeking this type of feedback, I wasn't mature enough to handle the truth. This flaw was rooted in my unhealthy desire to please people.

Though that was an incorrect way to approach feedback, it's important that you not avoid criticism all together. Usually, there is some truth to any criticism, though not all of it may be true. The person giving criticism is probably allowing their bias and opinions to taint their words. I encourage you to listen to the criticism, briefly evaluate yourself with the feedback, then let it go. Let the criticism go and let go of the desire to want to please everyone around you. I know that's easier said than done, but the more balanced your desire to please others becomes, the more socially secure you will be.

4. Don't compare yourself to others.

This last point is probably the most important one, but it's also the most challenging. Avoiding comparison is difficult. I chose not to be on social media for over 10 years because of my struggle with comparison, and I'd probably still avoid it today if I didn't need it as a tool for content creation and delivery.

Social media, many times, feeds unhealthy comparison. Comparison triggers social insecurity in people more quickly than anything else. We read all of the great things and the highlights that are happening in other leaders' lives, and we wonder why it feels like we can't make it to their level. They seem to have all of these amazing things happening to them and their organizations while problems constantly bombard us. This creates an unhealthy desire to compare ourselves with others. When we succumb to the comparison trap, feelings of resentment, worthlessness, and unacceptance can easily make their way into our hearts. Comparison puts a filter over our eyes and distorts how we see the world.

We often view others through the facade they present on social media—and there you're only seeing the highlights of their lives, the happy times and pretty pictures. They have extremely tough things to go through as well. Everyone does, without exception. We all, all of humanity, have struggles, insecurities, and various risks to deal with. That's just life.

We have all suffered from social insecurity at some point, but it is important that we not allow our insecurities to interrupt the calling God has given us. Invest in your emotional health, humbly accept constructive criticism, avoid comparing yourself with others, push through those difficult insecurities, and build productive relationships in your life. If you will implement these practices, you can overcome the social insecurities that keep you from reaching your full potential in Christ. I know you can do it; the Lord has given you what it takes.

A big part of our insecurities point back to conflict in our relationships. Normal, healthy people don't enjoy conflict. Therefore, being able to have good, hard conversations with others, especially when your opinions differ, is a big part of social intelligence. I'll give you some insights as to how to argue in the best possible way.

How to Argue the Right Way With Social Intelligence

I don't have strong opinions about anything. Ah, yeah, right. Actually, I know exactly what this world needs. I'll tell you with a big grin on my face. It needs fewer people who know exactly what the world needs. When team members have a difference of opinions, it can easily create conflict. Many people don't like conflict, but it creates boundaries and holds people accountable. Conflict is a healthy dynamic of leadership, but it must be handled in a healthy way. When tensions rise, it's easy for our emotions to get out of control. I want to give you some suggestions that will help you argue and deal with conflict in the right way with social intelligence.

You may think that it would help if we just had less conflict. I will argue against that thought process. We don't need less conflict; we just need the right kind of conflict. When there is no conflict, several unhealthy scenarios occur. First of all, only a few people get their way while the majority of people's opinions go unheard. Second, the practice of passive-aggressive behavior prohibits direct communication and open sharing of the truth.

Passive-aggressive behavior is actually very common in churches because those who possess great compassion often avoid direct conflict. When someone is deeply compassionate, they often struggle with voicing hard truths. It's very important to deal with difficult issues openly and in a timely manner in churches and other organizations in order to have productive relationships. This is where social intelligence can help.

One of the first things we need to remember when confronting behaviors is that we're dealing with real relationships. Some of those relationships—such as those with family members, coworkers, or fellow workers in ministry—are extremely important. These are real people, and we need them in our lives.

We also need to remember that we don't always have to win arguments. I am very competitive, but I know that if I'm going to consider the feelings of those I love and care about, I have to be comfortable with a resolution of the disagreement, even if that means the other person wins. The goal is not for me to win; the goal is for us both to win. I can't approach situations thinking that I'm always right and the other person is wrong. I can't believe that I will always change the other person's mind. If I do this, that person will most certainly resist.

If I approach the situation with a true desire to understand what the other person is feeling and thinking, I can be calm, and the other person will feel heard. I can respond in a peaceful and compassionate way that will decrease the tension between us. Proverbs 15:1 says, *"A soft answer turneth away wrath: but grievous words stir up anger."* A soft answer doesn't equal weakness. It takes someone with a great amount of self-control to regulate their reactions when tensions are high, and this will generally lower that tension in the room.

What if the argument takes a wrong turn and the other person becomes angry and raises their voice? If this happens, there's usually no way that you can speak sensibly to a person who is emotionally outraged. As I've mentioned previously, the only thing you can do in that moment is listen to the person and tune-in to their emotions. If you respond to the behavior, you will only make the situation worse.

When you listen to the other person, make sure you label the emotion that you're seeing or even restate what they are saying to you. For example, you could say, "Ryan, you're obviously very angry," or "Ryan, you seem upset about this situation," or "Ryan, it sounds like you are upset about..." This may sound overly simple, but it's the height of social intelligence. Practicing these techniques really works to diffuse stressful situations.

Responding with anger, trying to control the situation, or even trying to reason with an overly agitated person is not going to help you improve the situation. The person needs to know that you hear what they're saying, and you understand. Otherwise, they will likely continue to be angry until the situation explodes or they finally feel heard. If you're going to get anywhere with this person, you don't have to agree with them, but you do have to show them that you're on their side in resolving the conflict well.

I mentioned earlier to just stay curious. Don't push your agenda in order to save time or your reputation. Get curious and ask questions about why the person you're talking to is so passionate in their opinions. You're likely to come to a much greater understanding, and it's possible you could even change your mind about the situation.

At the least, the other person will see that you truly want to understand their point of view. This will help them calm down and open their mind to your perspective. Trying to force someone to change their mind doesn't work; they may submit to your authority, but I guarantee they will submit with resistance. Instead, try to use social intelligence so that you can have great conversations that lead to true, healthy resolutions.

Social intelligence is about understanding the social dynamics in us and around us so that we can function well when we interact with others. It just helps us learn how to manage relationships and build an effective network with people. I encourage you to work hard to improve your social intelligence. The greater your understanding and use of social intelligence, the better chance you have in regulating your interactions with those you lead. We will cover that next.

chapter 16

Increase Your Self-Regulation

† James 1:2–4: *My brethren, count it all joy when ye fall into divers temptations;*[3] *Knowing this, that the trying of your faith worketh patience. 4But let patience have her perfect work, that ye may be perfect and entire, wanting nothing.*

Have you ever found yourself in an overly stressful and challenging circumstance where your social intelligence just didn't seem to be working—a time where your emotions took control of your logic? It can be hard to know what to do or how to act in those moments. It's even possible that our worst side could surface in certain events. Self-regulation allows you to control your emotions and impulses with honesty and integrity.

Controlling your emotions does not mean you don't feel emotions, it simply means that you know how to channel them in helpful ways. Self-regulation allows you to think about the consequences of your actions before you act. This kind of self-control and self-management creates circumstances for greater relationship building and higher productivity. It can create opportunities to build trust with others as a leader. There are times, however, when the stress gets out of control and you need a plan to be able to release the pressure. Keep reading to learn how to hit the release valve on your anxiety.

How to Hit the Release Valve on Anxiety

During the summer of 2020 in central Louisiana, where I live, we prepared for an enormous hurricane that was sure to bring significant wind damage and power outages. While preparing for the hurricane, I went to my garage to make sure my gas cans were full in case we lost power and needed to run our generator. I grabbed one of the gas cans and realized it only had a small amount of gas left. It was very hot in my garage, and the entire can was swollen like a balloon from the heat. When I hit the button on the top of the can to open the lid, a big burst of air came out, acting as a release valve for the pressure that had been building in the can.

When people have so much stress that they can hardly breathe, many times they tend to eliminate the very things that will actually bring the greatest relief to their circumstances. Then the stress builds even greater. This stress actually turns into anxiety and emotional exhaustion. The person finally reaches their limit. The anxiety and emotional fatigue create unhealthy leadership behaviors, such as moodiness, passive-aggressiveness, cynicism, detachment, or host of other negative actions.

When you're under prolonged or constant stress, the unhealthy parts of you will begin to manifest in various areas of your life, including your leadership. Your spouse, kids, and those closest to you will probably see the greatest impact, but others that you work with on a routine basis will probably get a glimpse of the negative behavior as well.

You may even be able to control the negative behavior to some extent. Perhaps when you're somewhat rested at the beginning of you day, you are able to find a sense of composure; but as you tire through the day, you may notice how you lose your self-control. If you find yourself close to the point of losing your composure, it's important to know how to hit the release valve and try to self-regulate.

Of course, this is much easier said than done. However, you have to remember that when you find yourself exhibiting these unhealthy behaviors in these circumstances, you can quickly deteriorate or erode the very relationships that you need in your life to keep you moving forward. You can quickly destroy your influence with the most important people in your life.

Everyone is a little different, so I want you to take a minute to consider these questions for yourself. What can you do to decrease your anxiety when it's at the highest point that will not be abrasive to the people around you? What's your healthy release valve? What takes the pressure off you in a healthy way? I'll give you a few practical examples that have helped me hit the releases valve:

1. Release the stress.

Physically step back and breathe deeply and slowly until you feel the anxiety decrease. You may need to take a short break from people. Don't detach, don't disappear; but take a break, and then come back a little later and work through the problem.

2. Turn to the key relationships in your life.

Maybe you have a person or a few people who can help you process things, someone who can help you gain a different perspective. It's amazing how someone we trust can give us an entirely different viewpoint on a situation. In the next two chapters, I'll share more on this topic when I tell you about how to expand your empathy and grow your personal support team.

3. Read scripture.

Scripture can work wonders in diffusing tension and anxiety. For instance, Philippians 4:7 says, *"And the peace of God, which passeth all understanding, shall keep your hearts and minds through Christ Jesus."* As we read that, it can give us a reassurance that the peace of God is going to help calm the situation we may be in. Another example is 2 Timothy 1:7 as it states, *"For God hath not given us the spirit of fear; but of power, and of love, and of a sound mind."* When we're having trouble regulating, it can be a fearful thing. It's great to be reminded that we don't have to be consumed with the spirit of fear. We can rest assured that he gives us power, love, and a sound mind to help us regulate in the toughest of times. It's incredible what scripture can do for us. Make a list of go-to scriptures that you can refer to quickly, and put them in your phone or somewhere you can grab them when you need them.

4. Take time to pray.

This can be the best and most important thing you can do to relieve stress and anxiety. Prayer will allow you to free yourself of the inner turmoil, effectively releasing the pressure built up inside so that you can receive the peace of God.

There are many things you can do to help decrease your anxiety and stress, but here's the key, you can't wait until the pressure is high to try to figure out those release valves in your life. It can be too late at that point. You must prepare ahead of time. Find your release values for the stress and anxiety. When the pressure becomes high and starts to impact your key relationships, learn to hit the healthy release valve.

If you find yourself having to hit the release value too often, this could be a strong indication that you need to refocus your overall self-regulation. For a leader, times of tiredness, stress, and even elevated anxiety are inevitable and normal, but how can you tell where there's an issue? It's not always easy for a person to recognize their own struggle with self-regulation. I want to give you an easy solution to evaluate yourself.

This One Sign Will Tell You If You're Struggling With Self-Regulation

If a person is going to be an effective, relational leader, it is so important that they learn to routinely self-regulate in the presence of others when the stress and anxiety of life is peaked. A significant part of self-regulation is knowing what it looks like in your life when you aren't self-regulated. If we can't properly regulate ourselves, it is likely to lead to an internal imbalance, lack of fulfillment, burnout, or possibly even derailment of a person's leadership. Those internal consequences will eventually lead to an external manifestation where we actually struggle to regulate the negative responses with others. Often, this begins to happen without a leader even realizing it.

I can look back now and remember my struggles in the earlier years of my leadership. I was working a full-time job in nursing management in a hospital and trying to help lead a church plant in northern Virginia. The pressure was high as I juggled my responsibilities at the hospital and at the church. The hospital was money hungry and required heavy productivity with as little staff as possible. The church was small and had a million things to do with very few people to spread the load to. It was stressful! I had people and circumstances pulling the life out of me, but I had no idea how to refuel myself through relationships at the time. I could feel myself moving toward burnout more days than not. This led me to act out with anger, moodiness, or frustration with people at times. Though I was successful in many ways, I would sometimes have a trail of blood behind me because I had no clue as to how to healthily regulate myself. Even worse, I thought this was the normal way to operate and I had no idea just how it was impacting my leadership effectiveness. I had a lot to learn about how to regulate my chaotic emotions.

Often, a leader has an idea there's a problem but just doesn't know how the lack of self-regulation is truly impacting his or her effectiveness. If a person can easily be blinded to the damage, then what would bring more awareness to this area of a person's life? How would you even know if this is affecting you? It's amazing how scripture usually gives us the answer to our questions, and this one is no exception. Matthew 7:16 says: *"Ye shall know them by their fruits."* Then, verse 17 goes on to say: *"Even so every good tree bringeth forth good fruit; but a corrupt tree bringeth forth evil fruit."* I don't believe there are many Christian leaders who are literally corrupt and producing evil fruit. However, the principle still applies. Christian leaders will know whether or not their lack of self-regulation is causing issues by the fruit they are producing in their personal lives. In other words, the people closest to the leader will experience unnecessary frustrations and fears. There will be unresolved conflict that unhealthily pushes people away. This often creates a feeling of disconnect and eventually feelings of loneliness by the leader and others closest to the leader.

On the other end of the spectrum, when a leader is self-regulated, there is usually a unique vulnerability and transparency with others. A self-regulated leader has the ability to work through conflict with team members and other close relationships. They are able to love and connect with others without fear that problems will arise. When the leader is pressed the most, he or she can regulate the emotions within and feel a sense of relational balance and stability.

Here's the problem: Sometimes you are so conditioned to see that particular negative fruit in your life you literally become desensitized to the effects of it. It becomes "normal" for you. You may not even realize it's there. I was working with a pastor recently who couldn't understand why he felt so empty inside. No matter how much he prayed and spent time with God he couldn't really shake the emptiness and the aloneness he felt. He was surrounded by people—his spouse, his leadership team, and church members—he even had the presence of God with him, yet he still had an overwhelming feeling of aloneness. To make it worse, it seemed like when the loneliness felt the deepest was when he struggled with anger issues and other negative emotions that would just push people further away. He passed the blame on to others for many years and thought it was just part of the grind of leadership.

Together, we identified this client's negative fruit as emptiness, feelings of being alone, and the lack of energy. As we started diving deeper into trying to figure out what was actually going on with him, we realized he had lots of acquaintances he called friends. He even supplied a lot of their needs. However, he never engaged with them on a deeper level. He never allowed anyone to see those most intimate parts of himself. It was a defense mechanism he created in his early years of life to protect himself from relational pain and hurt. He didn't even realize it had become his pattern. The result was an emptiness and a lack of energy to do the functional things needed as a pastor. On occasions of high stress and anxiety, it would show up as passive-aggressive behavior and moodiness as he struggled to regulate himself. Over time, these things eroded the relationships that he desperately needed to be an effective leader.

We started prying into this and raising his awareness of what was really happening. Just bringing an awareness seemed to help him tremendously. Then, as we began to focus on the foundational issues in the soil of his relational life in our coaching sessions, he very quickly began to see some changes in his energy levels. He began to feel a sense of fulfillment he had not felt in a long, long time—if ever. Most of all, the awareness, increased energy, and better rhythm of life (all principles of *The Christian Leader Blueprint*) led to a greater ability for him to regulate himself in the toughest of times. He learned why he was experiencing these negative things and he learned how to use the power of relationships to regulate himself.

Based on Matthew 7:16, I encourage you to evaluate your life. What negative relational fruit are you producing in your personal and leadership life? The answer to this question will tell you if you are struggling to self-regulate or not. Keep in mind as you are evaluating yourself, negative fruit may not be extreme and overly terrible; it may show up as something mild, such as moodiness or detachment. However, if you really want to go to the next level of success in your leadership life, it's important to regulate yourself in these more subtle things as well. If you're seeing negative relational fruit in your life, it's important to trace that negative fruit back to the source and determine what is disrupting the soil.

Once you have identified the fruit and the source of the fruit, then it's important to begin taking steps to mature and grow. If you're struggling with self-regulation, there's some key methods and solutions that will help you no matter what circumstances you may face. Essentially, you need to learn to healthy control your negative emotions.

How to Healthily Control Your Emotions

Unhappiness, fear, anxiety, uncertainty, anger, loneliness, confusion, depression, emptiness, disconnectedness—these are all real feelings; and if you're like me, you've probably experienced some or all of these emotions and others as you've walked uncertain paths and experienced changes in life. God made us so that we could "feel" our feelings. He never intended for us to ignore them.

We're natural feelers, but there are times when these feelings and emotions can disrupt our lives. Perhaps you get a little more anxious or overwhelmed than you should. Proverbs 4:23 says, *"Keep thy heart with all diligence; for out of it are the issues of life."* Because I know your mind is occasionally disrupted by the issues of life, I want to give you practical steps that will help you know how to "keep your heart with all diligence," or in other words, help you know how to control your emotions when you're living through a difficult time.

1. Ask yourself: What am I feeling?

You're not going to control or temper anything that you can't identify. So, ask yourself, "What am I feeling?" Sometimes, it's hard to name those feelings. I struggle to identify my emotions. You may think it's funny, but I actually have a "feelings chart" in my phone that helps me name the emotion I'm experiencing when I struggle to do so on my own. Believe it or not, most of us struggle to identify our feelings. It's important that you take time to name your emotions. If you're aggravated or sad or tired or frustrated, verbalizing what is going on inside of you will help relieve the pressure of what you're feeling, making those emotions more manageable.

2. Ask God to help.

I often process my emotions in prayer. I'll figure out exactly what I'm feeling, and I'll tell God, "Lord, I'm mad. I'm scared. I'm overwhelmed." I ask God to help me with my emotions. The brain loves for you to identify what's going on inside of you and speak it out. Just by verbalizing those feelings to yourself and to God will help in bringing order to your chaotic emotions.

3. Get back to your normal routine.

After you identify your emotions and pray about them, try your best to go about your normal routine. I'm not saying you need to ignore the emotions, but many times emotions are fluid and will dissipate with time. If you're not experiencing intense emotions, then it's not worth spending extra time dwelling on them. By naming those emotions and moving on with life, your negative feelings will likely dissipate with no problem and your established structure and routine will help you get through the emotions you experience. However, if these methods don't work and your anxiety is persistent, then move on to step four.

4. Ask yourself why.

You feel emotions for a reason. The negative feelings that you're experiencing are the byproduct of a problem in your life. Maybe you didn't get enough sleep for too many nights in a row and you're feeling irritated. Perhaps you have to make a life-changing decision in the coming days or weeks and the stress is causing a tremendous amount of worry within you. A wide range of things could cause these negative emotions. Your feelings are actually telling you that there's a problem within you. So, ask yourself, "Why am I feeling this way? Why am I having such a strong emotional response?" Asking yourself these questions will usually bring understanding to what is causing you so much anxiety. Recognizing what is triggering your emotions will often help deflate that stress.

5. Take action.

Once you discover and understand what the source of your stress and anxiety is, you can take action to alleviate it. Maybe you need to simply get more sleep and rest. Fatigue can bring out the worst of our emotions and cause us to be moody and egotistical. Perhaps you need to apologize to those closest to you who have borne the brunt of your emotional distress. If you'll do what's necessary to assess the causes of your emotional distress and work to solve the root of those problems, your stress and anxiety will likely decrease. If you can't do anything about the issues that are contributing to that stress and anxiety, move on to step six.

6. Resource from others.

As I have on many occasions throughout this book, I strongly advocate having a support team and resourcing from other people for emotional regulation and energy. If you're not able to get your emotions under control yourself by following the first five steps, then it's important that you're able to get help from the safe people in your life. You probably don't need your safe person to give you advice or suddenly become your counselor. More than likely, you simply need someone who can be there for you and listen to you vent about what you're going through.

In the Bible, Job endured some incredibly tough circumstances. In Job chapter 2, Job's friends saw his anguish and poor emotional state. His friends sat with him without even saying a word for seven days and seven nights. Scripture says, "... *for they saw that his grief was very great*" (Job 2:13). Often, all we need to help us overcome our emotional distress is to know that someone is there with us and understands what we're feeling.

These actions really do work—they've worked wonders for my life. They're biblical, and they can help you successfully navigate the tough circumstances of life. I hope that these six steps can help you regulate your emotions and bring order to your feelings. Because when we are able to regulate ourselves, it not only helps us, but also makes it much easier to use the power of empathy in our leadership efforts. Next, we'll learn more about expanding our empathy.

chapter 17

Expand Your Empathy

✝ Galatians 6:2: *Bear ye one another's burdens, and so fulfil the law of Christ.*

With good internal regulation, we are able to more easily engage in the use of empathy, which is one of the most important leadership tools. Empathy is a relational tool that allows us to feel what others around us are feeling. It's understanding or being sensitive to what another person is experiencing from their point of view. Some people have a naturally strong ability to empathize, but many of us must foster and grow the ability to use empathy with others.

Empathy is one of the most impacting skills that a leader can learn. The people you lead need to know you hear them, understand them, and care about them and what's going on in their lives.

When people are empathetic, they avoid stereotyping or judging so that they may live in a more open and honest way. Empathy has the ability to make a significant positive impact on an organization's culture. When team members know that their leader understands how they feel and wants to share in their pain or frustration, they will better trust their leader's decisions. Ultimately this leads to happier, healthier, and more productive team members.

Empathy is an amazing tool for leadership because it sets the stage for personal growth and healing. It's also just as life-giving and necessary for the leader as well. We all need empathy in our lives. It provides a rich, non-judgmental atmosphere that brings us near to each other, allowing us to bond in a way that promotes growth and healing. I'll explain more in this first part.

Leadership Growth and Healing Through Empathy

At our core, we all want to be understood, which is why everyone, leader or not, needs empathy. When we take the time to truly listen and tune-in to the needs of another person, we can create a dynamic level of connection and feeling of being understood. This is critical for true relational growth and healing.

Empathy helps the people we may be leading, but we also need to be on the receiving end of it. We can't just give from an empty tank; we have *to receive* empathy from others in order to continue *to give* empathetically. Because of the growth and ongoing healing that comes from empathy, embracing this dynamic will allow us to remain effective in what we do as leaders for many years to come. This is a reality for me personally as well.

There are times when life gets chaotic and my vision is suddenly clouded by circumstances. I may even suffer from relational hurts and pains occasionally. Thankfully, I have a few close friends who understand empathy well and are able to provide it for me when I need it the most. These friends are able to tune-in to what's going on within me by the power of empathy and help me see my issues more clearly.

At one time in particular, I was struggling with insecurities related to the podcast content that I produce. Through a series of events and a rejection from an important person in my life, I was feeling inadequate and unworthy to share my knowledge on a podcast. Negative emotions in that moment had replaced my normal, logical thinking.

After I realized what I was feeling, I reached out to a close friend and he listened as I voiced my concerns. He then reflected on the content and the emotion he saw within me. I began to feel relational closeness, acceptance, and reassurance of our friendship through the empathy he displayed. Together, we talked through the underlying emotions and circumstances causing my feelings of inadequacy and we figured out why I was experiencing those emotions. Thankfully, I uncovered some deeper things that I didn't even realize were there, and it created opportunities for forgiveness, relational healing, and character growth. I was able to work through my circumstances and push past those negative emotions in a productive and healthy way.

It's amazing that I was able to learn so much about myself just by having someone truly tune-in, listen to me, and verbalize understanding of what I was going through. The power of my friend's empathy gave me the opportunity to have significant growth and healing in that moment. As a leader, I need to be able to give empathy, but it's even more important that I'm able to embrace it in my own life in a reciprocal way when opportunities like this arise.

There's not a normal person alive who doesn't routinely find themselves in an emotionally tough situation. Life is full of disruptive occurrences. The people you lead will sometimes need you to be there for them the same way my friend was there for me. If we interact with someone in an excessive emotional state of mind, we must realize that they can't be met with logic, facts, and perspective. Emotion needs to be met with more emotion. Let me say it another way—meeting a negative emotion like anger, sadness, or disappointment with advice, logic, or confrontation usually causes people to shut down and increases their frustration. These people first need to be heard and accepted. They need empathy. They need to know that someone is willing to connect with them in a deep and understanding way. Things like advice can come after the connection is made.

When we slow down to provide this for people in need, we give those individuals life-changing relational nutrients. They'll feel a connection that can't come any other way. This creates a great environment for significant life change—healing and character growth. When two people communicate with their feelings, true bonding can take place and that is when we are most open for change. As leaders who seek to be influential and help develop people, we must interact and bond with people from a wide variety of different cultures, characteristics, and opinions. To do this effectively, we need this common language of empathy.

Paul says in Ephesians 4:1–2, *"I therefore, the prisoner of the Lord, beseech you that ye walk worthy of the vocation wherewith ye are called,² with all lowliness and meekness, with longsuffering, forbearing one another in love."* It's very clear from this scripture that what we do in our vocations is deeply connected to the way we relate to each other in love. We have to learn to connect and love each other in a way that is more like Christ. The Lord gave us empathy to be able to make this happen.

Empathy provides a rich, non-judgmental atmosphere that brings us near to each other, allowing us to bond in a way that promotes this relational growth and healing. Empathy makes it possible for true relational transformation to actually happen. Now that you understand the growth and healing that's possible through empathy, you can put it into a simple five-step process to ensure you are interacting with people in an empathetic way, encouraging growth and healing.

A Five-Step Process to Use Empathy

I once took a very powerful assessment that said I possess an extremely low level of empathy. I argued with this assessment. How could I be a pastor and an executive coach but have so little empathy? It was ludicrous for me to think about and, honestly, very disappointing. I didn't feel as if I could be an effective minister without a high level of empathy.

As my executive coach examined the results of the assessment with me, we concluded that the evaluation was correct. I am naturally inclined to be cold toward people's issues and have a hard time understanding what they may be going through. There is nothing wrong with me; this is just my personality. Thankfully, I've worked to overcome this inadequacy, and I want to share with you how I've done that in a five-step process. First, I need to give you the back story.

I mentioned earlier that I went to a Townsend Institute Conference in California a few years ago. Though I had no idea what to expect, I believed it would be like most conferences I'd been to. I would sit in a crowd of people and listen to a speaker as I learned from his or her message. There was some of that, but what the conference really focused on surprised me.

I spent hours in a small room with a cohort group of 11 people and a coach, none of whom I had ever met. In process groups we were taught about the growth and healing that can come from the use of empathy. We learned how to accommodate one another and tune-in to each other's emotions as we practiced these exercises for many hours.

I must admit, I thought the experience was odd at first. I had never experienced anything like it before; but when we left the conference, I had a new, amazing realization of the power of empathy through the experience of process groups. I walked away with an extremely useful skill. Though it was not one of my natural gifts, I learned how to use empathy in a way that I didn't know was even possible prior to that experience. It changes lives. When you truly relate to someone's experience, it powerfully connects you to the hurting person and can potentially bring emotional healing in a unique way.

Romans 12:15 says, *"Rejoice with them that do rejoice, and weep with them that weep."* This is just one of many scriptures that speak of empathy. Empathy is discussed all throughout the Bible. Honestly, even though I had read those verses many times, they really didn't come alive for me until after the learning process of the Townsend Institute Conference. I had experienced empathy in my life from people who were naturally good at it, like a good counselor and close friends. I had seen empathy practiced all of my life, but because empathy was not one of my natural giftings, I really didn't understand the impact it could have. I understand now just how powerful it can be to a person.

I love the power of empathy. It's the greatest tool that I use in coaching, pastoral counseling, and the relationships of everyday life. I want to teach you how to use empathy and tune-in to what other people experience. You can always enroll in Townsend Institute; that's where I learned it, but I don't think that's necessary for everyone. Some of you are naturally empathetic; and that's a tremendous gift to have. But I bet that many of you are like me and need a little help. The good news is that you don't have to overcomplicate things. Here are some practical steps to help you integrate empathy into your relationships.

1. Get out of your own thoughts and listen.

What is the person saying? What does their body language communicate? What sort of facial expressions are they presenting? Does their body language line up with what they're saying? Get out of your own head, set aside your own thoughts, and listen to what the other person has to say.

2. Name the emotion that you're seeing.

Is it anger? Frustration? Sadness? Incorporate what you see into dialogue. For example, say, "You seem like you're happy today." Another example is to say something like, "John, it looks like you're really sad right now." Don't be concerned about being right; simply identify the emotion you see.

3. Wait for confirmation or clarification.

If John isn't sad, he won't be upset that you tried to name what he was feeling and got it wrong. He will simply correct you. He may say, "No, I'm actually frustrated that I'm having to deal with the same thing over and over." It doesn't matter if you get the emotion right or not; naming the emotion with sincerity allows you to connect and bond with the person. The person's confirmation or clarification may be the first time this person has ever used words to describe what they're feeling inside, and you helped them do it.

4. As you're listening, reflect on the words the person speaks and say something like, "Tell me more."

Reiterate to the person what you heard them say. For example, say, "I'm hearing you say that you're frustrated because you're dealing with the same thing over and over." Then, "Tell me more" will help draw out the deeper meaning of his or her words.

5. Pause and let the person talk.

When you pause and reflect, the person will usually tell you more. He or she will give a deeper explanation about the situation if there is trust present in your relationship. This time allows the person to talk about those things which are obviously very difficult for them, helping them break free of their own thoughts as they begin to release their stress and anxiety in the form of words. This is where they begin to gain a greater understanding of what they are experiencing and often times some level of growth and healing will take place.

This is the five-step process for implementing a greater amount of empathy into your life. The process is obviously not going to happen exactly like this every time, but as long as you push against your desire to give perspective, insight, or advice and simply be present with the person and tune-in with what's going on inside of them, they will most likely walk away from the conversation feeling connected and satisfied. It's not just about the warm, fuzzy feeling, though. You're actually giving them the relational nutrients needed to help them overcome the problem they're experiencing. You're giving them the profound solution they didn't even know they were seeking.

As a pastor, I often have people come into my office wanting me to "fix" things for them or give them advice. In years past, I was quick to give a piece of my mind in the form of good advice and guidance. People would leave with an answer that they generally already knew before they even came to speak with me. Then, they would go away with a sense of confirmation to move forward, but I didn't provide what most people were truly seeking emotionally. Ecclesiastes 3:7 says, *"A time to rend, and a time to sew; a time to keep silence, and a time to speak."* There are times when giving advice is needed, but I think there are more times when being there for a person while providing emotional support is even more important.

Proverbs 17:27 tells us, *"He that hath knowledge spareth his words: and a man of understanding is of an excellent spirit."* One of the most effective ways to have empathy is to spare the number of words you would speak and allow the other person to use their own words to express what they are experiencing. During this time, it's your job to listen and tune-in to what you are hearing.

Another powerful scripture in Proverbs says, *"Counsel in the heart of man is like deep water; but a man of understanding will draw it out"* (20:5). Most of the time, the things presented on the outside of a person are not the true picture of what they are really experiencing. There are usually deeper issues and needs that should be addressed. As I've mentioned, there is needed growth and healing within us all. Truthfully, we all really want and need certain relational nutrients from the key individuals in our lives. We want people to connect with us without judgment and to understand the significance of what we're going through. At times, we want someone to identify with us as they share a similar story.

When we provide empathy for those important relationships in our lives, we can connect to those close to us in a way that allows them to become relationally full. When I learned this truth and made the shift in the way that I connect with people, it transformed my relationships and improved the results of my connections. I can now bond with an individual, and they go away feeling warm and full. I give most of the credit for that success to the use of empathy.

The most important component of empathy is having the ability to effectively listen—the first step of the process. There's nothing worse than someone talking *at* you instead of *to* you, where it's hard to even get a word into the conversation. This type of relational environment is opposite of the rich environment that empathy creates. On the other hand, there's nothing better than having a good conversation where the exchange of information flows freely between two people and both parties actively listen to each other. This kind of conversation is the foundation of empathy because it creates a very powerful connection and bond where leaders can learn to truly listen to the people they lead. I want to share more with you on the power of active listening in leadership.

The Power of Active Listening in Leadership

I have a friend who starts talking as soon as I answer his call. I have to admit, for me, this is one of the most frustrating things a person can do in a relationship. This type of behavior makes me not even want to answer the person's call. Now, in defense of my friend, I know he is a wonderful person, and he would probably take a bullet for me. However, in normal, daily conversations, his behavior usually makes me think he's not very interested in knowing what's really going on in my life. Because he doesn't know how to listen well, I definitely don't feel any sense of empathy from him, but it's even hard to have an effective relationship as well.

Do you know anyone like this in your life? Or could it be that this behavior describes *you*? The truth is that most of us often struggle to some degree. Your issues may not be as severe as those of my friend, but you probably struggle to practice active listening at times. Most of the time, we are thinking about how we're going to respond when the other person stops talking. We worry more about getting our own point across than hearing what the person has to say. We rarely slow down to just listen. Even though it's foundational to empathy and leadership, we seldom use the true power of active listening in our conversations. It's vital to the five-step process we outlined, but it's important for everyday communication as well.

Active listening is not easy, but it is simple. When you practice active listening, it's important to listen for two things: content and emotion. When listening for content, try to understand what the person is really telling you. When listening for the emotion that the person is expressing, try to figure out what type of emotion the person is experiencing in that moment. Is it frustration, anger, joy, or something else?

After you listen for both content and emotion, share what you observed with the person. Doing this will allow them to feel empathy from you. They will believe you understand them and usually begin to trust you in that moment. From there, you will then be able to grow the relationship in a deeper way.

These steps may sound overly simple, but many people struggle to use them when they are most needed. Active listening is actually a great deal of work, and for most people, it takes *too* much work. I want you to understand though that it would be almost impossible to engage in intense, active listening all of the time. Here's how it can work for you—if you're in an intense conversation with a person you lead and that person's emotions are out of control, you may struggle to know what to say in the situation. Active listening will help you connect with the person in a very powerful, life-giving way. It will make a huge difference in calming that person down and helping to resolve the issue they're facing. Active listening will allow the person to feel the empathy from you. People want to be understood in all relationships. When you truly and actively listen to a person, they'll feel understood and connected with you in a way that's not possible without active listening.

Going forward, I challenge you to practice active listening while it's fresh on your mind. Next time you're with a close friend, ask them this question, "Can you tell me something you're grateful for?" While they're giving you their answer, listen for the content and details of their story. Listen for the emotions that they are feeling, then share what you hear with the person. When you learn to actively listen, you will positively impact the conversations you have and grow the relational connections with the people you lead. Again, active listening is a foundational aspect of the use of empathy.

With empathy, you can facilitate more productive relationships in a much quicker way. It will assist you in leading your team more effectively, but it has the power to give back to you in an amazing way as well. Empathy is something that can be reciprocal in a healthy relationship. As you are attempting to grow your personal support team, you will find reciprocal empathy come into play. In this next chapter, I want to share with you concepts related to a personal support team.

chapter 18

Grow Your Personal Support Team

✝   1 Thessalonians 5:11: *Wherefore comfort yourselves together, and edify one another, even as also ye do.*

Many leaders are good at giving things like care and empathy to others, but they often struggle to allow others to give to them. It's amazing how many leaders go through life surrounded by people, yet they still feel lonely. I've heard it said for many years that it's lonely at the top. Though this is true for many leaders, it doesn't have to be that way. In fact, for a leader to thrive in this day and age, it's vital that they develop significant relationships. In the midst of our failures and flaws, we as leaders need people in our lives who accept one another without judgment. Having a support team is vital to healthy leadership and life.

Though the structure of a personal support team can look quite different from one person to the next, there are some characteristics that are necessary for the structure to truly be considered a personal support team. In his book, *People Fuel*, John Townsend defined a support team as "an intentionally selected set of people who become your primary source for relational nutrients."[41] This is also my view of a personal support team, but I would add that it's a set of people who also connect without judgment. I'm so grateful for the people in my life who have become a support to me and are able to provide key relational nutrients without judgment. They have allowed me to live a much more healthy and stable life these last number of years.

Even Jesus had a support team. Jesus had a group of emotionally safe friends that knew and embraced everything about Him. Though Jesus didn't have any weaknesses, He still was transparent and raw to a few select people. Jesus ministered to thousands, was followed by a few hundred, discipled 12, but He had an inner circle of three. 1 Peter 1:22 says, *"Seeing ye have purified your souls in obeying the truth through the Spirit unto unfeigned love of the brethren, see that ye love one another with a pure heart fervently."* Simon Peter, who was part of the inner circle of Jesus, said key words that fit perfectly in the mix of Personal Support Teams. He said, *"unfeigned love"* and *"love one another with a pure heart fervently."* With all sincerity and enthusiasm, we are instructed to love and support one another.

So I ask you today, who is in your inner circle? Who is part of your personal support team? When we don't embrace consistent and life-giving relationships, it can lead to all sorts of emotional, spiritual, and even physical struggles in our lives. When people struggle to relationally connect and starve themselves of key relational nutrients, it leads to feelings of burnout. I'll share with you the dynamics of why we experience these negative emotions and then give you a glimpse of what it takes to overcome it by embracing a personal support team.

---

41 John Townsend, *People Fuel: Fill Your Tank for Life, Love, and Leadership* (Grand Rapids: Zondervan), 2019.

This is Exactly What Leads to Burnout

One of the most consistent issues I see with leaders is a sense of stress and anxiety that eventually leads to a physical and emotional burnout. Unfortunately, you may be feeling this type of stress and anxiety right now. Burnout is a real thing. Leaders and other people all over the world are experiencing burnout right now. They blame it on the world's circumstances and turmoil. Yes, perhaps on the surface those things may be the immediate causes; they definitely are contributors. However, I believe there's another reason—a better reason, a deeper reason—why so many are feeling burnout. I feel sure that the greatest reason people are feeling this burnout for long periods of time is because of the lack of relational support in their lives.

Let me explain. We're good at showing love and care and empathy to others. Yet, we rarely allow others to come in close to us to show us the same love and care. Most people generally don't realize that it's the process of reciprocal love and care that will keep us from those feelings of burnout or to help a person recover from it. Burnout is a symptom of a deeper-rooted problem that usually can only be addressed by receiving key relational nutrients from safe people in our inner circle. This is only one reason we withhold our needs from others. Even if there's another reason for you, the fact of the matter is that we all tend to distance ourselves relationally from people in general.

There are lots of reasons why we would avoid this relational support. Some are more serious and complicated than others. However, a very common reason is we don't like to be perceived as needy. When we ask for relational support, it feels needy. We all know someone who is so needy everyone runs from them. Right? We see them come through the doors of our church or organization and we quickly find someone to talk to—or we duck out and go to the restroom—any direction except toward that person. Just admit it! You know what I'm talking about because you've done it! No one really wants to be labeled or perceived as needy because these are the people who give the word "needy" a bad rap.

Here's the problem, though: It's impossible to build an inner circle of "safe" people if we don't allow others to truly know our vulnerabilities and needs. This was a foreign concept for me most of my earlier years of life. I would guard myself from anyone seeing what was truly under the surface. This would limit my ability to get close to people and get my own needs met. Christian leaders are usually really good at helping others and meeting the expressed needs of other people. It brings fulfillment and satisfaction to our lives as Christians. However, we have to allow people to give to us as well. If we are going to have life-giving relationships, it is vitally important for us to be "needy." We need to share our needs in a reciprocal way. We give, but we must also receive.

The Bible is full of examples of our need for others. Consider Genesis 2:18: *"And the LORD God said, It is not good that the man should be alone; I will make him an help meet for him."* This scripture is often used in the context of marriage. Yet the crux of this scripture is that man nor woman should be alone. We need people. Even Jesus asked Peter, James, and John to "tarry ye here, and watch with me" in the Garden of Gethsemane. Jesus knew He needed others around Him to provide support during one of the darkest times of His earthly life.

There are a lot of similar scriptures to these. The bottom line is simple: We need to be needy. We need each other. Jesus modeled this so well for us. As I mentioned, He surrounded Himself with the twelve and then brought three of them even closer.

Earlier in this book, I referenced a concept called "relational nutrients" that explains what being needy actually looks like. Relational nutrients are similar to food nutrients in that they feed us relationally. Relational nutrients include things like acceptance, encouragement, validation, comfort, respect, and more. These are all things that we must have in life in order to feel relationally connected and fulfilled. Even if a person has never heard of relational nutrients, he or she will accidentally give and receive a portion of these nutrients all throughout life. However, the more we are aware of our needs and understand how to get them met the more we are able to have a thriving relational diet.

As I previously mentioned, we are much better at giving relational nutrients than receiving them. If we are only giving to others and not allowing others to give to us, we will quickly find ourselves in a deficient relational state. By not allowing the relational nutrients you give out to be replenished by others, we can and will eventually run dry and begin presenting signs of burnout. If it goes on too long and we don't take necessary measures to take care of ourselves, the burnout feelings will eventually lead to a derailment of our leadership and other areas of our lives.

I want to give you an alternative to these feelings of burnout. It is possible for you to know your relational needs and actually seek them from safe people in your life. When you supply the needs of others and, in turn, you allow them to supply your needs, there's a phenomenal, life-giving, life-replenishing connection that happens. We need to allow ourselves to need other people and not be afraid to show it. We need each other. It's God's design. Having someone supply our needs is not a luxury; this is a basic necessity of life.

We first must become aware of what we need. Then, we must allow people in our lives to help supply those needs. It's important that we develop the capacity to be able to make those relational connections. Do you want to be effective in the Kingdom of God for many years to come without burning out? Then you need to be needy now! We need those healthy, deep, and meaningful relationships in our lives; they will sustain our ministry life for many years to come.

I was once working with a pastor in executive coaching who was deeply struggling to pull people in close. He had a phenomenal interpersonal sensitivity that was likely one of his greatest strengths, definitely much greater than mine. However, he allowed people to feel that warmth and compassion from him to a certain extent, then those around him would invariably relationally hit a wall with him. It was as if he wouldn't allow them to get any closer than arm's length. This began to create disfunction on his team and lead to regular feelings of burnout.

As I worked with him, we realized that the primary disconnect was that he was not allowing people to meet his needs. He had no support team and was not deeply connected to anyone on his leadership team. He would attempt to provide for the needs of his leadership team; yet he was not being appropriately vulnerable and transparent with his own needs. The top tier leadership team in his church, the team that he desperately needed for a healthy organization, would literally feel the relational wall he put up.

As he worked to become more aware of his tendencies and to educate himself on relational nutrients, he slowly began asking for his relational needs to be met. First, he became more intentional with the first few people he asked to be on his personal support team, then he began to appropriately open up to his leadership team. This immediately impacted the connection and bonding that was felt on the team. The transparency and vulnerability of asking for his own needs to be met drastically improved and lessened his routine feelings of burnout. In addition, it was the missing piece to the cohesiveness of the overall team.

I want to reiterate to you the bottom line: It is God's design for you to need others and allow them to supply your relational needs. Hebrews 10:24–25 says, *"And let us consider one another to provoke unto love and to good works;[25] Not forsaking the assembling of ourselves together, as the manner of some is; but exhorting one another: and so much the more, as ye see the day approaching."* Though I feel assembling together in a church service is important, I believe this scripture is so much more than just that. It's about gathering in intimate relationships of transparency and vulnerability. It's about supplying the relational needs of others through love and exhortation. I also love the way this scripture ends by reinforcing that we will need this sort of interaction even more as we approach the last days.

If you're a Christian leader, I know you must be a phenomenal person who cares deeply for others. In all probability, the people closest to you know you care, feel your support, and know you want to encourage them. My questions for you today, though, are these:

1. In times of high stress and burnout, do you have a couple of individuals who can provide the relational support that you may need in the moment?

2. If you have these support people in your life, do you utilize them to get you out of tough emotional places?

3. What's one step you can take this week to move a little closer in sharing your personal needs with safe people around you?

We need a relationship with God every day of our lives. However, God created a system wherein we not only need Him, but we also need one another. We need to be needy. We need those healthy, deep, and meaningful relationships in our lives. Take a chance with the people in your closest circle and I promise it will make a big difference in the enjoyment and fulfillment of your life. It is the answer to those feelings of burnout. It will also make a difference in the longevity of your service in the Kingdom of God. Now that I've introduced a Personal Support Team to you, I want to share some more details of what that looks like in my life and how it can develop in your life in a practical way.

What Does This Personal Support Team Look Like?

As I mentioned, there are so many Christian leaders who go through life with people all around them, yet they feel a loneliness that just won't go away. This can easily lead to burnout and other negative emotions. In addition, it is actually fairly common to find a leader who is easily triggered by an event or circumstances and can find themselves spiraling emotionally in the moment. A Personal Support Team is the solution to this relational loneliness and/or the extended, negative rollercoaster of emotions. In this section, I want to give more details on what a Personal Support Team can look like, including some of the mistakes I've made along the way.

One of my good friends and coaching clients considered me to be part of his personal support team. He texted me late one Wednesday night and asked, "Why do I beat myself up after a sermon?" I was literally lying in bed almost asleep, exhausted from my day, and honestly, there was no gas left in my tank. I knew I was scheduled to meet with him the next day, so I just bypassed his question and asked him if he was still able to meet me the next morning. When he said "yes," I said, "Good! We can discuss this in the morning." I put up my phone and went to sleep.

Yikes! What a great leadership coach, right?! My friend needed a relational nutrient in that moment. Realistically, it wouldn't have taken me long to engage in a brief and encouraging discussion with him. However, I was too focused on how tired I was and how close I was to going to sleep. Instead of just pausing for a minute and giving him that relational nutrient, I put him off until the next day. That was not my best moment in ministry.

You may ask, "As a person on his support team, what could you have said to him, Ryan?" He asked, "Why do you think I beat myself up after a sermon?" Even though it seemed he was asking for advice, in that particular moment he didn't really need or want advice or an answer to the "why?" Because I know him so well, I knew in that moment he really just needed acceptance. He had just poured out all he had in the pulpit, and he needed someone he trusted to give him the relational nutrient of acceptance.

Sometimes, even in the midst of our failures and flaws, we just need someone to accept us as we are. I know that may sound overly simplistic, yet it is a powerful and profound need within every one of us. When I woke up the next morning rested and in my right mind, I knew my friend simply needed relational nutrients. I wished I had given them to him in the moment. However, I was able to somewhat make up for it by apologizing to him and then giving him the acceptance he needed when we met in person the next day.

Another friend who would consider me to be part of his personal support team called me a week later. He understands the relational nutrients concepts. He said, "Ryan, thank you for taking my call. This shouldn't take long, but I really need your help right now. I'm feeling down because I haven't made much progress on my goals these past few weeks. Can you tell me that you accept me anyway and maybe encourage me a little?" So, I immediately put my Support Team hat on. In a short period of time, I gave him the acceptance and encouragement he needed in that moment. It literally took about 10 minutes.

I had a scheduled meeting with this friend later in the week where we met and evaluated our lives as we do quite often. It was amazing the difference that acceptance and just a few days had made for him. He was already moving forward again in accomplishing the things needed in his ministry and life. The right relational nutrient at the right time has such a healing power that it can change a person's mindset in an instant.

I just shared with you two stories that involved me providing relational nutrients to two different friends—for one of them I struggled to provide nutrients and for the other I provided quickly and thoroughly. However, both situations had a positive and life-giving result. This is the primary purpose of a Personal Support Team. At various times, I've had to call my Personal Support Team members and ask for attunement, validation, hope, clarification, perspective, or any number of relational nutrients vital to me as a person and a leader. A support team can easily provide these types of nutrients when we find ourselves in a place of need.

I can tell you from my own experience, it is truly amazing how much better I am doing in my life relationally, spiritually, and emotionally since I established my Personal Support Team a few years ago. If I experienced a major rejection or ministry issues, for most of my life it would create an unusual and unhealthy amount of stress and anxiety. Sometimes it would even trigger something in me that could cause me to spiral emotionally for days. What I have experienced may resonate for you. Now, after establishing my Personal Support Team, if I do get triggered, the spiral time is usually just an hour or two, and I find it much easier to get back to a normal pace of life. This is only because I understand the value of a team of people who know how to provide those relational nutrients that are so vital to life. You could have this same sort of support.

In 2022, as I was working on this book, I had six primary Support Team members who know just about everything there is to know about me. This includes my wife, Angie, who is my most important Personal Support Team member (note: It wouldn't be fair to Angie for me to put all of my emotional ups and downs solely on her, so that's why I have a team). I meet with one of them every week and the rest I meet with routinely about every three to four weeks. I also have a number of people within a slightly bigger circle of close friends who can easily step in and help at times if needed. With the exception of a few individuals, these people are not coaches. I haven't hired them to help with my growth and development. These are my comrades. Most are fellow ministers engaged in a mutual growth process with me. They either already knew about relational nutrients and how to provide them, or I took time to teach them. Now, we can come to our scheduled meeting times and mutually provide for one another exactly what we need in the moment.

I want you to take in what Jesus has to say about this: *"Henceforth I call you not servants; for the servant knoweth not what his lord doeth: but I have called you friends; for all things that I have heard of my Father I have made known unto you"* (John 15:15). Jesus called them friends because He had a true transparency when them. My Personal Support Team are friends who I don't have to hide anything from. They know me—they know my vulnerabilities, they know my weaknesses, and yet, they still love me. I can tell them things that feel embarrassing, knowing they will still love me. They can handle the raw and undesirable parts of me. They know my dark side and failures and yet they just "get" me. They understand me and accept me. They don't ignore me, detach from me, or judge me. They love, help, challenge, give advice, and encourage me. This is the value of a Personal Support Team.

I would like you to consider a few practical questions as we close this chapter:

1. Name two people in your life you think you can be completely transparent with AND they would still love you.

2. Make a to-do item for yourself to reach out to those two people this week and ask them to join your Personal Support Team.

I realize this is a bold move. For some of you, it feels really tough and unusual, but this kind of relational connectedness is what the family of God is intended to be for one another. If you will step out and make a few small steps toward building your Personal Support Team, I promise you will be glad you did!

conclusion

What Comes Next?

My heart's desire is to see you learn and master the skills you need to grow your leadership effectiveness and enjoyment. I hope this blueprint has brought clarity and understanding for ways to better structure your personal growth. I desire to help you lead your ministry or organization forward with even greater success and fulfillment. Remember, this is a process that will take time and effort to fully understand in order to accomplish and implement these principles.

As I interact with Christian leaders every week, it's clear that many people are struggling to grow themselves because they have no plan. Unfortunately, this stifles their growth and the growth of their church or organization.

This was me a few years ago. My growth plan was based on whatever happened to accidentally land in my inbox or whatever book was at the top of the business development list at the time. This often left me floundering as I wasted time and energy that I didn't have to give. Leadership growth doesn't have to be that way.

In *The Christian Leader Blueprint*, you just went through a framework with four pillars. You learned about establishing a better rhythm of life, seeing yourself more clearly, leveraging your strengths, and building more productive relationships. Here's the truth that I've learned from working with many clients over the years—if you systematically and continually work through these four pillars, you have a *proven* plan that will help you maximize your effectiveness as a leader for years to come. Ultimately, I believe you'll crush the results of your organization and even enjoy the work of leadership at the same time.

You can continue to use this blueprint as a guide and dive deeper into these topics on your own. There are a million books and resources available on each of these subjects. However, I would love to be a more consistent part of your journey. So, I'm inviting you to choose one (or several) of the following methods to assist in moving you along in your personal growth with ideas, support, and regular interaction on these subjects:

- Visit *ChristianLeaderMadeSimple.com* to check out current offerings to assist in your leadership development
- Follow me on Instagram, Facebook, LinkedIn, or YouTube (@ rnfranklin)
- Subscribe to my regular email content offerings
- Subscribe to The Christian Leader Made Simple Podcast on YouTube or wherever you consume podcasts
- Enroll in on-demand online courses and community coaching
- Enquire about one-on-one executive coaching
- Join a mastermind or coaching group
- Request team coaching for your existing teams

Visit **ChristianLeaderMadeSimple.com** *or get in touch at* **info@ryanfranklin.org** *and we'll figure out a way to work together!*

Afterword

USE THIS BOOK TO DRIVE A CULTURE OF LEARNING AND DEVELOPMENT.

Get a copy of this book for each member of your team, ask your team members to read a chapter a month and explore the topic using resources from Christian Leader Made Simple, and enjoy the results that come from a team of value-driven professionals. Visit christianleadermadesimple.com for more information on how I can help with other services, such as one-on-one coaching, group coaching, team coaching, courses, workbooks, assessments, masterminds, and other community building opportunities to help you deepen these concepts in your life.

USE THIS BOOK AS AN ON-RAMPING TOOL FOR YOUR CHURCH OR ORGANIZATION.

Instruct all new hires or volunteer leaders to go through this book as an on-ramping protocol. Within a year, your employee or volunteer will be a much more effective leader than the way you found them. Did you buy a copy for your entire team? Reach out to me at ryanfranklin.org for ways that I can personally help your team through team coaching.

Acknowledgments

This book has been the culmination of a lifelong journey of learning and help from others. Thanks to the small, extremely talented Christian Leader Made Simple team, Gentry Needham and Bethany Fontenot-Miller, for believing in what we are doing to bring clarity and more effectiveness to leaders' lives. You've supported me and kept me afloat throughout the process of writing this book. You two are truly awesome!

Thanks to the late Pam Nolde, who encouraged me to write this book and helped me get started. I miss you, Pam.

Thanks to my wife, Angie, for putting up with me throughout the intense process of writing this book. I have felt the love and support all along the way.

Thanks to Bishop Anthony Mangun and Terry Shock, who took a chance on me in 2005 as a young pastoral assistant at The Pentecostals of Alexandria (POA). Then, again, Bishop Anthony Mangun took a chance in 2016 as he promoted me to an assistant pastor. He gave me leadership opportunities in ministry that others only dream of having.

Thanks to Sharon Turner for introducing me to emotional health concepts that changed my life many years ago. Thank you to Dr. Brian Epperson who was my first executive coach and coaching mentor. He was instrumental in believing in me and showing me the path to becoming a successful executive coach. Thanks to the Townsend Institute team, an amazing executive coaching program in Southern California, for introducing me to so many of the concepts that make up this life-changing model.

Thanks to the POA pastoral team, Senior Pastor Gentry Mangun, Associate Pastor Andrew Cox, Executive Pastor Gary Maxwell, and Student Pastor Garen Stanley, for supporting me during this intense season of writing.

Thanks to my life team, a group of six people, for helping me through one of the most challenging years of my life (for many reasons and not just this book). You've been there for me when I needed you. Words can't express how grateful I am for you.

Thanks to my first few years of clients that gave me the opportunity to begin practicing and developing my coaching skills and these concepts. I couldn't have done it without you believing in me.

And last, and most importantly, I want to thank Jesus Christ for being the rock that you claim to be in scripture. You've never failed me. You've always been right on time. Your guidance is perfect. Thank you for loving me.

Visit christianleadermadesimple.com for more learning opportunities.